HOW TO WIN AT
FANTASY
FOOTBALL

HOW TO WIN AT
FANTASY
FOOTBALL

INCLUDES THE **Sun**'S DREAM TEAM

RICHARD NEALE

JOHN BLAKE

Published by John Blake Publishing Ltd,
3 Bramber Court, 2 Bramber Road,
London W14 9PB, England

www.blake.co.uk

First published in paperback in 2007

ISBN: 978 1 84454 469 1

British Library Cataloguing-in-Publication Data:

A catalogue record for this book is available from the British Library.

Design by www.envydesign.co.uk

Printed in the UK by CPI Bookmarque, Croydon, CR0 4TD

1 3 5 7 9 10 8 6 4 2

Papers used by John Blake Publishing are natural, recyclable products made
from wood grown in sustainable forests. The manufacturing processes
conform to the environmental regulations of the country of origin.

Every attempt has been made to contact the relevant copyright-holders,
but some were unobtainable. We would be grateful if the appropriate
people could contact us.

ACKNOWLEDGEMENTS

Many thanks to Will Hagerty, without whom this book would not have got off the ground, and to Dream Team guru Tony Warner, for his help with the statistics.

CONTENTS

INTRODUCTION   ix

1.   HOW TO PLAY DREAM TEAM   1
2.   DON'T BERATE THE RATINGS   13
3.   WHEN HOMEWORK IS A GOOD THING   23
4.   FINDERS KEEPERS: PICKING A GOOD
     GOALIE IS A GIVEN   29
5.   THE CASE FOR THE DEFENCE   35
6.   THE MIDFIELD OF DREAMS   47
7.   FORWARD PLANNING   55
8.   TIME TO PUT ON YOUR SUNDAY BEST   59
9.   GET IN FORMATION: BUT IS IT 4-4-2 OR 4-3-3?   67
10. IN A LEAGUE OF YOUR OWN   71
11. THE GOLDEN GAMBLE   75
12. TRANSFERS: A WINDOW OF OPPORTUNITY   79
13. KING HENRY THE FIRST   95
14. THE FOREIGN LEGION   101
15. DREAM TEAM MOVERS AND SHAKERS   105

16.	POINTS PER MILLION: THE WAY TO PICK A WINNER	117
17.	LET'S GO ON A BARGAIN HUNT	129
18.	THE YELLOW PERIL	149
19.	EUR ON TO A WINNER WITH EXTRA GAMES	153
20.	THE CUP THAT CHEERS	157
21.	FINAL FANTASY XI: THE CONCLUSION	161
22.	STATISTICALLY SPEAKING: 2006–07 DREAM TEAM STANDINGS	167
23.	THE DREAM TEAM CHAMPIONS	209
24.	MORE TOP TIPS TO GET YOUR TEAM IN TIP-TOP SHAPE	245
25.	OTHER FANTASY FOOTBALL GAMES	261

THE PRE-GAME INTRODUCTION

Fantasy Football fever is a phenomenon that has gripped the nation in ever-increasing numbers over the past decade and more. Everyone thinks they can do a better job than their own club or national manager and many itch for the chance to prove it. Fantasy Football gives you that chance to pit your wits against millions of other similar hopefuls. It is fun and it can be lucrative, with £1 million-plus in prizes on offer to punters who tasted success in 2006–07. The biggest of the lot is the *Sun*'s Dream Team, which offered £300,000 in prize money in 2006–07 and which continually attracts more than half a million entrants. It is the biggest and the best in Britain and everyone wants to win it. Only one person can, but there is no reason why that person cannot be you, now that you have this guide to give you some pointers along the way. So what are the secrets, the do's and don'ts and the pitfalls you may want to avoid? This book guides you through the process step by step from the moment you decide you want to see just how good you really are in Fantasy Football management.

Most of the book concentrates on Dream Team, because it is the UK's most popular Fantasy Football game and offers the biggest prize. But later on we do have a look at some of the other games out there, some of which are free and others which do involve an entry fee but which carry a more-than-tasty prize which would take a chunk out of your mortgage, or simply because they are a lot of fun and good practice for beginners. Each game has its own subtle keys to victory, but the general principle behind them all is the same. Identify which attributes each individual game rewards best: is it clean sheets, goals or assists?

There is as little or as much in this book as you want or need. If you are after ten quick tips to help you pick a better team and ensure you're not counting down the days until the first transfer window, then you'll find it here. It should put an end to those office jibes of 'Your Dream Team's not doing very well' or 'You're still the strongest team in our Mini-League because you are holding all the rest up'.

If, however, you want to go deeper and start doing a little bit more homework, then hopefully this book will cater for you, too. It might inspire you to come up with your own method for getting to the top.

And, as for you Statto-types out there, hopefully there are enough tables in this book to keep you occupied, and quite a few that you will never have seen anywhere else before.

Some people are not into number crunching. Sara James, who came so close to being our first female winner in 2004–05 (she missed out by a single point) had a much simpler philosophy; players were picked according to one of three criteria: skill, looks or value for money.

I don't quite subscribe to that philosophy – looks don't do it for me, I'm afraid – but there is much to be said for the other two.

If you are doing your pre-season homework and researching players you are going to pick for the latest Dream Team game come July, you might as well put that knowledge to other use as well.

Wayne Rooney might be the top-priced player in the *Sun* game, which puts you off buying him, but he could be comparatively cheaper elsewhere.

Fantasy Football can take over your life. If it does, it is obvious that you enjoy pitting your wits against other managers. The aim of this book is to help you do so more competitively and hopefully win you some money. At the end of the day, though, it is down to you to decide who you want to play in your team. The wonderful thing about the Premiership is that everyone has their favourites and everyone sees the game differently, otherwise there would be 500,000-plus Dream Team managers with identical teams all sharing out the prize money at the end of the season – and that would be no fun for anyone.

This book is aimed at everybody, from the Dream Team novice to the seasoned veteran who is looking for the one tip that might make all the difference. So, for the newbies, we take a look at the rules of Dream Team and how you score points, and then we'll give you a few tips on how to get your information on players before the start of the season.

We then look at goalkeepers, defenders, midfielders and strikers in turn and evaluate how important each of these positions is in the overall quest for first prize, the always-fun Mini-Leagues and the Golden Gamble.

There is an in-depth look at how to make the most of your transfer windows and get your side back on track, before we focus on some of the stars who should be at or near the top of your shortlist. Just as importantly, there is a section on whose Fantasy Football stock has dropped the most over the past couple of years.

What is Points per Million? The serious fantasy gamers swear by it and reckon it is a recipe for success – we explain it, as well as how to uncover those bargain-basement players that are another ingredient of Dream Team success.

Do you know how bookings, European football, and the FA and League Cups affect your chances? If you don't, you will after reading this book.

We look at the stories of our past winners, how they landed the Dream Team jackpot and how it changed their lives.

Finally, we check out some of the other Fantasy Football games available and offer you some tips on how to turn your underperforming side from non-league into big time or, if you prefer, from Chelmsford City into Chelsea.

CHAPTER 1

HOW TO PLAY DREAM TEAM

DREAM TEAM ACTUALLY made front-page news in the *Sun* when it hit Britain on Saturday, 29 January 1994. The unsuspecting punters were greeted with these immortal words: 'It's a dream come true. Your chance to win an amazing £100,000 in a great new soccer game. The *Sun* is launching Dream Team soccer, where you are the boss in the big-money world of the football elite. Players like Ian Wright, Andy Cole, Ryan Giggs, Alan Shearer, Chris Sutton and Les Ferdinand can make *you* rich. This is the Premiership of the dream soccer craze sweeping Britain. It is your chance to prove you can do a manager's job better than the professionals and cash in, big time.'

The game did not start until 12 February, so there were only three months for players to gain points and, with only two points for a goal (it's five these days) and no cup competitions, it's little wonder that the finishing totals were small.

First-year winner Andy Grinter's team managed a total of 250 points. Thierry Henry used to manage a lot more than that on his own: he bagged an incredible 393 in 2003–04.

It seems a long time ago, and it was, but top-priced players at £5 million were goalkeepers David Seaman (Arsenal) and Tim Flowers (who was from Blackburn – your granddad might have told you about them: they are the Lancashire side that won the Premiership before the Big Four took over).

Six strikers would also set you back a fifth of your £25-million total budget: Manchester United pair Giggs and Eric Cantona, Wright of Arsenal and his BBC pundit pal Shearer of Blackburn, together with Shearer's future Blackburn team-mate Sutton (then Norwich) and Cole (Newcastle).

The Premiership stars may have changed and the scoring may have been tweaked a little over the years (in the early days players were actually deducted three points each time they did not play in a match: there was no squad rotation in those days and, had Sir Alex Ferguson rested one of his players, you would have been ready to lynch him – it could have cost you tens of thousands of pounds).

So are you up for a challenge? Do you fancy trying to prove you have what it takes to be a truly great manager? Look no further: the *Sun*'s fabulous Dream Team is the game and, if you do turn out to be the Special One, you can expect to find yourself handsomely rewarded!

For those of you deciding to have a bash for the first time, here are the rules. Dream Team could hardly be easier to play, as there are only a few, easy-to-follow steps. It's deciding which 11 players are going to land you the title that's the complicated bit.

HOW IT WORKS

Each year we produce a list of the players we expect to feature in the upcoming Premiership season. From July, that list is regularly published in the *Sun* newspaper and it is always available to peruse on our award-winning website: www.dreamteamfc.com.

As the manager, you must pick an all-conquering Premiership side of 11 players without exceeding the fantasy budget of £50million. We assign each of the players in our game a value, partly based on how they have done in the game previously and how well we might expect them to do in the upcoming campaign. Although it bears no real resemblance to their actual value in the transfer market, you can expect to pay more for established internationals and top stars. Be warned, Steven Gerrard, Frank Lampard and Wayne Rooney do not come cheap.

Your main job is to decide who you think will perform best over the whole season. The players come in the usual four groups: goalkeepers, defenders, midfielders and strikers.

Once you have selected your 11 stars, they earn or lose points for every match they play in the Premiership, FA Cup, Carling Cup, Champions League or UEFA Cup throughout the 2006–07 season.

We like to make our scoring system as easy as possible and you will find full details later on in this chapter. But it rewards the things you would expect, such as goals, clean sheets and good performances, and it punishes leaky defences, bookings and red cards.

Don't worry if your potential world-beaters do not quite perform up to expectations on the pitch. You get chances to dump up to three of your duffers at a time in each of the two transfer windows, which are usually open in early October and the end of January.

Choosing your side

There are three main rules:

1. Your team's value cannot exceed £50 million.
2. You must pick no more than two players from any one Premiership side.
3. Your 11-man team must have one goalkeeper, four defenders, three or four midfielders and two or three forwards, so either a 4-3-3 or a 4-4-2 formation.

How your side scores points

HOW TO SCORE IN DREAM TEAM	
Action	**Points**
Ratings of seven or more	3
Named Star Man	5
Goal	5
Hat-trick bonus	5
Clean sheet (goalkeeper/defender)	5
Clean sheet (midfielder)	2
Conceded more than one goal (goalkeeper/defender)	-1 per goal
Penalty save (goalkeeper)	3
Booking	-1
Sent off	-3 in total
Season's top points-scorer bonus	20
News of the World best in position	8
News of the World team of the day	2

1. Players who appear in the official Dream Team list score points in Premiership, Champions League, UEFA Cup, FA Cup and Carling Cup matches from the opening day of the Premiership season to the last game of the season, which can either be in the Premiership, the FA Cup final or, if it involves an English team, the Champions League final. Qualifying rounds for the Champions League do not count – nor does the Intertoto Cup or any other fixtures. Players not picked for any reason score zero points for each game they miss.

2. Three points are awarded to a player given a mark of seven or more in the *Sun* newspaper's individual ratings carried with every match report. A five-point bonus is awarded to the *Sun*'s Star Man.

3. Eight points are awarded to four players (one goalkeeper, one defender, one midfielder and one striker) chosen by the *News of the World* as the best in their position each Saturday.

4. Two points are awarded to the other seven players chosen by the *News of the World* each week in its team of the day.

5. Five points are awarded for a goal scored. A player scoring three or more goals per game gets five additional bonus points. A player who has been awarded points as described above will retain those points regardless of whether a goal is attributed to another player at a later date. Any player who is subsequently awarded a goal will not receive the points retrospectively, nor will the original scorer lose points.

6. A goalkeeper or a defender who keeps a clean sheet scores five points. If they concede one goal, they score 0 points, two goals -1, three goals -2 and so on.

7. A midfielder whose team keeps a clean sheet scores two points. Midfielders are not penalised if their side concedes goals.

8. Any player who is booked loses a point. A player who is sent off loses three points in total. Any player that loses points for a booking or sending-off will not have those points reinstated if the offence is rescinded on appeal.

9. A goalkeeper who saves a penalty scores three points. A 'save' is defined as a goal not being scored directly from the penalty spot (e.g. if the ball rebounds off a post, then that is a 'save'). Penalty save points are awarded even if a goal is scored subsequently from the rebound.

10. Any player who comes on as a substitute at any time scores or loses points as if he had played all 90 minutes. So, if a defender comes on as a substitute with four minutes to go and his side are already losing 4–1, he will score -3, the same as his defensive team-mates who have been on the pitch all game. Players subbed off also score or lose points in normal fashion regardless of how long they were on the pitch.

11. The season's top individual scorer earns a 20-point bonus. In the event of a tie, each of the tied top-scorers will get 20 points.

12. There will be two mid-season transfer windows. During each one, you can swap up to three players, providing you do not break any of the existing rules – making a total of

six changes in total over the course of the season. The first window will be in October, the second in January.

13. Any player transferred from one Premiership club to another continues to score points. For the purposes of the game, he stays registered with his original club. If a player leaves the Premiership, his points are frozen until such time as he returns.

14. The rules remain the same for games involving extra-time. A match that is 0–0 after 90 minutes must be 0–0 after extra-time for goalkeepers, defenders and midfielders to keep clean sheets. Penalty shootouts do not count, either for goals scored by outfield players or for spot-kicks saved by goalkeepers. Replays are counted as separate games.

Note: All the match statistics that affect the game's scoring are checked by us with the individual clubs and, where appropriate, the Premiership. In the case of a disputed goal, for example, Dream Team officials would, after viewing the recording, approach both clubs involved and make an immediate decision based upon these discussions.

This is preferable, because managers know instantly where they stand. If we did not do it this way, it could lead to some managers having their prizes taken away at a later date. The Premiership's dubious goals panel, for instance, can take several weeks to decide on contentious goals. Its decisions, therefore, are generally made too late for the conduct of the game.

Who can play?

Entrants must be 16 years old or over.

When you've picked your side

Give it a name – keep it clean – and make it funny, because there are prizes on offer for the most hilarious, and choose which of the 20 Premiership sides you want to link your Fantasy XI to. This does not score you extra points, but it does put you in that team's Supporters' League for the season and gives you another chance of winning a cash prize.

HOW TO ENTER

The easiest way is to register through the *Sun*'s very user-friendly website, www.dreamteamfc.com. There are two ways to pay on the website, either by entering valid debit- or credit-card information (18 years old and over only) or by phoning the *Sun*'s Dream Team telephone line and getting a ten-digit PIN, which you then input on the payment page when you register your team online. The cost should be the same: £5. Keep an eye out on the website because there are sometimes fabulous offers allowing you to enter extra teams for free.

The second method is to enter via the *Sun*'s official Dream Team telephone line, details of which you will find published regularly in the newspaper from July in the run-up to the start of the new season. You need a touchtone telephone and will need to have the three-digit numbers of each of your players ready so they can be successfully registered (again, you will find these details either in the newspaper or on the website).

THE GOLDEN GAMBLE

To maximise your points-scoring potential you should enter your team before the start of the season. But for the latecomers – and those who like a little more excitement – there is a Golden Gamble option, which allows you to enter a team up to three weeks after the start of the season.

So, if your star striker gets injured on the opening day of the season and is ruled out for the next six months, or if a team buys a star player after the season has kicked off and you are desperate to have him in your Dream Team, then the Golden Gamble is there for you.

Note, though, that your team only starts scoring points from the first match of the Saturday *after* you have entered it: you do not gain points for matches already played.

THE TRANSFER WINDOWS

There are *two* transfer windows in Dream Team: generally one is in early October and the other at the end of January.

This allows you two chances to change up to one, two or three of your players who are not performing. Of course, if things are going well you can opt to keep your team as it is, but you will find that is rarely the case. At all times after making the transfers, your team must again conform to the three simple rules: it can cost no more than £50 million; it can have no more than two players from the same Premiership club, and it must conform to either a 4-3-3 or a 4-4-2 formation.

Players only start scoring points for your side once they have joined your team; you do not get the points they had already accumulated and, similarly, you get to keep the points of those underperformers you have discarded up to the point they are summoned into your manager's office and given their P45s.

Transfers cost £1.50 to make in each of the two windows in 2006–07, regardless of the number of players switched.

PRIZES

In 2006–07, there were 100 ways to win a prize from an incredible £300,000 prize pot, which boasted a mind-boggling £125,000 first prize, the biggest in British Fantasy Football. There is even more exciting news planned for the 2007–08 season, so make sure you check out the *Sun* newspaper from early July and log on to www.dreamteamfc.com.

Remember, even if your side is not in with a chance of winning the overall first prize, there is still every reason to keep playing.

Just take a look at some of the prizes that were on offer in 2006–07:

1st prize: £125,000
2nd prize: £50,000
3rd prize: £10,000
4th prize: £6,000
5th prize: £5,000
6th prize: £4,000
7th prize: £3,000
8th prize: £2,000
9th prize: £1,500
10th prize: £1,000

Manager of the month: £3,000 to the manager whose team scores the most points in a single calendar month and £750 for the runner-up. This competition runs from the end of August through to the end of April.

Manager of the week: £1,000 to the boss whose team has moved the most places up the league in the previous seven days, running from midnight Thursday through to 11.59pm Thursday, UK time. In a week where there are no games affecting the Dream Team scores (for example, when players are involved in international duty), and so no points scored, there will be *no* weekly prize awarded. Instead, that week's prize will be rolled over to the following week, doubling the weekly prize to £2,000. There were 34 weekly prizes in 2006–07, netting the winners a total of £34,000.

Mid-game prizes: £1,000 to the manager whose team has scored the most points when the first transfer window opens. The manager whose team has scored the most points when the second transfer window opens also gets £1,000.

Best Mini-League: £4,000 to the manager who set up the best-performing Mini-League to share as he or she sees fit. The end-of-game Mini-League prize will be awarded to the creator of the Mini-League whose average score (determined by the total scores of each team divided by the total number of teams in that Mini-League) is the highest. There were also prizes down to fifth as well as nine monthly prizes of £1,000 to the best-performing Mini-Leagues from the end of August to the end of April. **Note:** each Mini-League must have a minimum of five teams to qualify for Mini-League prizes.

Supporters' Leagues: £250 to each of the 20 winners of the Supporters' Leagues.

Best Team Name: £300 to the manager whose team has the best name, in the opinion of our judging panel, with £200 to the runner-up.

There is also a host of other great goodies on offer just for entering the game. The prizes on offer in 2006–07 included stylish and compact Sagem mobile phones, 32-inch HD-Ready LCD televisions and PlayStation football video games.

SMS UPDATES

If you cannot wait to buy the newspaper or cannot regularly log on to the website, there is an option for managers to receive weekly and/or monthly SMS text message updates on their mobile phone to tell them how their team is performing. In 2006–07, texts cost 25p per message including VAT. See www.thesun.co.uk/mobile for full details.

CHAPTER 2

DON'T BERATE
THE RATINGS

ONE OF THE things that make the *Sun*'s Fantasy Football game different from most of the others is that players earn points for how they are perceived to have performed in the game, not just for their goals and clean sheets.

Sun reporters at every game give each player a mark out of ten, the score reflecting the journalist's opinion of their performance. If a player scores seven out of ten or better, he earns three Dream Team points. The player with the highest mark is awarded the Dream Team Star Man, or the reporter nominates that man-of-the-match award if two players are tied on the same score. Earn a Star Man award and that is another five points.

So, if your player collects a Star Man award with a rating of seven or higher, he will earn eight points. That's more than if your striker scores a goal or if your goalkeeper keeps a clean sheet, so it's quite obviously an important scoring component of the game and plays a big part in deciding the overall winner.

At the beginning of the season each reporter is issued with strict guidelines. The criteria are:

1. Involvement in the game: If during the overall course of a game a player does not make a positive contribution to his team, then he should not normally get a rating greater than six.

2. Inspirational play: A positive effect on other team members merits a higher rating. Because Dream Team points are allocated for specific events – goals, cautions, clean sheets, etc. – there is no need to take these into account in the player rating, unless they stem from the specific positional consideration given below. By way of example, a striker might score two goals in a single game and gets ten Dream Team points for doing so. However, both goals could have been complete flukes and, those aside, the striker had no other material involvement in the game. In this case, he would not merit a rating of seven or more.

3. Goalkeepers: Ratings for goalkeepers take the following specific positional criteria into consideration:
- Confidence and concentration
- Command of the box and set-piece control
- Aerial effect
- Shot stopping
- Minimising the goal as a target
- Building offence from defence

4. Defenders: Ratings for defenders take the following specific positional criteria into consideration:

- Protection given to the goal
- Confidence
- Clearing the ball from the danger area
- Set-piece performance
- Aerial ability
- Tackles made and possession won
- Building offence from defence

5. Midfielders: Ratings for midfielders take the following specific positional criteria into consideration:

- Defensive contribution
- Winning and retaining possession
- Offence building and creation of goal-scoring opportunities
- Work-rate and work off the ball
- Attacking power
- Goal attempts

6. Strikers: Ratings for strikers take the following specific positional criteria into consideration:

- Work-rate and work off the ball
- Offence creation
- Positional awareness
- Creation of goal-scoring opportunities
- Achieving one-on-one situations
- Attacking power
- Goal attempts

All criteria have both positive and negative elements and the final rating awarded by a reporter reflects a combination of these. The Star Man award goes to the player deemed to have made the greatest contribution to the performance of the team.

Occasionally there might be ratings you disagree with. Middlesbrough lost 1–0 at home to Notts County in the second round of the Carling Cup in September 2006, but Boro striker Mark Viduka – who was held scoreless by the Magpies' defence – got the Star Man award with a rating of six. But, like dodgy penalties given against the club you support and the blatant handballs the referee misses in the penalty area when your team attacks, these debatable decisions all tend to even themselves out over the course of the season.

Football is all about opinions. It always has been and always will be. Rather than complain about how subjective the ratings are, why not use it to your advantage by identifying who tends to collect the Star Man awards and the ratings of seven or better. Who collects the Star Man awards? That is easy: it tends to be strikers because they score more of the goals and therefore tend to catch the eye of the reporter. Often, there is little to choose between three or four of the best players on the park, but if one of them has scored the winning goal then that makes him the obvious choice. It is probably worth noting here, though, that, if you have a team full of superstars, then expect the man-of-the-match accolades to be spread about a bit more over the course of a season, because all the players do their bit for the team, such as has been the case at Chelsea in recent years. But, at Liverpool, Steven Gerrard often appears head and shoulders above anyone else on the pitch in terms of talent and, when he produces his best (which is often), he is more than capable of turning a game on his own. West Ham found that out to their cost in the 2006 FA Cup final. Little wonder that Gerro collects the bulk of the Star Man awards for the Reds. Consider that with other sides, too: is there one player who stands out and will frequently catch the reporter's eye? And something else to ponder: the Star Man award will rarely go to a player who ends up on the losing side unless he has produced an absolutely standout performance, so don't expect many awards if you pick players from teams who are down at the wrong end of the table.

– STAR MAN AWARDS 2006–07 –

Player	Club	Position	Awards
Wayne Rooney	**MANU**	**STR**	**10**
Dimitar Berbatov	**TOT**	**STR**	**10**
Frank Lampard	**CHE**	**MID**	**10**
Michael Essien	**CHE**	**MID**	**10**
Paul Scholes	**MANU**	**MID**	**9**
Cristiano Ronaldo	**MANU**	**MID**	**9**
Tomas Rosicky	**ARS**	**MID**	**8**

Here, in table form this time, is why your outfield superstars pile up so many Dream Team points over the course of a season and why goalkeepers seem to score so comparatively poorly. Remember, it's three points if your man gets a rating of seven or above in a game. Steven Gerrard scores a rating of seven at least 75 per cent of the time he steps on the pitch, but it's a different story for members of the goalkeepers' union.

7+ RATINGS 2006–07 (selected players)					
Player	Club	Pos	Games	7+	% 7+
Cristiano Ronaldo	**MANU**	**MID**	53	41	77
Frank Lampard	**CHE**	**MID**	61	46	75
Steven Gerrard	**LIV**	**MID**	48	36	75
Paul Scholes	**MANU**	**MID**	45	33	73
Ryan Giggs	**MANU**	**MID**	44	31	70
Jose Reina	**LIV**	**GK**	47	27	57
Brad Friedel	**BLA**	**GK**	53	24	45
Petr Cech	**CHE**	**GK**	36	16	44

Fair enough, you might say, but the ratings don't make that much of a difference to how many points a player scores over the course of the season, do they? I don't have to worry about them. Want to bet? Here's another table below showing some of the leading players from 2005–06 and breaking them down to show how they got their points. Note that only goalkeepers and defenders lose points for conceding goals and that strikers do not score points when their teams keep clean sheets. It's five points for a clean sheet for goalkeepers and defenders and two for midfielders, while a goalkeeper scores three for a penalty save. To explain some of the headings across the top of the table:

RP = points scored in total for ratings of 7+ and for Star Man awards

Gls = points for goals scored (five points per goal)

Disc = points lost for red and yellow cards

CS = points scored for team keeping clean sheets

GA = points lost for team conceding goals

Points breakdown for leading Dream Team players 2005-06								
Player	Club	Pos	RP	Gls	Disc	CS	GA	Pts
Henry*	ARS	STR	152	175	–4	N/A	N/A	**343**
Gerrard	LIV	MID	190	75	–6	50	N/A	**309**
Terry	CHE	DEF	150	35	–7	130	–6	**302**
Lampard	CHE	MID	113	100	–6	50	N/A	**257**
Carragher	LIV	DEF	139	0	–9	140	–14	**256**
Rooney	MANU	STR	175	90	–13	N/A	N/A	**252**
Hyypia	LIV	DEF	98	10	–4	140	–14	**230**
R Ferdinand	MANU	DEF	97	15	–5	120	–14	**213**
D Bent	CHA	STR	91	110	–2	N/A	N/A	**199**
Toure	ARS	DEF	90	5	–5	115	–8	**197**
Lehmann**	ARS	GK	81	0	–6	115	–10	**188**
Finnan	LIV	DEF	65	0	–2	135	–12	**186**
van der Sar	MANU	GK	85	0	0	115	–15	**185**
Gallas	CHE	DEF	65	25	–11	110	–5	**184**
Reina	LIV	GK	63	0	–6	135	–11	**181**
Nolan	BOL	MID	91	55	–10	38	N/A	**174**
J Cole	CHE	MID	81	55	–9	44	N/A	**171**
Stelios	BOL	MID	74	60	–4	40	N/A	**170**
Yakubu	MID	STR	74	95	–1	N/A	N/A	**168**

* Henry's total includes 20-point bonus as top individual points-scorer
** Lehmann's total includes six points for two penalty saves

What do we notice? How big a part the Dream Team ratings play in the game. Steven Gerrard scored eight fewer goals than Frank Lampard and both kept 25 clean sheets and were booked six times. But Gerrard scored 77 more points for his ratings from *Sun* reporters and so finished well clear of Lamps as the leading midfielder. Another thing to notice: if you think Wayne Rooney is not a prolific goalscorer, you are right, but his all-action performances certainly catch the eye of the gentlemen of the press. No fewer than 175 of Roo's 252 points came courtesy of the ratings; that's more than two-thirds of his total. Yakubu (down at the bottom of the table) actually scored one more goal than the Manchester United youngster, but accumulated 101 less points from the ratings and finished well adrift, even allowing for all the points Rooney lost for his ten yellow cards and one red card!

England midfielders Lampard and Gerrard again featured prominently in 2006-07 , but this time the Chelsea man came out top of the pile, in no small measure to the 188 points he collected courtesy of 10 Star Man awards and 46 ratings of seven or better in the 61 games he played. Michael Essien may have scored only six goals, and had to fill in at centre-back and right-back at various stages of the season due to an injury crisis at Stamford Bridge, but his work did not go unnoticed by the *Sun* scribes and he still made it into the top 10.

Player	Club	Pos	RP	Gls	Disc	CS	GA	Pts
Lampard*	CHE	MID	188	110	-7	64	N/A	**375**
Drogba	CHE	STR	155	175	-12	N/A	N/A	**318**
Ronaldo	MANU	MID	168	115	-5	36	N/A	**314**
Rooney	MANU	STR	152	120	-9	N/A	N/A	**263**
Berbatov	TOT	STR	143	115	-3	N/A	N/A	**255**
Gerrard	LIV	MID	138	55	-1	50	N/A	**242**
Essien	CHE	MID	155	30	-10	56	N/A	**231**
Carragher	LIV	DEF	113	0	-5	130	-19	**219**
McCarthy	BLA	STR	106	120	-11	N/A	N/A	**215**
Carvalho	CHE	DEF	79	20	-8	130	-10	**211**
Terry	CHE	DEF	92	5	-7	115	-4	**201**

Title row: **Points breakdown for leading Dream Team players 2006-07**

* Lampard's total includes 20-point bonus as top individual point scorer

One real benefit of the ratings is that it involves more players in the game and gives you a wider choice. Many Fantasy Football offerings reward goals, assists and clean sheets, but little else, meaning that expert, but defensively minded, midfielders are penalised and might as well not be in the game. In Dream Team you can still plump for an Essien (or, in previous seasons, a Patrick Vieira) and still be in with a chance of that player registering a useful score.

CHAPTER 3

WHEN HOMEWORK IS A GOOD THING

THE DREAM TEAM player list usually comes out in July, giving you plenty of time to do the research over the summer that could put you in a position to mount your title challenge. If you are not a football fanatic who follows every kick during pre-season, you may miss important news about players you are going to pick, but you can soon catch up both quickly and easily, but only if you know where to look.

The arrival of the Internet has been a blessing to Fantasy Football fans because there is an ever-increasing host of sources from which to gather your information.

There are way too many to list, but here are just a few of the more useful ones to help you on the way to picking that title-winning team.

BREAKING NEWS/TRANSFER GOSSIP
www.thesun.co.uk/sport

The *Sun*'s own website is always on top of breaking news stories during the day. But of even more value, particularly before the season begins and then again coming up to transfer-window time, are the stories linking players with moves to other clubs.

The newspaper is full of them, especially during the transfer windows, and, if you can't get your hands on a copy, you should find many of them posted on the *Sun*'s website.

It is an idea to save all your useful Fantasy Football website links in one folder so that you can access them quickly and easily, so let's do that before we start surfing the web seriously.

To add your first website – www.dreamteamfc.com – follow these instructions:

In Internet Explorer

1. When you have accessed the Dream Team website, click on the word 'Favourites', near the top of your browser page (it's normally the fourth word along, after File, Edit and View).
2. Click on 'Add to Favourites'.
3. Click on 'New Folder'.
4. Give the New Folder a name, like 'Fantasy Football'.
5. Hit the 'OK' button. You should now have that webpage saved as one of your favourites in a folder called Fantasy Football. With all subsequent websites you find useful, repeat steps one and two and, instead of clicking on New Folder, simply find the folder called 'Fantasy Football' in the 'create in' window and hit OK.
6. As a short-cut, you can also right-click anywhere in a page and select Add To Favourites from the menu.

In Netscape Navigator

1. Select the 'Bookmarks' option from the Window menu to open the bookmarks window.

2. Go to 'Item' and select 'Insert Folder'. Type 'Fantasy Football' for the folder name and leave the description field empty. Click on the OK button and you have saved the folder, which should now appear in the Bookmarks window.

3. When you come across a website you want to save in the Bookmarks submenu, select 'Add Bookmark' or 'Add Current Page'.

4. As a short-cut, you can also right-click anywhere in a page and select Add Bookmark.

There are scores of excellent football websites out there for breaking news and you'll gradually get to know your favourites if you don't have them already.

Among mine are http://soccernet.espn.go.com, which has scores of breaking news stories, and www.sportinglife.com/football/news, which provides equally good coverage.

PLAYER NEWS ARCHIVE

To follow how individual players are getting on, you can obviously monitor 20 different official club websites if you have the time, but it can take ages to trawl through the site if you are looking for the latest news on why a particular player is out of action. A much better option is the very impressive offering from Sky Sports. Go to http://home.skysports.com/football. Find the 'Team Pages' dropdown menu on the right-hand side and choose the team you are interested in. Click on 'Squad List' when the page opens and you have a list of the club's players; from there click on the ones you want to find out more about: you have an archived list of all the stories Sky has written about that player over the past days, weeks, months and years at your disposal. It really is a fantastic resource and I'm amazed it has not been copied more elsewhere.

STATISTICS

If it is facts and figures you are after, the soccernet site http://soccernet.espn.go.com/stats/topscorers?league=eng.1 &cc=5739 has as many team and individual player statistics as you would probably want. For more on team trends – such as winning runs, monthly records and much more besides – see http://stats.football365.com, while www.soccerbase.com gives a game-by-game and season-by-season log for every club in the league and, most impressively, for every player.

INJURIES

There is nothing more frustrating than picking a player and finding he is either injured or suspended for any length of time. This can be avoided with a little homework. The site www.physioroom.com has an up-to-date Premier League injury table (it's often buried halfway down the page on the right-hand side), which lists every top-flight player who is currently on the treatment table, what injury he has and, most importantly, when he is expected to return to action. If you are really sad, physioroom also allows you to read up on injuries like the one Michael Owen suffered in the World Cup to his anterior cruciate ligament to get a better understanding of why he spent so long on the sidelines.

SUSPENSIONS

If you want to find out if any of your players have been suspended, the FA is the best place to go for the definitive list. Check out www.thefa.com/TheFA/Disciplinary/SuspensionLists and click on 'Premiership'. There is also a secondary pending list – www.thefa.com/TheFA/Disciplinary/SuspensionLists/Pending Players.htm – of players who will be serving suspensions shortly.

UNDERSTANDING THE ODDS

If there is one thing I have learned in my 40 or so years on this earth, it is that bookmakers do not like losing money. Obviously, they do make the odd mistakes with prices, which generally happens when they have too many markets to cover or when they are covering a fringe sport and do not have the background knowledge or form of the players or teams involved to be able to make cast-iron predictions. The Premiership does not fall into this category: bookies know their stuff and, if you don't, why not use some of their expertise to cut off a few corners for yourself. Not sure how the newly promoted sides from the Championship are going to perform this season? Well, hop along to either www.oddschecker.com or www.odds.bestbetting.com before the start of the campaign.

These two sites compare the odds of all the major

bookmakers and give you an indication of how clubs might fare. Is a striker on your shortlist among the top five to be leading Premiership scorer? That's a good sign. And compare the odds of the leading goalscorers against their values in the Dream Team game – that might throw up a bargain or two. But do some of your defenders figure in one of the three sides the bookies are predicting will leak the most goals? It might be worth thinking again. I am not saying change your mind just because the bookies do not agree with you. If you know something they don't and if you are sure you have done your homework, then stick with the courage of your convictions. But, if your selections are based solely on a hunch without any hard facts and figures to back it up, it may be worth reconsidering.

CHAPTER 4

FINDERS KEEPERS: PICKING A GOOD GOALIE IS A GIVEN

EVERY GOOD TITLE-WINNING side has a solid man in goal and your Dream Team outfit should be no different. But should you pick a gloveman from one of the Big Four – Manchester United, Chelsea, Liverpool or Arsenal – or can you risk looking elsewhere?

Chelsea and Liverpool have been the two sides with the best defensive records in recent years (you'll find more detailed tables in our next chapter, 'The Case for the Defence', which will prove the point). Managers may feel that by not selecting a goalkeeper from one of these two clubs then they are already behind the eight ball. Well, let's take a look at who our recent winning Dream Team managers have picked, which should provide a clue...

	WHO OUR WINNERS PICKED IN GOAL				
Year	**Goalie**	**Club**	**Value**	**Pts**	**GK rank**
2006–07	Jose Reina	LIV	£5.0m	150	2nd
Top GK:	Brad Friedel	BLA	£4.5m	159	1st
2005–06	Jussi Jaaskelainen	BOL	£3.0m	140	7th
Top GK:	Jens Lehmann	ARS	£4.0m	188	1st
2004–05	Brad Friedel	BLA	£2.0m	139	3rd
Top GK:	Petr Cech	CHE	£4.0m	201	1st
2003–04	Tim Howard	MANU	£2.5m	136	5th
Top GK:	Shay Given	NEW	£4.0m	164	1st
2002–03	Paul Robinson	LEE	£2.0m	169	1st
2001–02	Shay Given	NEW	£2.5m	159	4th
Top GK:	Jerzy Dudek	LIV	£4.5m	230	1st

So, in the six seasons from 2001 to 2007, only one manager selected the top points-scoring goalkeeper of that season. The boss in question, John Bell in 2002–03, did his homework and got a little lucky because he went for Paul Robinson, who was available at a bargain £2 million because he was the Leeds reserve goalkeeper at the time. The expected first-choice stopper at Elland Road, Nigel Martyn, was available for double that amount, having scored 191 points the previous season, while Robinson had sat on the bench all year scoring zero. Martyn, an experienced England international, lost his place under Terry Venables after refusing to go on the club's pre-season tour to Australia. Robinson stepped in and Bell had fitted the first piece of a puzzle that would go on to net him a cool £100,000 at the end of the season.

It is worth pointing out that the modest £3 million spent

by 2005–06 champion Chris Marshall on Jussi Jaaskelainen was the most of any of our five featured winners until our 2006-07 winner Ian Preedy broke the mould by forking out £5million for Liverpool stopper Jose Reina.

Looking at the points tables, you might think that 2004–05 winner Gary Utting and Christopher Hartley, the 2001–02 champion, would already be out of the running before we even get to the ten outfield players. Utting was already 62 points behind anyone who had Chelsea's Petr Cech in their side and Hartley plumped for the always dependable Shay Given of Newcastle, whose 159 points was more than respectable, but which put him 71 behind top-ranked Jerzy Dudek. Liverpool's Polish international stopper set a Dream Team record for a goalkeeper that season by registering an incredible **230 points**!

Other factors should also prevent you from plumping for a goalkeeper from one of the top four teams. Because you are limited to a maximum of two players from one Premiership side, picking a top-drawer goalkeeper means that you can only have one of his big-name team-mates. So go for Petr Cech and you are forced to make a choice between only one of Frank Lampard, John Terry and Didier Drogba. Similarly, at Liverpool, if Jose Reina is the first name on your teamsheet, you can still have Steven Gerrard if you like, but that means no Jamie Carragher, who has been one of the biggest-scoring Dream Team defenders in recent seasons.

There's something else to consider, too: goalkeepers playing for the big clubs tend to have a quality defence in front of them. So, although they might let in fewer goals, they also have fewer shots to deal with in the first place. Fewer saves means fewer chances to impress the *Sun* reporter at the match doing the Dream Team ratings and, therefore, not as many man-of-the-match awards. In 2005–06, Arsenal's Jens Lehmann, the top-ranked goalkeeper, collected three Star Man awards. Edwin van der Sar of Manchester United, who finished just a point behind the German, managed two. Jose Reina of Liverpool and Petr Cech from champions Chelsea did not pick up a single Star Man award between them. These keepers played in 182 games, kept a remarkable 95 clean sheets and managed a total of five Star Man awards between them. *Five in total!* Paul Robinson of Tottenham and Mark Schwarzer of Middlesbrough did the best in this category with four each. But, by comparison, it was not as many as defenders John Terry of Chelsea (six) and Liverpool's Jamie Carragher (five). Incidentally, top in this bracket were Liverpool's mercurial midfielder Steven Gerrard and star Manchester United striker Wayne Rooney with 14 Star Man awards, one more than Arsenal's Thierry Henry.

It's the same when you look at the marks out of ten goalies get. Now we know Lehmann, van der Sar, Cech and Reina are no mugs between the sticks, as they are all experienced international goalkeepers, but none of this quartet managed a rating of seven or better in at least half of their games in 2005–06. Tottenham's Paul Robinson, an eye-catching and dynamic goalkeeper who can produce miraculous saves at his best, netted at least a seven rating in 25 of his 40 games, some 62 per cent of his matches. Here are some numbers to conjure with: John Terry, 40 ratings of 7+ in 49 games (81 per cent); Wayne Rooney, 35 ratings of 7+ in 47 games (75 per cent); and Steven Gerrard, 40 ratings of 7+ in 46 games (almost 87 per cent!).

As a general rule, don't pick goalkeepers from sides that have been promoted for the same reason you should not plump for their defenders either – they tend to concede too many goals and their points total suffers accordingly. This is explained in the next chapter on picking your back four.

But remember, also, that with an extra scoring criterion being added to the game this year (explained fully in Chapter 8) goalkeepers should become a more valuable commodity whose importance should not be overlooked.

Conclusion: Do not necessarily think you have to pick a goalkeeper from the top four sides, as you are limited to picking just two players from one club and you will probably find bigger points-scorers playing in different positions. Value for money should be your top priority in picking your goalkeeper. Look to spend around £3 million or £3.5 million and for your goalkeeper to earn somewhere in the 135–150-points bracket. If you spot an even cheaper keeper who is going to earn you more than 100 points, then snap him up. Check out the statistics section of this book for a list of the top Dream Team goalkeepers over the past six seasons.

CHAPTER 5

THE CASE FOR THE DEFENCE

NOW THAT WE'VE installed a safe pair of hands to guard our goal and give us a solid start, we need to find four reliable defenders to keep him company. Dream Team does not distinguish between full-backs or centre-backs as some Fantasy Football games do, so you can choose four central defenders if you like. In fact, you do not even have to know where in defence they actually play, although some knowledge about your potential new recruits will be a big help. Full-backs are generally preferred in games that reward points for assists, because they get forward more down the flanks to support the attacks and create goals from crosses. There can be lots of arguments over what is and is not an assist and, because we like to keep it simple, Dream Team players score nothing extra if they create a goal for a team-mate.

WHAT TO LOOK FOR

Plain and simple, you need defenders who play for teams who keep clean sheets. In recent seasons, this has generally meant the Big Four – Manchester United, Chelsea, Liverpool or Arsenal – with Chelsea and Liverpool being particularly mean when it comes to conceding goals. The Anfield club had a blip in 2004–05 when Rafa Benitez first took over, because the players were somewhat confused by the zonal marking system he introduced, but normal service was resumed in 2005–06, and the Koppites were equally impressive in 2006-07, as witnessed by the table below. It shows each team's defensive record in their 38 Premiership games. The 'GA' heading is how many goals in total they conceded and the numbers 0 to 7 show how many goals they conceded in each game. So Liverpool, for example, kept 20 clean sheets, let in one goal 11 times, two goals five times and three goals twice, making a grand total of 27. The number really to take note of, though, is the one in bold, titled Df Pts. With five points for a clean sheet and minus one for each goal apart from the first that a team concedes in a game, it calculates how many points a defender would have scored for his side if he had played for them in every Premiership match.

				Dream Team defensive records 2006/7							
Club	GA	0	1	2	3	4	5	6	7	DF Pts	MF Pts
MAN	27	16	17	5	0	0	0	0	0	75	32
CHE	24	22	8	8	0	0	0	0	0	102	44
LIV	27	20	11	5	2	0	0	0	0	91	40
ARS	35	12	20	4	1	1	0	0	0	51	24
TOT	54	6	19	5	7	1	0	0	0	8	12
EVE	36	14	16	5	2	1	0	0	0	58	28
BOL	52	12	12	7	3	3	1	0	0	34	24
REA	47	13	9	11	4	1	0	0	0	43	26
POR	42	12	16	5	4	1	0	0	0	44	24
BLA	54	8	16	8	4	1	0	1	0	16	16
AST	41	13	14	6	5	0	0	0	0	49	26
MID	49	9	15	9	4	1	0	0	0	25	18
NEW	47	7	16	14	1	0	0	0	0	19	14
MNC	44	14	12	6	4	2	0	0	0	50	28
WHM	59	9	13	9	2	4	0	1	0	15	18
FUL	60	7	15	7	6	2	1	0	0	6	14
WIG	59	10	10	7	9	2	0	0	0	19	20
SHU	55	9	11	11	6	1	0	0	0	19	18
CHA	60	11	6	13	5	2	1	0	0	22	22
WAT	59	9	11	9	6	3	0	0	0	15	18
SUN	47	17	17	7	4	1	0	0	0	67*	34*
BIR	42	18	19	5	3	1	0	0	0	76*	36*
DER	46	15	19	10	1	1	0	0	0	60*	30*

*Statistics relate to 2006-07 Championship season

So, not allowing for Dream Team ratings or bookings, Chelsea defenders would each have scored 102 points (22 clean sheets = 110, minus eight penalty points for goals conceded) and Liverpool 91. Fulham would have gone through the whole season and had six points to show for their efforts. Hardly worth turning up, was it, lads? And take a look at Tottenham. They managed to finish fifth in the Premiership despite leaking 54 goals and keeping just six clean sheets in 38 outings. The season before, with a fit Ledley King in central defence and Michael Carrick positioned in front of the back four they conceded just 38.

It should also be noted how quickly things can change from season to season. Portsmouth defenders scored a total of minus four points in 2005-06, but improved out of all recognition to register 44 points just 12 months later, due in no small part to the arrival of Sol Campbell in central defence and David James in goal.

The figures down the bottom show the Championship record of the two sides automatically promoted, Sunderland and Birmingham, and Derby, the winners of the playoff final at Wembley. Two things to note about these statistics (hence the asterisks); the Championship is a 46-game season, not 38, and it is a whole lot easier to keep clean sheets in the lower divisions. As we will see later, a general rule is to avoid picking defenders from newly promoted sides.

For those of you who can handle a few more numbers, here is a table showing the best Dream Team defences of the past five seasons. Dream Team points in the Premiership over the past five seasons, added together, again with five for a clean sheet and one away for every goal conceded in a match after the first one. Who comes out on top? The sides that normally fill the top four positions in the Premiership.

Dream Team's best defences							
	2006/7	2005/6	2004/5	2003/4	2002/3	2001/2	TOT
Chelsea	102	96	123	92	52	60	**525**
Liverpool	91	101	25	61	53	80	**411**
Man United	75	76	88	59	56	45	**399**
Arsenal	51	71	66	72	36	58	**354**
Everton	58	41	44	21	33	25	**222**
Blackburn	16	60	55	11	55	19	**216**
Aston Villa	49	27	30	42	27	27	**202**
Middlesbrough	25	20	36	42	34	39	**196**
Newcastle	19	48	5	42	46	22	**182**
Fulham	6	20	10	52	32	54	**174**
Bolton	34	57	26	22	27	4	**170**
Charlton	22	35	28	27	14	37	**163**
Man City	50	14	43	12	24	N/A	**143**
Tottenham	8	52	49	13	-4	17	**135**
Birmingham	N/A	28	28	50	25	N/A	**131**
West Ham	15	19	N/A	N/A	15	33	**82**
Portsmouth	44	-4	-1	16	N/A	N/A	**55**
Wigan	19	26	N/A	N/A	N/A	N/A	**45**
Sunderland	N/A	15	N/A	N/A	-3	31	**43**
West Brom	N/A	20	5	N/A	-3	N/A	**22**
Derby	N/A	N/A	N/A	N/A	N/A	3	**3**

But it's not quite as simple as that, because defenders don't come cheap nowadays, especially ones from the top teams: £8 million could have bought you John Terry and Wayne Bridge in 2003–04, both scored over 200 points and both were in the team of the season. Terry alone cost £8 million in 2006–07. So, once again, it's necessary to strike a balance between good players who are going to score you big points and value players who will not cost you a ransom but who can still tally somewhere in the region of 100–150 points. If you spot a potentially good defence, look to get two defenders or a goalkeeper and a defender in from the same club. That means you collect ten points every time their side keeps a clean sheet and your Dream Team will receive a great boost.

Whatever you do, you must steer clear of defenders from sides that you think will struggle for survival. The table below shows what defenders and goalkeepers would have scored playing every Premiership game in sides that were relegated at the end of the season. So if you were unfortunate enough to have a Leeds defender in your side in 2003–04, simply allowing for goals conceded and five points for a clean sheet, he would have netted -29 points had he played all 38 games. Just think, if you had doubled up and gone for two Leeds defenders, that's -58! Game over.

Points scored by relegated defences			
2006/07		**2005/06**	
Sheff United	19	Birmingham	28
Charlton	22	West Brom	20
Watford	15	Sunderland	-15
2004/05		**2003/04**	
Crystal P	16	Leicester	9
Norwich	-15	Leeds	-29
Soton	0	Wolves	-11

Don't think salvation lies ahead in plucking little-known defenders from sides that have been newly promoted out of the Championship, either. This next table shows the goals conceded by sides in the season they won promotion and the number they conceded the season after in their first year in the top flight. Only West Ham conceded fewer the following year, but generally (and not surprisingly) promoted sides leak more goals, and occasionally at an alarming rate. West Brom let in just 29 the year they won promotion in 2001–02, but let in 65 – more than double – the following year. Wolves and Leicester both conceded 77 goals in their one season in the Premiership, which led to negative returns for their defenders. Reading, head and shoulders the best team in the Championship in 2005-06, also adapted best to life up with the big boys, and even though they conceded almost 50 per cent more goals (47 compared to 32 the season before) some of their defenders represented excellent value for money in Dream Team terms.

Goals conceded by promoted sides		
	Championship	Premiership
Manchester City	52	54
WBA	29	65
Birmingham	49	49
Portsmouth	45	54
Leicester	40	65
Wolves	44	77
Norwich	39	77
WBA	42	61
Crystal Palace	61	62
Sunderland	41	69
Wigan	35	52
West Ham	56	55
Reading	32	47
Sheffield United	46	55
Watford	53	60

We are ruling out lots of possibilities here, but look on the bright side: if you do this, you will cut down on the number of defenders to choose from before selecting your final XI. But, having just laid down a golden rule not to pick defenders from promoted sides, I am just about to break it. Defenders from promoted sides are usually among the most cheaply priced in the game, often at £1 million or £1.5 million. So there may be bargains to be had and, if you feel the side in question is not going to have a total collapse, then it could be worthwhile taking one on, if they are on offer at a real bargain-basement price.

Check out the stats below on two West Ham defenders from 2005–06, their first year back in the Premiership. Hayden Mullins was priced at just £1 million and Danny Gabbidon was on offer at £1.5 million. West Ham's defence was not spectacularly good that year: Mullins let in 56 goals in 41 games in all competitions, but he played in almost every game, enjoyed a good cup run – though he missed the FA Cup final through suspension – and slowly accumulated points steadily throughout the season. It was not a spectacular return, but, as we will find out later, 89 points from a player available for £1 million is just the sort of return we are looking for.

– Hayden Mullins (West Ham) –

Achievement	Totals	Points
7+ ratings	21 (in 41 games)	63
Star Man	1	5
Goals	1	5
Clean sheets	9	45
Conceded	56	-24
Bookings	2	-2
Sent off	1	-3
	TOTAL POINTS	**89**

– Danny Gabbidon (West Ham) –

Achievement	Totals	Points
7+ ratings	21 (in 38 games)	63
Star Man	1	5
Goals	0	0
Clean sheets	10	50
Conceded	49	-21
Bookings	2	-2
Sent off	0	0
TOTAL POINTS		**95**

Every year, we calculate a Dream Team of the season, which is the absolutely best team you could have picked at the start of the season, not allowing for transfers. Goalkeepers and defenders for the last six seasons are listed below. It is interesting to note that, to strike a balance and fit everyone in, the top point-scorers of the season do not always make it into the best team because they are sometimes too expensive. Stephane Henchoz made the 2001–02 best team with 258 points, a fantastic total, but his central defensive colleague at Anfield, Sami Hyypia, actually finished as top defender with 279. Hyypia, though, was one of the two most expensive players of that season, costing £6 million, while Henchoz would only have set you back £4.5 million and the £1.5 million you saved there could have been better spent elsewhere. Also, look at the fact that these best-of-the-best teams are not choc-ful of top-price defenders. There are some good ones and some cheapies, though also remember that your budget went up to £50 million in 2006–07, previous teams listed below were when Dream Team managers had a paltry £40 million to spend. Also notice the doubling up we talked about: two from Liverpool in 2006-7, two from Blackburn in 2004–05, two from Chelsea in 2003–04, two from Aston Villa in 2002–03 and two from Liverpool again in 2001–02.

2006–07 team of the year (defences)				
Player	Club	Pos	Value	Pts
James	MCY	GK	3.0	145
Carragher	LIV	DEF	6.0	219
Toure	ARS	DEF	5.5	178
Agger	LIV	DEF	4.0	189
Lescott	EVE	DEF	2.0	135

2005–06 team of the year (defences)				
Player	Club	Pos	Value	Pts
Lehmann	ARS	GK	4.0	188
R Ferdinand	MANU	DEF	5.5	213
Hyypia	LIV	DEF	4.5	230
Mullins	WHM	DEF	1.0	94
Chimbonda	WIG	DEF	1.5	131

2004–05 team of the year (defences)				
Player	Club	Pos	Value	Pts
Friedel	BLA	GK	2.0	139
Terry	CHE	DEF	6.0	368
El Karkouri	CHA	DEF	1.5	114
Todd	BLA	DEF	2.0	147
Carragher	LIV	DEF	4.0	198

2003–04 team of the year (defences)				
Player	**Club**	**Pos**	**Value**	**Pts**
Howard	MANU	GK	2.5	136
Bernard	NEW	DEF	3.0	132
Mellberg	AST	DEF	3.5	133
Terry	CHE	DEF	4.0	249
Bridge	CHE	DEF	4.0	206

2002–03 team of the year (defences)				
Player	**Club**	**Pos**	**Value**	**Pts**
Robinson	LEE	GK	2.0	169
Barry	AST	DEF	2.0	180
Mellberg	AST	DEF	2.5	150
Geremi	MID	DEF	2.5	160
Gallas	CHE	DEF	3.5	200

2001–02 team of the year (defences)				
Player	**Club**	**Pos**	**Value**	**Pts**
Dudek	LIV	GK	4.5	230
Henchoz	LIV	DEF	4.5	258
Terry	CHE	DEF	2.5	214
Weir	EVE	DEF	2.5	167
Finnan	FUL	DEF	2.5	153

Check out the statistics section of this book for a list of the top Dream Team defenders over the past six seasons.

CHAPTER 6

THE MIDFIELD OF DREAMS

FOR A LONG time, midfielders were the poor relations in Dream Team. You had to pick a goalkeeper, even though they generally scored poorly, and you invested the big cash in your strikers and, to a lesser degree, your defence, because that is where you would find the really big points-scorers. Midfielders were the list you scoured last to hunt down the bargains to fill out the rest of your 11-man team. But now that midfielders are rewarded with two extra points if their team keeps a clean sheet, all that has changed. Playing a 4-4-2 formation (with four midfielders and two strikers) is now equally as good as a 4-3-3 (with three midfielders and three strikers) and, because they are priced more modestly on the whole, midfielders generally represent better value and you certainly get more for your money.

These should be at the top of the list of criteria you use when picking your three or four midfield generals:

1. Value.
2. Playing regularly (expected to feature in at least two-thirds of his side's matches).

3. Flair player who impresses the judges and collects frequent Star Man awards.

4. Goalscorer.

5. Playing for a team that keeps plenty of clean sheets.

6. Disciplinary record.

If your midfielder takes penalties and direct free-kicks, like Everton's Mikel Arteta and Cristiano Ronaldo of Manchester United, then that is a very welcome bonus as it should boost his goals and points tallies. But remember, there is nothing at all in Dream Team for an assist, so a flashy run down the wing, beating three players and putting the ball on the head of the centre-forward to score will earn your man nothing, only a plus from the *Sun* reporter when he comes to handing out the ratings at the end of the game. Here are the midfielders who featured in our team of the season from 2002–03 through to 2006–07.

2006–07 team of the year (midfielders)			
Player	Club	Value	Pts
Lampard	CHE	8.0	375
Ronaldo	MAN	5.0	314
Scholes	MAN	4.0	192

2005–06 team of the year (midfielders)			
Player	**Club**	**Value**	**Pts**
Bullard	WIG	1.0	124
Jarosik	CHE	1.0	116
Gerrard	LIV	6.0	309
Steven Davis	AST	2.5	153

2004–05 team of the year (midfielders)			
Player	**Club**	**Value**	**Pts**
Scholes	MAN	5.0	202
T Cahill	EVE	2.5	150
Lampard	CHE	6.5	342
Gravesen	EVE	2.5	122

2003–04 team of the year (midfielders)			
Player	**Club**	**Value**	**Pts**
Lampard	CHE	4.5	250
S W-Phillips	MNC	2.5	148
Nolan	BOL	2.5	135

2002–03 team of the year (midfielders)			
Player	**Club**	**Value**	**Pts**
Scholes	MAN	4.5	219
Murphy	LIV	4.0	193
Okocha	BOL	2.0	124

You will see that in 2005–06 there were two £1-million midfielders who both topped the century mark, representing outstanding value for money. The bargain buy of the season was Jimmy Bullard, who played for Wigan at the time: 124 points was an outstanding contribution and would have delighted any Dream Team manager. But, with all due respect to Jimmy, it is surprising to see how his points mounted up even though he was not particularly outstanding in any Dream Team category. Most of his points came from earning a mark of seven or better from the reporter in nearly two-thirds of his games. He only earned one man-of-the-match award in 42 outings and his total of four goals was not particularly special either. Wigan kept 12 clean sheets that season, again not particularly outstanding, to give Bullard another 24 points. What is most noteworthy is that he played 42 times and it was being a regular on the pitch and turning in solid, but not breathtaking, displays week in, week out, that saw his points total slowly mount up. You should look for players like Jimmy Bullard in your team.

– Jimmy Bullard (Wigan) –

Achievement	Totals	Points
7+ ratings	25 (in 42 games)	75
Star Man	1	5
Goals	4	20
Clean sheets	12	24
	TOTAL POINTS	**124**

Team-mate Graham Kavanagh was another bargain buy as a midfielder, also costing just £1 million. He managed 83 points even though he achieved a rating of seven or better in less than half of his games, lost a point for each of his nine bookings and failed to score a single goal!

– Graham Kavanagh (Wigan) –

Achievement	Totals	Points
7+ ratings	17 (in 42 games)	51
Star Man	3	15
Goals	0	0
Clean sheets	13	26
Bookings	9	-9
	TOTAL POINTS	**83**

The key to Kavanagh's success was that he was another one of the mainstays of the Wigan side, either from the start or off the bench, and with such a low price tag he could hardly put a foot wrong as long as he was in the first-team picture.

Midfield clean sheet points		
	CS	Points
Man Utd	16	32
Chelsea	22	44
Liverpool	20	40
Arsenal	12	24
Spurs	6	12
Everton	14	28
Bolton	12	24
Reading	13	26
Portsmouth	12	24
Blackburn	8	16
A Villa	13	26
Middlesbrough	9	18
Newcastle	7	14
Man City	14	28
West Ham	9	18
Fulham	7	14
Wigan	10	20
Sunderland	17	N/A
Birmingham	18	N/A
Derby	15	N/A

Remember that clean-sheet table we showed you in the section on defenders? Here it is again as it relates to midfielders. The men in the middle, remember, collect two points for each shutout, but do not lose points for goals conceded. So what do we note? Clean sheets are not really that big a factor for picking midfielders, more of a welcome bonus. Chelsea, one of the Premiership's best defences in 2006–07, kept 22 clean sheets in the top flight, which equates to 44 Dream Team points. But even a bottom-half-of-the-table side like Manchester City managed 14 clean sheets for 28 points, a difference of only 16 points on the season's champions. That deficit is not a big one among players scoring 200 points, but it becomes more crucial in the bargain end of the market, so you should give clean sheets more thought if you are shopping for a £1.5-million or £2-million midfielder you are hoping will get you around 120 points. Also use it as one of the deciding factors if you have two otherwise equally matched players and cannot choose between them: who do you think will play for the better team defensively? Remember, the clean-sheet totals for Sunderland, Birmingham and Derby relate to their promotion season from the Championship.

Check out the tables of the best-performing midfielders in recent years if you need any clues for your shortlist; for a list of the top Dream Team midfielders over the past six seasons check out the statistics section of this book.

CHAPTER 7

FORWARD PLANNING

TRADITIONALLY, STRIKERS HAVE been the biggest points-scorers in Fantasy Football, but the main problem is that you usually have to pay a higher price to pick them. Furthermore, if you pack your side with expensive forwards, it destroys the balance of the rest of your team and you are left with a comparatively small amount of your original budget to invest in other areas of the side.

So what to do? Although strikers are still a very important ingredient in the winning formula, they are not quite as vital as they once were. As we have already seen, since midfielders started scoring points for clean sheets in 2004–05, their total scores at the end of the season have risen dramatically, making them just as important a component as their forward partners and, generally, more generously priced.

If a bargain does not jump out at you as a third striker, then take a look in midfield, because this is where you tend to get more value for your Dream Team pounds and it could be worth plumping for 4-4-2 instead of 4-3-3.

Do not automatically think you have to go for the top-priced strikers to make your side a winner. You should look at perhaps landing a mid-range player in the £3.5–5million price bracket, who will fulfill one of our keys to Dream Team success: value for money. The 2004–05 team of the season (that's the highest-scoring team you could have picked within the budget available) featured two £4million stars – Jermain Defoe of Tottenham and Crystal Palace's Andrew Johnson – who each tallied around the 200-point mark. Here are the strikers that made our team of the season between 2003 and 2007, with Arsenal ace Henry featuring three times.

2006–07 team of the year (strikers)			
Player	Club	Value	Points
Drogba	CHE	4.5	318
Berbatov	TOT	4.5	255
McCarthy	BLA	3.5	215

2005–06 team of the year (strikers)			
Player	Club	Value	Points
Henry	ARS	8.0	343
D Bent	CHA	3.0	199

2004–05 team of the year (strikers)			
Player	Club	Value	Points
Defoe	TOT	4.0	201
A Johnson	CPA	4.0	175

2003–04 team of the year (strikers)			
Player	**Club**	**Value**	**Points**
Henry	ARS	7.5	393
Saha	FUL	3.0	183
Angel	AST	3.0	183

2002–03 team of the year (strikers)			
Player	**Club**	**Value**	**Points**
van Nistelrooy	MAN	7.0	359
Henry	ARS	6.5	335
Beattie	SOT	3.0	204

With five points on offer for a goal it is a no-brainer that your choices should be regular scorers, but the marks awarded by the *Sun* journalists can play a part as well. Wayne Rooney was hardly prolific in front of goal in 2005–06, but his all-action style of play caught the eye of the scribes and his Dream Team total was boosted by a host of Star Man awards and ratings of seven or better.

If you are short of cash, take a closer look at some of the Premiership's more threadbare squads. Fewer players means less squad rotation and more games for your selections, either because the squad is small in the first place or because the club in question is experiencing an injury crisis. And try and pick strikers who are clearly regarded as the best or second best in the position at their club. It is always tough making your mind up when you have a situation such as with Spurs in 2006–07 when Dimitar Berbatov, Defoe and Robbie Keane all produced generally excellent performances when selected by manager Martin Jol. But three into two will not go and, although the trio all performed well enough in Dream Team, their hauls could have been so much higher with less competition for places at White Hart Lane.

Ideally, you want proven goalscorers who have hit the target regularly over a number of seasons. Check out the statistics section of this book for a list of the top Dream Team strikers over the past six seasons, as well as the leading Premiership goalscorers.

CHAPTER 8

TIME TO PUT ON YOUR SUNDAY BEST

FOR SEVERAL YEARS now, scoring in Dream Team has remained largely unchanged, allowing participants to hone their managerial skills before, hopefully, arriving at a tried and tested recipe for success.

This season, however, things are slightly different.

For the first time in the history of the most popular Fantasy Football game in Britain, the *Sun's* sister newspaper, the *News of the World*, will have an input into Dream Team scoring.

Every Sunday throughout the football season, the *News of the World* will publish what it considers to be the best team from all the Premiership players who were in action the previous day.

One goalkeeper, one defender, one midfielder and one striker will each be awarded EIGHT points for being deemed the best at their position on the Saturday, as judged by the newspaper's journalists covering the matches and by its Sports Editor.

An 11-man team of the day will also be chosen, either in a 4-4-2 or 4-3-3 formation. In addition to the four star players already mentioned above, the other seven Premiership footballers picked in this side will collect TWO Dream Team points.

One thing to note here is that this team is only selected from the Saturday games. So if your player's club has no fixture, then he obviously will not be considered for the team of the day. It's something to think about.

The following table shows how many games each Premiership club played on a Saturday out of their total matches for the 2006/7 season, which as well as the league includes those in Europe and the two domestic cup competitions.

WHO PLAYED WHEN IN 2006/07			
Club	Tot games	Saturdays	Sat %
ARS	57	27	47%
AST	42	22	52%
BLA	53	22	42%
BOL	43	25	58%
CHA	43	25	58%
CHE	63	23	37%
EVE	42	23	55%
FUL	43	24	56%
LIV	55	26	47%
MAN	60	25	42%
MCY	44	22	50%
MID	47	30	64%
NEW	53	19	36%
POR	42	25	60%
REA	44	25	57%
SHE	41	30	73%
TOT	59	19	32%
WAT	46	29	63%
WHM	43	22	51%
WIG	40	23	58%
TOTAL	**960**	**486**	**51%**

Ok, so what information can we glean from this?

Let's look first at the teams that played the fewest games on a Saturday. Two in particular stand out: Tottenham and Newcastle did not even manage 20 matches.

The main reason? The UEFA Cup. Club sides involved in

the Champions League's poorer cousin tend to play their European games on a Thursday night. That means the Premier League switches these clubs' Premiership weekend fixtures to a Sunday to give their players extra time to rest. They may not arrive back in the UK until well into the early hours of Friday morning if they have been involved in an away game.

On the flip side of the coin, who saw the most action on a Saturday last season? Sheffield United and Middlesbrough both played 30 games and Watford 29.

Two of those sides ended up being relegated and one could speculate that perhaps the TV executives did not think these teams would attract enough viewers to switch their games as frequently to a Sunday, which is when many of the Premiership games are televised.

Partly because of a ruling from the European Commission, Sky Sports lost its exclusive rights to televising top-flight games from 2007/8. But even though rival Setanta successfully bid for two of the six packages available, you will see from the list below that the times and days earmarked for the live televised games should not be drastically affected. Here is how the deal, effective for three years up until the end of the 2009-10 season, breaks down:

Sky (92 matches a season)

Package A: 23 matches shown at 16:00 on Sunday
Package B: 23 matches shown at 13:30 on Sunday
Package E: 23 matches shown at 12:45 on Saturday
Package F: seven to 13 matches on midweek evenings or

Bank Holidays, 10 to 16 (making a total of 23) at 12:45 on Saturday and 16:00 on Sunday

Setanta (46 matches a season)
Package C: minimum of 12 matches at 20:00 on Monday, the rest (up to a total of 23) either at 13:30 on Sunday or 17:15 on Saturday or other times
Package D: minimum of 18 matches at 17:15 on Saturday, the rest (up to a total of 23) either at 13:30 on Sunday, 20:00 on Monday or other times

So it appears that nothing much will change for football fans, just the channel you turn to/have to subscribe to in order to get your fix of live Premiership action.

Back to the points scoring courtesy of the *News of the World*, then, what does in all mean for Dream Team? Here are a few statistics:

550 Dream Team Star Man awards were handed out in 2006/7 in games across the Premiership, the FA Cup, the League Cup and in Europe. Remember, players score five points for a Star Man and 99 per cent of the time are awarded a rating of seven or better, meaning they score an additional three points (a total of eight).

The *News of the World* will be allocating its equivalent of 'Star Man' points to four players (the best goalkeeper, defender, midfielder and striker) once a week for 38 weeks of the season, meaning, in effect, that it will be handing out 152 eight-point bonuses (38 weeks x 4 players) over the course of 2007/8, well under a third of the total of man-of-the-match awards players will receive from the *Sun*.

Some 2,736 players were allocated points by the *Sun* in 2006/7, while if the *News of the World* scoring system had been in place, an additional 418 players (a 15 per cent increase) would have garnered points.

And 24,818 points were earned by players in Dream Team last season. Had the *News of the World* scoring been in effect there would have been an extra 1,748 points available, boosting totals by just less than seven per cent.

It's all very well throwing numbers at you, but what's the bottom line?

Conclusion
The number of points available from the *News of the World* in proportion to the game as a whole is so relatively small that it should not affect your overall strategy unduly.

European games boost a player's total points considerably, as we will see in a later chapter. So do not ignore these players just because they might be playing more often on a Sunday as a result and not picking up as many points courtesy of the *News of the World*. Quite often players find it difficult to raise their game at the weekend following a big European match anyway and their performance suffers. And just as frequently the top sides can rest some of their big names on a Saturday to keep them fresh for a vital Champions League clash the following midweek.

Ian Preedy's Wot Not To Wear team won last season's £125,000 jackpot with 2,324 points. But because of the increased number of points on offer, players' total will increase across the board, meaning you will probably need a total approaching 2,500 to collect the big prize in 2007/8.

Because there are fewer goalkeepers to select from, their role in the game will become a little more important because they are more likely to collect the eight-point award on offer from the *News of the World*. It's only logical. Say there are six games on a Saturday, one of 12 goalkeepers will win the bonus, while the eight-pointer will go to one of 48 defenders.

CHAPTER 9

GET IN FORMATION: BUT IS
IT 4-4-2
OR 4-3-3?

AS WE HAVE seen in the rules, you can select one of two formations for your all-conquering Dream Team side, either 4-3-3 or 4-4-2. You always have to select one goalkeeper and four defenders, so the choice really boils down to: do you pick three strikers and three midfielders, or two strikers and four midfielders? This decision always used to be a no-brainer. Strikers traditionally got bags more points than midfielders and even if they cost more money you simply knew there had to be a freak occurrence for anyone picking a 4-4-2 formation to be in with a chance.

Times have changed, and it all boils down to a scoring change that was introduced ahead of the 2004–05 season, which recognised the work midfielders also do in defence and gave them two points for every clean sheet their team kept. With teams like Chelsea and Liverpool blanking opponents 20 or more times a season in the Premiership alone, this was a 40- or 50-point boost and it suddenly levelled the playing field. Check out the following table:

Year	Points	GK	DF	MD	ST	TOT
2002–03	100+	12	28	24	25	89
	200+	0	2	1	6	9
	300+	0	0	0	2	2
2003–04	100+	12	24	18	26	80
	200+	0	2	2	4	8
	300+	0	0	0	1	1
2004–05	100+	12	30	36	22	100
	200+	1	1	3	2	7
	300+	0	1	1	0	2
2005–06	100+	9	29	34	20	92
	200+	0	4	1	2	7
	300+	0	1	1	1	3
2006–07	100+	10	26	27	21	84
	200+	0	3	4	4	11
	300+	0	0	2	1	3

This is a season-by-season list from 2002 to 2007 showing how many players in each position have crossed the three thresholds of 100 points, 200 points and 300 points. To take 2002–03 as an example, there were 12 goalkeepers who scored 100 points or more out of a total of 89 Dream Team players who reached the mark, but no goalkeeper managed a score of 200 or better (that has only happened three times, Chelsea's Petr Cech was the last to do it in 2004–05, following the Liverpool pair of Sander Westerveld in 2000–01 and Jerzy Dudek the following season). The really interesting bit here, though, is when you compare midfielders and strikers. In 2002–03, 24 midfielders scored 100 or more points and 25 strikers managed the same feat. The strikers won hands down the following season, 26 to 18. But then came the rule change – two points for a midfield clean sheet – and suddenly it was hip to be in the centre of the park. Midfielders beat strikers hands down in 2004–05, 36 to 22, and it was the same story in 2005–06, where 34 midfielders made it to 100 points and only 20 strikers. They completed the hat-trick in 2006–07, coming out on top by 27 to 21.

So what do you draw from this? You no longer have to be worried over which formation you choose, either 4-4-2 or 4-3-3 should serve you equally well. If your side underperforms, it will not be the formation at fault, but your choice of personnel. Pick the players you want in your side first and then the formation that best allows you to include more of them. Midfielders generally tend to be slightly cheaper than forwards. But there are bargains to be had among the strikers as well, so don't rule out a 4-3-3 and, most importantly of all, when the transfer-window period comes around, remember that you don't have to stick with the formation you picked when you originally entered your team. If you set out with a 4-3-3, there's nothing stopping you from bringing in a midfielder for one of your underachieving strikers and switching to a 4-4-2.

CHAPTER 10

IN A LEAGUE OF YOUR OWN

ONE OF THE best innovations in Fantasy Football over the past few seasons has been the advent of the Mini-League. If you've never taken the plunge before, this means that, as well as competing against the half-a-million-plus other managers bidding to win the main game, your team can also be entered into a separate league involving just you and your buddies. You can have a little wager with your mates as to who will finish top of the league and it keeps the game interesting from the first week of the season to the last.

Come April, we can't all be in with a chance of landing the Dream Team first prize, but there should always be something to play for in the Mini-League, whether it is to finish top, beat your boss or simply to haul yourself off the bottom of the table and avoid a summer of jibes or insulting emails asking whether you will be entering the Championship version of Dream Team after your relegation from the top flight. (Note for Dream Team virgins: there is no such game, currently.)

As well as the fun factor, there are some very good prizes on offer for magnificent Mini-Leagues as well. At the end of the 2006–07 season, the manager who set up the best-performing Mini-League walked away with a tasty £4,000 to share as he or she saw fit. The end-of-game Mini-League prize is given to the creator of the Mini-League whose average score is the highest at the end of the season: this is calculated by adding the total scores of every team in the league and dividing that figure by the total number of teams. The runner-up in the final Mini-League table collected £2,000 and the third-placed Mini-League creator £1,200, with £750 for fourth and £300 for fifth. Between August and April, there was also a £1,000 monthly prize awarded to the Mini-League whose teams had the highest points average over the course of the previous month.

There are a couple of things to bear in mind. You must have five or more teams in a Mini-League for it to qualify for a prize and the maximum number of teams allowed in one league is 2,500. You can check how you are doing in your Mini-League at any time, by simply going to the website, www.dreamteamfc.com, keying in your username and password and clicking on the 'My Mini-League' button. There's your team highlighted with its position in the table for everyone to see. The other thing is that to qualify for prizes the teams all have to be entered by different managers and they must all be different. Duplicate entries (teams or managers) can invalidate your Mini-League and render you disqualified from collecting a prize.

HOW DO I SET UP A MINI-LEAGUE?

After you have registered a team, log in with your username and password or 12-digit PIN number. On the 'My Team' page click on the 'Create Mini-League' link. You will then be taken through the simple process of setting up your own Mini-League. You will be asked to input a name for your Mini-League and a password, which will be accepted as long as it's clean and hasn't already been taken. Your team will immediately be entered into your Mini-League and you will have the opportunity to invite others to join it.

HOW DO I INVITE OTHERS TO JOIN MY MINI-LEAGUE?

If you supply Dream Team with the names and email addresses of your friends or colleagues, they will automatically be invited to register a team or teams and then join your Mini-League. They will be sent your league name and password, or you can also give your league name and password to your friends as well. Or, if you like, you can register teams on their behalf and then enter them into your Mini-League.

HOW DO I JOIN A MINI-LEAGUE THAT HAS ALREADY BEEN SET UP?

First register a team or teams. Then log in with your username and password or 12-digit PIN number. On the 'My Team' page click on the 'Join Mini-League' link. You will then be prompted to enter the league name and password to the Mini-League you want to join.

WHEN IS THE LAST CHANCE TO SET UP OR JOIN A MINI-LEAGUE?

You can set up or join a Mini-League at any time up until registration closes, which is generally four weeks after the start of the season, the same time as the Golden Gamble finishes.

CHAPTER 11

THE GOLDEN GAMBLE

TO MAXIMISE YOUR points-scoring potential you should enter your team before the start of the season. But for the latecomers – and for those who like a little more excitement – there is a Golden Gamble option, which allows you to enter the competition up to three weeks after the Premiership campaign is under way.

So, if your star striker gets injured on the opening day of the season and is ruled out for the next six months, the Golden Gamble is there for you.

Another advantage of taking the Golden Gamble is that it allows Dream Team bosses to wait until the Premiership transfer window has closed at the end of August, so they get the advantage of picking up the last-minute big-name players that clubs who are desperate to strengthen often sign in what is their last chance before January. Late transfers can also throw your careful planning into turmoil, for instance, if a side buys a big-name striker, then suddenly the bloke you have in your team goes from being a certain first choice to spending most of the season on the bench. And you may find that, although you rate the player you picked, his manager does not and leaves him on the sidelines. A Golden Gamble is there to get you out of this jam.

Note, though, that your team only starts scoring points from the first match of the Saturday *after* you have entered it. You do not gain points for matches already played. And if you enter, say, on a Tuesday morning and there are games on the Tuesday and Wednesday evenings, these will *not* count towards your score. You will miss points-scoring opportunities and you should know what they are before taking a late plunge.

The Premiership season does not always kick off in the same weekend in August, but here is how taking the Golden Gamble would have affected you in 2006–07, which started on 19 August:

Enter up to one week late: Ten games on the first weekend of the Premiership season, plus eight games the following midweek (there is not a full midweek league programme because two teams are generally in action in the third qualifying round of the Champions League, trying to reach the lucrative group stages. These Euro qualifiers do *not* count for Dream Team).

Matches missed: 18

Rough estimate of points lost: 40–60

Comments: Although it is a fair head start, past winners have come back from far bigger deficits to take the Dream Team title.

Enter up to two weeks late: Ten games on the second weekend of the Premiership season, but no midweek matches.

Matches missed: 28

Rough estimate of points lost: 70–100

Comments: Not an insurmountable obstacle, but we are starting to get into the realms of unlikely if you gift your opponents a 100-point-plus start.

Enter up to three weeks late: No additional Premiership matches because of international fixtures.

Comments: No additional games missed, no more points lost, with the position exactly the same as the previous week.

Enter up to four weeks late: Ten games on the fourth weekend of the Premiership season, with midweek matches for four Premiership teams in the Champions League and five more in the UEFA Cup, all counting towards Dream Team totals.

Matches missed: 47

Rough estimate of points lost: 120–160

Comments: Time to concentrate on the monthly and weekly prizes.

Note: The 2005–06 season was a little different. It kicked off a week earlier, so the first midweek matches and the Champions League qualifiers took place after clubs had played two weekend games. This also meant that a Premiership break for international matches came on the fourth Saturday of the season instead of the third as it did in 2006–07.

Golden Gamble is like giving everyone a head start – it's always worth doing with the *Sun* game because there are tasty monthly prizes, but there comes a point when it doesn't make sense if you're looking to win the whole thing because you are already too far behind.

CHAPTER 12

TRANSFERS: A WINDOW OF OPPORTUNITY

THE GREAT THING about Dream Team, unlike the Premiership, is that none of your players will hand in a transfer request. You, the manager, are in total control of your team. If one of your players leaves, it is because *you* want him out because you think he has not lived up to your expectations, not because he thinks the grass is greener elsewhere.

Most of our winners will tell you: if you want to triumph in Dream Team, the transfer windows are absolutely crucial, because this is where the game is won and lost. There has been the odd exception, most notably in recent years courtesy of Dream Team 2003 winner John Bell, a serviceman in the RAF who was posted to the Falkland Islands for five months and forgot his PIN, therefore making it impossible for him to change his team. On that occasion, John's starting XI was so good it lasted the pace.

For the rest of us mere mortals, however, two transfer-window periods are available which allow us to cover up for those costly spur-of-the-moment decisions, or even just plain bad luck. Players can get injured, lose form or find themselves out of the picture if their side gets off to a bad start to the season or if a new boss comes in who has a different philosophy and different favourites.

Every manager in the Premiership makes player personnel mistakes at times and it is the same in Dream Team. What is important is that you make more good choices than bad ones. The earlier you make the good ones – and the more of them you make – determines whether or not you are in contention. If things do not start out well in August and September, be patient. Console yourself with the thought that picking the perfect team from the start is a rare exception and always will be. That's why the transfer windows are there: to strengthen your side and get it back on track.

As you will see later in our section on the Dream Team winners, the 2006 champ Chris Marshall picked Bradley Wright-Phillips and Anthony le Tallec in his original selection. The pair had amassed a grand total of 14 points combined by the start of the first transfer window, with Chelsea star Shaun's younger brother hardly getting a game early in the season and failing to trouble the scorers. Yet, even though Chris was nowhere to be seen on the leaderboard come October, he made some smart moves at the first window and gradually turned things round, further strengthening his position when the second transfer window came around and ultimately finishing up with a side that netted him a cool £125,000.

There are *two* transfer windows in Dream Team: one in early October and the other at the end of January. This allows you two chances to change one, two or three of your players who are not performing. Of course, if things are going well, you can opt to keep your team as it is. At all times after making the transfers, your team must again conform to the three simple rules: it can cost no more than £50 million, it can have no more than two players from the same Premiership club and it must conform to either a 4-3-3 or a 4-4-2 formation.

Players only start scoring points for your side after they have joined your team; you do not get the points they had already accumulated and, similarly, you get to keep the points of those underperformers you have discarded up to the point that they are given their P45s.

Should you bother paying your £1.50 and making transfers even if it appears you are out of contention? Absolutely. It could turn you into a winner like Chris Marshall, and there are examples of players who have finished in the top ten of Dream Team who would have scooped the big prize had they made changes. But, even if it does not net you the ultimate title, the monthly and weekly prizes are still worth winning in their own right. There was a £3,000 prize on offer to every monthly winner in 2006–07 and £750 for the runner-up, together with a £1,000 cheque for the weekly winner. And then there's the glory of beating your mates in your Mini-League (or should we say avoiding the humiliating experience of finishing bottom!).

These are the things you should consider before each transfer window:

BEFORE THE FIRST TRANSFER WINDOW

1. How many of your players are no longer playing in the Premiership?

Some of your selections could have been farmed out on loan to the lower leagues or moved on altogether.

2. How many of your players are injured and unlikely to play much again before the next transfer window at the end of January?

Ditch the crocks first if they are likely to be sidelined for any length of time. But be more patient with the more expensive players in your line-up – such as Wayne Rooney or Frank Lampard – because you might have to waste a transfer bringing them back into your line-up come the second transfer window.

3. How many of your players are not first choice at their club and is the situation likely to change?

If it was something you considered at the start of the season and you still back your man to win through, then stay put. But if someone was brought in after the start of the season whom you had not bargained on and who has been setting the Premiership alight, is your player likely to see much action? If the answer is 'probably not', then it is time to make a change.

4. Are your defenders earning points for you or do you find they are playing in sides that have been unexpectedly leaking goals?

As we have seen, the Big Four sides generally have solid defences and you can count on them to sort things out even if they have the odd blip. But, as for the rest, if things are not turning out as planned then it could be time to make a switch. Spurs kept 13 clean sheets in 2005–06, but struggled spectacularly to replicate that kind of form the following season, shutting out opponents just six times in 38 games, the worst in the Premiership. Even relegated Sheffield United, Charlton and Watford fared better than the White Hart Lane club and it is certainly something manager Martin Jol will be looking to address ahead of 2007-08. By contrast, Portsmouth – who conceded 62 goals in 2005–06 – let in just 42 in 2006–07 campaign, helped by the additions of Sol Campbell, goalkeeper David James, the team's player of the season, and the on-loan Glen Johnson to their backline.

5. How many of your players are still playing in Europe?

European football, as we have already seen, gives a terrific boost to your players' points-scoring potential. Your players get extra games and, therefore, a chance to score extra points. Take a look at the table below: it shows you how many matches a snapshot of the teams in the Premiership played in 2005–06. The top four sides were in the Champions League, Bolton and Middlesbrough were in the UEFA Cup – Boro reached the final – and Sunderland and Portsmouth were not in Europe and did poorly in both the League and FA Cups. The rows are split into games up to the first Dream Team transfer window 'up to T1'; 'T1-T2' is the number of matches between the first and second transfer windows and 'T2 to end', as you may have guessed, is the number of matches each team played between the second Dream Team transfer window and the end of the season.

The number in brackets shows how many of those games were in the Premiership. Arsenal, for example, played 27 games between the first and second transfer windows, 16 of them in the Premiership. Two things to note here are: look at the difference in how many games played between the teams who were in Europe and the ones that weren't. Champions League finalists Arsenal played 58. Middlesbrough (UEFA Cup finalists and semi-finalists in the FA Cup) played 64! Compare that to Sunderland, who played 42 games and Portsmouth (only 41). That is half as many games again.

The second thing to note is which part of the season these games arrive. Up to the October transfer window there is no difference in the number of matches played by teams in Europe and the also-rans. They all played a total of eight, nine or ten games (Arsenal and Liverpool played fewer league games because they had to take part in a qualifying round in the Champions League). But the period between the first and second transfer windows is the most crucial. Middlesbrough played 32 games, Manchester United 29 and Arsenal 27, while Sunderland and Pompey played just 18. It was the same again between the second transfer window and the end of the season, though the difference was not quite as marked. Manchester United's games' total tailed off because they finished bottom of their Champions League group and did not even have the consolation of a place in the UEFA Cup. OK, so what's the conclusion?

Get players from teams playing in Europe (Champions League or UEFA Cup - it does not really matter at this stage) and get them in your side in the first transfer window in particular, because they are going to be playing loads of games.

GAMES PLAYED 2005–06				
Club	**Up to T1**	**T1–T2**	**T2 to end**	**TOT**
Arsenal	9 (7 Prem)	27 (16)	22 (15)	58 (38)
Chelsea	10 (8)	23 (16)	20 (14)	53 (38)
Liverpool	8 (6)	23 (16)	22 (16)	53 (38)
Man United	9 (7)	29 (17)	16 (14)	54 (38)
Club	**Up to T1**	**T1–T2**	**T2 to end**	**TOT**
Bolton	10 (8)	23 (14)	20 (14)	53 (38)
Boro	10 (8)	32 (18)	22 (12)	64 (38)
Sunderland	9 (8)	18 (15)	15 (15)	42 (38)
Portsmouth	9 (8)	18 (16)	14 (14)	41 (38)

When the first transfer window arrives you already know which English clubs have made it through to the group stages of the UEFA Cup. They have generally played one of their four group games but are guaranteed at least three more, with a better-than-even chance of continuing on to the knockout stages. Conversely, if an English team has gone out early, like West Ham did in 2006–07, you may want to reassess how highly you value holding on to their players. English teams in the Champions League have generally played two of their six group games, so it's too early to make a call about offloading anybody, but with four more European games to go for these sides before the next transfer window, it could be worth trying to sneak an extra Champions League player in, if you have the budget to do so and if it is not going to destroy the balance of your team.

6. Are your players underperforming?

If you are in the enviable position of not having to ditch your duffers because they are injured or because they have lost their place in the team, you will still have some interesting choices to make. Now it's a case of deciding whether your 11 players are all performing as you hoped they would. Come the first transfer window especially, there are not an awful lot of points separating the players: the average players will be in the 20s or 30s and even the leaders might only be in the 50s or 60s. Having said that, Frank Lampard had already clocked up 81 points by the first transfer window in 2005–06, more than many midfielders score in a season. It was obvious he was on for another bumper season if he stayed fit. So how do you gauge whether or not your players are meeting your expectations? Your team as a whole might be underperforming, but, if your £2-million bargain-basement player has 20 points at the first transfer window and your £8-million star striker has 35, which is doing worse? If only there was a little table to show how many points you could expect your players to end up with if they kept playing at their current levels. A table, eh? Well this might do the trick...

CLUBS IN EUROPE			CLUBS NOT IN EUROPE		
End	T1	T2	End	T1	T2
60	11	41	60	14	39
80	14	54	80	18	52
100	18	68	100	23	65
120	22	82	120	27	78
140	25	95	140	32	91
160	29	109	160	36	104
180	32	122	180	41	117
200	36	136	200	45	130
220	40	150	220	50	143
240	43	163	240	54	156
260	47	177	260	59	169
280	50	190	280	63	182
300	54	204	300	68	195
320	58	218	320	72	208
340	61	231	340	77	221
360	65	245	360	81	234
380	68	258	380	86	247
400	72	272	400	90	260

And now an explanation. There are two tables here, side by side. The one on the left is for players still involved in European action come the first transfer window. It is based on an assumption that they will play 50 games in a season in all competitions. The one on the right (assuming a 40-game campaign in all competitions) is for players who have no European football to look forward to. Column one, entitled 'End', shows the number of points you were hoping your player would reach at the end of the season. Column two, titled 'T1', shows how many points the player should have by the start of the first transfer window if he is on course to hit that target. 'T2' is the same for the second transfer window. Because players not featuring in Europe do not play as many games, they need to score more points each match and get off to a quicker start, because they do not have Champions League or UEFA Cup games to boost their totals.

As discussed in chapter 15, 'Points per Million', ideally you want your players to score 50 points for each million of their Dream Team value (so a £2-million player = 100 points, a £4-million player = 200 points, etc.). So, if you take your £4-million player (Liverpool's Steve Finnan in 2005–06), what do you expect him to score? Answer: 200 points (4 x 50 points). Is he still in European action? Answer: yes. Therefore, look down the table on the left, look down the End column until you find his hoped-for total, 200, and look across to find that, to be totally happy, I would want Finnan to be on 36 points by the time the first transfer window comes around, and on 136 at the second.

Please don't make your transfer decisions determined solely by these tables. They are simply there for guidance and, like those financial ads on the TV, past performance is no guide to future results. Players have peaks and troughs of form during the season and can suddenly catch fire. It's spotting these stars who hit form just before the transfer window opens and bringing them in that is key to your success. We've said it before, but remember that, if your player has the pedigree and a proven points-scoring record in

Dream Team, the odds are that, if he is fit, he will come good again. Patience, patience.

7. Did you overlook someone at the start of the season?

Envy is a terrible thing. It is one of the seven deadly sins. It cost Gwyneth Paltrow dearly, you may remember, if you ever saw that excellent 1995 movie *Se7en*, with Brad Pitt and Morgan Freeman. As a well-balanced, cool, calm and calculating Dream Team manager, you must not lose your head and let envy rule your thinking. Just because some players have got off to a fast start and are leaving yours for dust does not mean they will continue scoring in the same vein. Stubbornness, however, may not be up there with greed, wrath or gluttony, but it can also be a deadly sin for a Dream Team manager. Take an impassioned view of your team at the first transfer window. Have you overlooked someone who is setting the Premiership alight? Is one of the players you had on your shortlist but who missed your final XI performing as well as you worried he might? That's what the window is there for: to allow you to admit to your mistakes and correct them. Just make sure you consider all the factors you covered when you originally picked your starting side to justify it as a calculated choice rather than just a knee-jerk reaction.

8. Don't forget you can change formation

You can have four defenders, four midfielders and two strikers or four defenders, three midfielders and three strikers. And just because you started the season with a 4-3-3 formation does not mean that you have to stay that way: you can always bring in a midfielder for one of your strikers and change to a 4-4-2, or vice versa, if that would fit your masterplan better.

BEFORE THE SECOND TRANSFER WINDOW

Consider all the points made above for moves in the first transfer window, then take into account a couple more:

1. Leading points-scorer bonus

There is a 20-point bonus to the Dream Team player who finishes the season with the most points. Is it crystal clear who this is going to be? Is he fit and likely to keep scoring heavily for the rest of the season? Can you get him into your team? Will it wreck the rest of your side if you do so? If the answer to these four questions, in order, is Yes, Yes, Yes, and No, then go for it and make the move.

2. Transfer-window bargains

The second Dream Team transfer window generally spans a week covering the end of January and the start of February, so it also arrives at the end of the real-life transfer window in the Premiership. That means players moving clubs, with many going out on loan to lower-league sides and an influx of new blood bought in by managers desperate to keep their jobs and retain their club's Premiership status. What it means for you is potential bargains. For some reason, players brought into the game at the second transfer window often provide real value for money. Two international-class strikers in John Carew and Vicenzo Montella were available at £2 million and £3 million, respectively, come the second transfer window in 2006–07. At face value, both were good buys, but both had come from abroad and were unproven in the Premiership and Carew had been dogged by injuries in recent seasons.

3. How are your rivals getting on?

If you are in the running for one of the major prizes, then it is worth scouting the opposition and seeing who they have in their team before making your final transfer moves. Where are your rivals stronger and who can you bring in to close the gap or keep them at bay are questions you will have to consider. Obviously, you cannot see the transfer moves your opponents have made until the window is officially shut and it is game on again. Remember, though, not to throw out the philosophy that got you into a good position in the first place. Rash, desperate moves are for people not in the running who are taking a gamble to get there because they have nothing to lose. People already sitting in the cash-prize positions should be more rational in their thinking.

It's the same in your Mini-League, only on a smaller scale. You might only have a fiver or maybe £50 riding on it, but if you are on the outside looking in your moves should be more imaginative and bolder unless you have been closing the gap over recent weeks and months.

ONE FINAL, GENERAL POINT

Remember you can bring in none, one, two or three players in each of the two transfer windows. If you are planning to make more than one change, then when you think you have made your choices, don't consider them one by one, but as a block and see which is going to earn you the most points. Say you were playing a 4-3-3 formation and were going to get rid of strikers Wayne Rooney and Francis Jeffers and defender Zat Knight in the second transfer window: Rooney because you wanted to chase the 20-point bonus available to the top points-scoring player and the other two because they had had disappointing seasons. Write down the values of the players you are planning to jettison and how many points you think they will score for you between February and May (see the table on the following page).

Your initial plan was to bring in Thierry Henry because he always goes goal-crazy in the final third of the season, and change to a 4-4-2, plumping for Antoine Sibierski because Newcastle were still in the UEFA Cup where he had been a frequent scorer, and Joleon Lescott because he had been sound all season for an Everton defence that does not concede many goals. Not bad – you guess they will score you 190 points in the final third of the season, almost double your estimate of 105 for the players that you originally had in your team.

But wait, you can do even better. Swapping to a 4-2-2 formation again you could bring in the ridiculously cheap Didier Drobga, along with Manchester United's free-scoring midfielder Cristiano Ronaldo. And Gael Clichy had been playing often in Arsenal's backline since Ashley Cole left for Chelsea. You've got three players who still have European competition to look forward to and you think their points total will surpass even what had been an impressive-looking trio of Henry-

Sibierski-Lescott. Suddenly, the winning combination is clear to you and you go to www.dreamteamfc.com to make some very confident changes.

Rooney	Jeffers	Knight	Total
£8.0m	£2.0m	£2.0m	£12.0m
90	5	10	105

Henry	Sibierski	Lescott	Total
£8.0m	£2.0m	£2.0m	£12.0m
120	35	35	190

Drogba	Ronaldo	Clichy	Total
£4.5m	£5.0m	£2.5m	£12.0m
110	100	40	250

TIMING IS EVERYTHING

Leave your transfer changes as late as you can, say until the day before the window is due to close. That way you can be sure to check that none of your intended choices has collected an injury, either in the final round of matches or in training. Don't leave it too late, though. Tens of thousands of people are trying to make their changes at the same time in the run-up to the closure of the transfer window, so save yourself the hassle and do it a day early to make sure you register your moves.

CHAPTER 13

A TRIBUTE TO KING HENRY THE FIRST

DREAM TEAM IS going to feel more than a little strange this year, almost as if we have lost a much-loved and respected friend of the family. The reason is that, for the first time since the 1998-99 season, there will be no Thierry Henry for managers to select from the player list. Henry, if you have been on Mars these past few months and missed the news, signed for Barcelona in a stunning £16million switch at the end of June 2007 that left Arsene Wenger and 500,000 Dream Team managers shaking their heads in disbelief.

When the news first broke of his imminent departure Sky Sports rolled out the clips of all those wonder-goals he scored during his time in the Premiership, leaving you in awe of a player who could do just about anything he put his mind to. Volleys from outside the area, mesmerising dribbles past whole defences from the halfway line, curling shots with the outside of his foot, deft back-heels through opponents' legs – it was a highlight reel that among players who have graced the Premiership, perhaps only Eric Cantona could get close to.

If ever there was a Dream Team Star Man, the mercurial Frenchman was it.

Henry's scoring statistics while in England were incredible, and it was just the same in Fantasy Football, where he was a Dream Team points-accumulating machine. Just check out the table below.

– THIERRY HENRY FACTOR –

Year	Points	Striker ranking	Overall ranking
1999–2000	153	9	13
2000–01	212	4	=9
2001–02	293	2	2
2002–03	335	2	2
2003–04	393	1	1
2004–05	279	1	3
2005–06	343	1	1
2006–07	113	16=	64=

The French international was simply a scoring phenomenon after arriving at what was then Highbury following an unhappy and brief spell in Italy with Juventus.

Henry took a little time to adapt to his new role of central striker under Arsene Wenger, but went on to buck one of our golden rules: don't pick a foreigner in his first season.

It took him eight games to break his scoring duck in the Premiership and 17 games into his first season he had only two goals to his credit, one of those against Swedish minnows AIK Solna in the European Cup.

Once he found his feet, however, Henry was unstoppable.

Listed below is his goalscoring record, with the number of games played in brackets:

Season	League	Europe	FA Cup	League Cup	TOTAL
1999–00	17 (31)	8 (11)	0 (3)	1 (2)	26 (47)
2000–01	17 (35)	4 (14)	1 (4)	0 (0)	22 (53)
2001–02	24 (25)	7 (7)	1 (5)	0 (0)	32 (37)
2002–03	24 (37)	7 (12)	1 (5)	0 (0)	32 (54)
2003–04	30 (37)	5 (10)	3 (3)	0 (0)	38 (50)
2004–05	25 (32)	5 (8)	0 (1)	0 (0)	30 (41)
2005–06	27 (32)	5 (11)	0 (0)	1 (1)	33 (44)
2006–07	10 (17)	1 (7)	1 (3)	0 (0)	12 (27)
TOTALS	**174 (246)**	**42 (80)**	**7 (24)**	**2 (3)**	**225 (353)**

Goals in every Fantasy Football game ever invented translate into points. In Dream Team, when you bag them by the bucket-load like Monsieur Henry, they also get you much more besides: ratings of seven-plus from the Dream Team reporters and more than your fair share of Star Man awards, too.

Henry also set a single season Dream Team points-scoring record back in 2003–04 when he piled up a mind-boggling total of 393, more than some DT bosses manage in a season with 11 players at their disposal. It's a record that will take some beating. His month-by-month totals are listed below.

THE RECORD-BREAKER	
Month	**Pts scored**
August	29
September	23
October	26
November	53
December	29
January	44
February	45
March	47
April	67
May	30
2003–04 TOTAL	**393**

Four of the five winners between 2002 and 2006 had Henry in their side. The exception, Gary Utting, had the Chelsea duo of Frank Lampard and John Terry instead and both of those players outscored the Frenchman that particular season.

– HOORAY FOR HENRY –

Year	Winner	Thierry?
2007	Ian Preedy	No
2006	Chris Marshall	Yes
2005	Gary Utting	No
2004	Michael Bayliss	Yes
2003	John Bell	Yes
2002	Christopher Hartley	Yes
2001	Danny Rofe	No
2000	Terry Gridley	No

For many Dream Team managers Thierry Henry was an automatic choice and the first name on their teamsheet, something they had done without question and fear of contradiction over the past seven seasons.

Those managers who risked omitting him from their side were nervously looking over their shoulder for the second half of the season, waiting for Henry to hit that red-hot streak that brought his customary avalanche of points. Bosses no longer need have that fear, instead they are left with the not-inconsiderable poser of who, if anyone, can be the next Thierry Henry. The nearest we have in terms of points-scoring potential is probably Wayne Rooney, but whether the Manchester United ace can ever match Henry's strike rate is open to question. Didier Drogba enjoyed a magnificent season in 2006-07, but can the Ivory Coast international reproduce that kind of form year in, year out, for the better part of a decade?

So what does Henry's departure mean? In a nutshell, that the game of Dream Team will be more wide open and more challenging than ever.

CHAPTER 14

THE FOREIGN LEGION

EVERY SIDE HAS had them – the players from abroad that a manager stakes his career on and who generally leave him both sorely disappointed and out of a job. They look unbeatable in continental Europe, but for some reason they fail to settle in the Premiership and end up being expensive misfits who generally do not last very long.

If you ever bump into a Leeds fan, a sure-fire way to wind him up is to ask about Thomas Brolin. He was one of the top marksmen in European football before his arrival at Elland Road, but the Swedish international failed to discover anything approaching his best form and became an overweight figure of fun to many opposition fans. It was hard to imagine that this was the same player who, only a year earlier, had been named in the team of the tournament at the 1994 World Cup.

The good news for Dream Team managers is that Brolin arrived in English football in mid-season and never made it into the game, but there are numerous cases each year of foreign imports who have driven Fantasy Football bosses to despair. Let me throw a few more names at you: Bosko Balaban, Diego Forlan, Steve Marlet, Albert Luque, Sergei Rebrov, Fernando Morientes, Juan Veron, Jordi Cruyff, Andriy Shevchenko and Jared Borgetti.

Still not convinced? How about we look back a little further at some of the other imports who singularly failed to make a mark on the Premiership:

William Prunier: French centre-back who played two games for Manchester United before being deemed surplus to requirements.

Stephane Guivarc'h: French World Cup-winning striker who cost Newcastle's Kenny Dalglish £3.5 million and scored just once before moving to Rangers.

Daniel Cordone and Christian Bassedas: Newcastle's answer to Ossie Ardiles and Ricky Villa, but the Argentinean duo flopped on Tyneside at the turn of the century.

Yoshikatsu Kawaguchi: Played in goal for Japan in the 2002 World Cup, but failed to make an impact at Fratton Park.

Massimo Taibi: Another goalkeeping catastrophe. Taibi was the Manchester United keeper who somehow let Matt le Tissier's weak shot sneak through his legs for one of the all-time comic goals at Old Trafford, proving in one fell swoop that he was not the answer as a long-term replacement to the legendary Peter Schmeichel.

Ali Dia: This one is my favourite. Purported to be a Senegal international (he was no such thing), Dia was signed by Southampton in 1996 partly on the recommendation of a man who phoned them up pretending to be World Footballer of the Year George Weah. He came on for his one and only appearance at Leeds, where he played 53 minutes as a substitute before being replaced himself and was released 14 days later. After a failed spell at non-league Gateshead, he disappeared into oblivion.

Foreign imports. In a word: **beware!**

We could carry on and make a list ten times the length of the one above, I am sure. All those mentioned are either world-class players or have shown themselves capable of playing at the highest level. All were far from impressive in English football, though you feel in Andriy Shevchenko's case that a man of his calibre has the ability to turn things around. But any manager who invested his or her Dream Team millions in the Foreign Legion above would have been left sorely disappointed.

Foreign players can and do adapt to the English game, but you need to give them time to do so. Didier Drogba might have got 12 Premiership goals in his first season, but he missed a bucket-load more and ended up with a very modest 115 Dream Team points, that's less than his Chelsea team-mate Hernan Crespo. I'm not saying, do not pick foreign players in their first season, just do not pick them in your original team.

Teams have played nine or ten games before the first Dream Team transfer window opens in October, which is plenty of time to run the rule over them and decide whether or not to take the plunge. If they are going well, they will have 40 or 50 points by then, whereas, if your alternative choice is performing poorly, he might have 20 or so and you are 20 points worse off than you might have been. But, if your instincts are proved correct, then you will not have to bother wasting one of your October transfers to undo the damage.

Tottenham's Jurgen Klinsmann and Tony Yeboah of Leeds were two early imports to prove you could do it in your first season in England. Ruud van Nistelrooy scored 23 Premiership goals in his first season and finished as Dream Team champion points-scorer with 329. With only one transfer window mid-season back in 2001–02, you would have been sick had you missed the boat and waited to see if he was going to settle. These days it is different: you can jump on the bandwagon in October and you are still very much in the running.

The 2006–07 season bucked the trend for foreign stars making a mark in their first campaign, with more of them than usual proving a hit. Blackburn's Benni McCarthy, Liverpool's Dirk Kuyt and Dimitar Berbatov of Spurs (and to a slightly lesser extent Obafemi Martins at Newcastle) have all seemed excellent acquisitions, players who look as though they have been playing over here their entire career. South African McCarthy settled immediately, with 48 points by the arrival of the first transfer window, while Martins (26 points), Kuyt (28 points) and Berbatov (just 11) were slow burners who had yet to catch fire. Each did, though, to differing degrees, with the Spurs ace in particular drawing admiring glances from bigger clubs after proving to be one of the buys of the season. However, if you pinned your hopes on Georgios Samaras, Mido or Bernardo Corradi, your season would have had more than its fair share of disappointments.

CHAPTER 15

DREAM TEAM MOVERS AND SHAKERS

NEED A LITTLE inspiration picking your Dream Team side? Here we list some of the players whose Dream Team stock should continue to rise in 2007–08, together with several players who will need to bounce back from disappointing campaigns before you consider drafting them into your team.

ON THE UP
Morten Gamst Pedersen

Morten Gamst Pedersen is no longer a secret and has been on the shortlist of many a shrewd Fantasy Football manager over the past season or two. He scored eight goals for Blackburn in his debut season in 2004–05 and was a £2-million bargain in his first Dream Team campaign the year following, with a very impressive 129 points. Pedersen loves to get forward and support the attack, is one of the deadliest takers of a free-kick in the Premiership from around the edge of the penalty area and is a frequent choice for the Star Man award. Blackburn manager Mark Hughes will do well to keep hold of one of his prize assets.

Nemanja Vidic

Nemanja Vidic made his name as a member of the Serbia and Montenegro defence who were dubbed the Famous Four after conceding just one goal in ten qualifiers for the 2006 World Cup finals. He joined Manchester United from Spartak Moscow in the January 2006 transfer window but failed to reproduce his best form in his first half-season at Old Trafford. His first full campaign, however, was a different story, as his consistently impressive displays earned him a regular starting spot in central defence. Vidic also showed himself to be one of the most dangerous headers of a ball at corners, often going upfield to score valuable goals and proving a constant threat. His only downside is that his totally committed and wholehearted attitude to tackling could get him into trouble with referees, particularly away from home.

Benni McCarthy

Benni McCarthy settled incredibly quickly after being signed by Blackburn from Porto in August 2006 and, despite being new to the Premiership, he ranked third among strikers behind Didier Drogba and Wayne Rooney at the January transfer window. The South African international hit six goals in his first ten games and represented a shrewd investment at only £3.5 million for those willing to take a calculated gamble in the October transfer window. Quick, skilful, agile and able to score with either foot, he is also his club's regular penalty-taker. Having found his feet so impressively in what traditionally is a difficult debut season for foreign imports, expect McCarthy to score even more impressively in 2007–08.

Aaron Lennon

A succession of niggling injuries meant the youngster's Dream Team points total in 2006–07 was not as high as it should have been. Check out his form (and his fitness in pre-season). If he steers clear of injuries, he is one to look out for in 2007–08. He will score more highly in Fantasy Football games where assists score points, which is not the case in Dream Team, but, even so, his manager Martin Jol has been getting the former Leeds youngster to be more decisive and less unselfish in front of goal and Lennon has responded by upping his goals total.

Steve Sidwell

Rejected by Arsenal earlier in his career, Sidwell proved he was a class act in Reading's runaway Championship success in 2005–06. He then showed himself to be Premiership class and started to attract the attention of the bigger clubs, who were all aware that his contract was up and that he was available on a free transfer at the end of the season. He was just the sort of player Dream Team managers should have been looking at last season as a potential bargain buy, priced at a modest £2.5 million and hungry for success. Sidwell subsequently joined Chelsea when his contract at the Madejski expired, so he is not quite as tempting a proposition, particularly as there will probably be better Dream Team buys to be had from the Bridge. Even so, this is the type of hungry player you should be scouring the three newly promoted teams for.

Joleon Lescott

Joleon Lescott had always been viewed as one of the outstanding defenders outside the Premiership during his time at Wolves. He finally got to the top flight with the Black Country club in 2002–03, only then not to play a single top-flight game after having knee surgery. Everton took the risk on him in June 2006 in a bid to boost what had been an ageing defence and Lescott proved he belonged in the big time by producing some assured performances both at left-back and in the centre. Priced at a very modest £2 million, he proved one of the Dream Team bargains of the season last time around and, if the price is reasonable again, he is one to consider in a safety-first Everton side that normally sets itself up around the priority of preventing opponents from scoring.

Matthew Taylor

Matthew Taylor scored some vitally important goals for Portsmouth as they mounted an unlikely but successful fight against relegation in 2005–06, showing himself to have nerves of steel from the penalty spot. Always an attack-minded full-back, the arrival of Glen Johnson (on loan) and Sol Campbell saw a rejigged Portsmouth defence with Dejan Stefanovic switched to left-back and Taylor pushed into a position on the left side of midfield, which he loved. He went on to enjoy an outstanding campaign, the highlight of which was a stunning strike from the halfway line against Everton. He is still the club's penalty-taker and is a real danger from free-kicks as well.

Obafemi Martins

Martins cost then Newcastle manager Glenn Roeder £10 million as an August 2006 addition from Inter Milan, though he was available to Dream Team managers for just £3.5 million. He was given the famous No. 9 shirt at St James' Park, but in the early days looked as though he might struggle to match the likes of Jackie Milburn or Alan Shearer who had worn the jersey before him. Martins managed just one league goal in his first ten outings, but gradually looked more at home as the season progressed and became a more regular scorer. He was helped by the fact that with the Toon beset by a number of injury problems – including the likes of Shola Ameobi – he was practically guaranteed a starting spot in attack. He should do even better this time around.

Dimitar Berbatov

Like Benni McCarthy and Obafemi Martins, Berbatov made a nonsense of one of our Dream Team golden rules: be wary of picking a foreign player in his first season in the Premiership. Berbatov looked a class act from day one, showing himself to be a deadly finisher but much more besides: mobile, skilful, unselfish and a player who helped bring team-mates into the game. He will probably not be available to Dream Team managers for the £4.5 million you may have snapped him up for in 2006–07, but stick him on your shortlist and see what value he is listed at come July. With Robbie Keane and Jermain Defoe also on the Spurs books, you could think he might struggle for games, but manager Martin Jol is very reluctant to partner his two 'little ones' (Keane and Defoe) side by side in the same starting line-up.

Michael Dawson

Michael Dawson was the one shining light in a Tottenham defence that looked less assured in 2006–07 after defensive midfielder Michael Carrick had departed for Manchester United and was no longer there to provide an additional protective barrier. Mature beyond his years, Dawson made light of the loss of England international Ledley King through injury to become the leader of the Spurs backline and will become a regular in the national team himself if he continues to develop. One nagging concern over Dawson could be his disciplinary record – he was sent off twice in the space of eight games in 2005–06, and his wholehearted approach does lead to him collecting more than his fair share of yellow cards.

Patrice Evra

Manchester United beat a host of other clubs to the signing of the attack-minded left-back from Monaco in January 2006, but must have wondered if they had made a big mistake, as the Frenchman endured a nightmare debut that month in the Manchester derby and a very ordinary first year. Evra's position at the start of the 2006–07 season was uncertain with Gabriel Heinze returning from a serious injury which had kept him out for most of the previous campaign, but his form was vastly improved to such an extent that, come the end of the campaign, his rival for the left-back spot was being linked with a move away from Old Trafford.

James Milner

James Milner was minutes away from completing a permanent move from Newcastle to Aston Villa before the start of the 2006–07 season before Newcastle had a sudden change of heart. It was a shrewd move, as the young wide midfielder turned into one of the most reliable performers in a squad that was decimated by injuries. He became the youngest-ever scorer in the Premiership at 16 years 357 days while with Leeds, before that record was surpassed by Everton's James Vaughan. Far from being a prolific scorer, Milner nevertheless demonstrated a taste for goals with four in seven games in January 2007 and showed he can strike a deadly free-kick. He will not amass massive totals in Dream Team, but is capable of topping 150 if he stays fit and is worthy of consideration for your team if the price is right.

ON THE FALL

Sami Hyypia

It is dangerous to write Sami Hyypia off too early. The big Finn has been one of the finest performers among Dream Team defenders over the past few seasons, and even finished as the top-ranked among all Dream Team players with a staggering 290 points back in 2001. Hyypia was actually the top defender for four straight years between 2000 and 2003, but his powers looked on the wane when 244 points in 2003 fell to 178 in 2004 and 134 in 2005. Hyypia bounced back with 230 points in 2006, though his 2007 total was down again as Daniel Agger and Jamie Carragher became Rafa Benitez's preferred pairing in central defence. Will Hyypia be able to regain his best form – probably not, he will be 34 early in the 2007–08 season.

Gabriel Heinze

The Argentine left-back or central defender was a very popular choice with 165 points in his debut season for Manchester United in 2005. But a serious injury ruled him out for most of the 2005–06 season and he netted just 23 points. Heinze recovered just in time to participate in the 2006 World Cup finals, but he lost his place at left-back at Old Trafford to the much-improved Patrice Evra in 2006–07 and was linked with a move away from Manchester.

Danny Murphy

Consistently ranked among the top-ten midfielders over the past five seasons, Murphy managed a very impressive 193 Dream Team points in 2002–03 ahead of Frank Lampard and Steven Gerrard and only behind Manchester United's Paul Scholes. He left Liverpool in search of regular first-team football in August 2004, choosing to join Charlton, but after initially impressing at The Valley he became unsettled and made a switch across London to Spurs in January 2006. Murphy has yet to win a regular first-team place under Martin Jol in a Tottenham squad overloaded with midfielders. Dangerous from free-kicks when he gets a game.

Steven Davis

The young Aston Villa midfielder was one of the Dream Team finds of the season in 2005–06, when he produced an incredibly consistent campaign which earned him 153 points. Priced at only £2.5 million, it made him one of the Dream Team bargains of the season. As with many promising youngsters, Davis fell prey to the 'season-after syndrome' and was a shadow of the player he had been the season before and even lost his place in the Aston Villa team for a while.

Philippe Senderos

The shaven-headed young Swiss defender looked like the answer to Arsene Wenger's prayers early in his Arsenal career when he produced some impressive displays and filled the gap left by the underperforming Pascal Cygan. Senderos managed 103 Dream Team points in 2005–06, but has struggled to replicate his early success and has proved a little suspect alongside the ever-dependable Kolo Toure. It would be no surprise to see Wenger invest in another centre-back, which would marginalise Senderos and finally allow the French manager to stop regretting his decision to sell Matthew Upson to Birmingham in January 2003.

Chris Riggott

The former England Under-21 international central defender had finally been starting to show the Boro fans what he was capable of after a somewhat indifferent start to his career on Teesside following a January 2003 move from Derby. After collecting 107 points in 2004–05, he raised the bar again the following season, ranking as tenth-best Dream Team defender with a haul of 154 points. With Gareth Southgate announcing his retirement to concentrate on managing the team, Riggott might have expected to have been a permanent fixture in the Middlesbrough side in 2006–07, but he damaged ankle ligaments in September 2006 and was ruled out for the best part of two months. When fit again, he found his way back into the first team barred by the excellent form of Jonathan Woodgate (on loan from Real Madrid) and Emanuel Pogatetz.

Mikael Silvestre

The French defender has been one of Sir Alex Ferguson's unsung heroes over the past few seasons at Old Trafford, always willing to fill in at left-back or in the centre of defence and generally producing sound performances when required. However, the impressive form of Nemanja Vidic at the heart of the United defence and of Patrice Evra at left-back meant that Silvestre's opportunities for first-team starts were greatly reduced in 2006–07 and with it his Dream Team points output. Manchester United defenders are never cheap, and if he is priced around the £4-million mark as he was in 2006–07 you can spend your money better elsewhere on someone who is guaranteed a starting spot.

Darius Vassell

The man once seen as the future for England has faded from the international picture since scoring with a spectacular volley on his debut against Holland in Rotterdam back in 2002. Vassell has never been a prolific marksman, but has possessed enough skill and intelligence to inspire the notion that he might just burst into life one season and turn into a

Dream Team bargain. But, after a career-high 130 points in 2003, his output has been modest at best and it is hard to see him grabbing 30 goals a season in a very ordinary Manchester City side. He only cost £3 million in Dream Team in 2005–06, but on recent form you could hardly say he was a bargain at any price.

CHAPTER 16

POINTS PER MILLION: THE WAY TO PICK A WINNER

I DON'T KNOW about you, but some of my Dream Teams in the past have not had an awful lot of thought behind them. One season, I seem to recall, it was just get Thierry Henry and Ruud van Nistelrooy in as my two top strikers and try and cram a team of cheapies around them.

I'm not saying, necessarily, that that is the wrong way to go about things, but you should be able to justify every player you pick in a way other than to say, 'Well, that's all the money I had left.' This is where Points Per Million, or PPM for short, comes in. The winner in 2005–06, Chris Marshall, scored 1,987 points with his £40 million. That's just short of 50 points for every £1 million he had to spend on his team. It was not much different the previous year, with Gary Utting's Super Furry Animals team totalling 1,971. Both managers scored around 2,000 points with their £40-million budget. So, if you can pick a team of players that gets you 50 points for every million of their price tag, you are not going to be too far short of winning the top prize.

There's a slight problem with this theory and it needs a little modification. Let me explain why. There's no point picking up a whole host of bargain-basement £1-million players in your team because, even though they fill the value-for-money criteria, your total is going to be way off the winning mark.

Jimmy Bullard (124 points for £1 million as a Wigan player in 2005–06) was an excellent purchase that season if you spotted him before the start of the season. But, even with 11 Jimmy Bullards in your side, you would only have amassed 1,386 points and only have spent £11 million, a fraction of your budget.

Jiri Jarosik (114 points for £1 million as a Chelsea player in 2005–06), incidentally, was not quite as smart a buy as Bullard, because, although he provided value for money scoring points while on loan at Birmingham, he actually counted as one of the two Chelsea players you were allowed in the game and thus prevented you from having two big hitters from the champions in your side, like John Terry *and* Frank Lampard.

Conversely, if you fill your team with top-dollar men like Steven Gerrard and Lampard, you are going to run out of money very quickly. So you must strike a balance between the two extremes.

Your Dream Team budget went up in 2006–07 and for the first time managers got to splash out £50 million instead of the £40 million it had been since 2001–02. That's inflation for you. But I'm not going to get into a debate about that one: politics and sport definitely do not mix and the only labour we will be talking about here is the work you will be putting in to pick your winning Dream Team. The £10-million hike in the money you had available to spend changed the dynamic of the game somewhat in that it gave you more options: you could choose more star players or better-quality bargain-basement players, or if you chose all mid-range-value players you would get more for your money there, too. I think the Americans call that a win-win-win.

But back to the 50-points-per-million theory and problem number two: there were six players priced at £8 million at the start of the 2006–07 season: Frank Lampard, Thierry Henry, Steven Gerrard, Wayne Rooney, Michael Ballack and John Terry. Pick them all and we have a meagre £2 million to spend on the remaining five members of our side. Impossible. So which to include and which to discount?

Hindsight is a wonderful thing, but it was easy to predict that, despite having a world-class pedigree, Ballack was always going to struggle in his debut season at Chelsea. With Frank Lampard already the first name on the teamsheet as the club's most attack-minded midfielder, something had to give and it was hard to see Ballack and Lamps both operating at their full attacking potential, a bit like Lampard and Gerrard rarely seem to play well in the same England side. If we went with the earlier premise of staying clear of foreign imports in their first season, then Ballack should have been the first off the list.

All the others were coming off stellar seasons. Henry needs no introduction. Terry had strung together back-to-back campaigns with more than 300 points. Lampard had totalled

250 or better for three straight years and Gerrard had netted 309 in 2006 having scored 212 in 2005 and 226 in 2004. Rooney managed 252 in 2006, and, yes, he had an impressive season, but his value rocketed from £5.5 million the year before and, in my opinion, he did not quite offer the same value at £8 million as the other four, who were all established winners in Fantasy Football teams year in, year out.

But where from there? You could have gone for all four of Henry, Gerrard, Lampard and Terry, but that would have eaten away more than half your budget. And, if one got injured (as, in fact, Henry and Terry both did), you were unlikely to see a full return for your money. If you are shelling out for one of the most expensive players on the list, you should be looking for a return of 250 points as a minimum.

DREAM TEAM WINNER 2007						
Pos	Player	Club	£m	Total	BR	PR
GK	Reina	LIV	5.0	150	76	23
DF	Agger	LIV	4.0	189	34	13
DF	M Dawson	TOT	4.0	143	71	33
DF	Evra	MAN	2.5	121	26	61
DF	Toure	ARS	5.5	178	91	17
MD	Barry	AST	3.5	175	19	18
MD	Lampard	CHE	8.0	375	36	1
MD	Ronaldo	MAN	5.0	314	6	3
ST	Drogba	CHE	4.5	318	3	2
ST	Berbatov	TOT	4.5	255	12	5
ST	B McCarthy	BLA	3.5	215	8	9

DREAM TEAM OF YEAR 2007						
Pos	Player	Club	£m	Total	BR	PR
GK	James	MNC	3.0	145	28	32
DF	Carragher	LIV	6.0	219	69	8
DF	Toure	ARS	5.5	178	91	17
DF	Agger	LIV	4.0	189	34	13
DF	Lescott	EVE	2.0	135	4	40
MD	Lampard	CHE	8.0	375	36	1
MD	Ronaldo	MAN	5.0	314	6	3
MD	Scholes	MAN	4.0	192	29	12
ST	Berbatov	TOT	4.5	255	3	2
ST	Drogba	CHE	4.5	318	12	5
ST	McCarthy	BLA	3.5	215	8	9

Let's take a look at the team of 2007 winner Ian Preedy (above) and compare it with the best possible side you could have picked with your £50 million had you not made any transfers from the start of the season. Note the two columns at the extreme right-hand side of the table: 'BR' shows the Bargain Rank of each team member compared to all off the rest of the players in Dream Team that season, basically dividing their points score by their price tag. Scott Carson, the Liverpool goalkeeper who spent the season on-loan at Charlton, was ranked as the bargain of the season, scoring 100 points and being valued at just £1 million in Dream Team.

The column 'PR' alongside stands for Points Rank, which represents where the player finished among the top Dream Team points-scorers that season. Frank Lampard, with 375 points, was top-scorer and therefore ranks first. Note how many players in both the winner's choice and the ideal choice rank in the top 20 of one category or other, and there is quite an even spread of value-for-money players and big points-scorers.

Pos	Player	Club	£m	Total	BR	PR
			**DREAM TEAM WINNER 2006**			

Pos	Player	Club	£m	Total	BR	PR
GK	Jaaskelainen	BOL	3.0	140	36	39
DF	Carragher	LIV	5.5	256	38	5
DF	Terry	CHE	8.0	302	74	3
DF	A Ferdinand	WHM	1.5	87	16	117
DF	Mullins	WHM	1.0	94	3	104
MD	Gerrard	LIV	6.0	309	22	2
MD	Bullard	WIG	1.0	124	1	55
MD	MG Pedersen	BLA	2.0	129	11	49
MD	Jarosik	CHE	1.0	116	2	67
ST	Henry	ARS	8.0	343	53	1
ST	Bent	CHA	3.0	199	10	9

DREAM TEAM OF YEAR 2006

Pos	Player	Club	£m	Total	BR	PR
GK	Lehmann	ARS	4.0	188	33	11
DF	R Ferdinand	MAN	5.5	213	69	8
DF	Hyypia	LIV	4.5	230	24	7
DF	N'Gotty	BOL	3.0	166	20	21
DF	Chimbonda	WIG	1.5	131	5	44
MD	Bullard	WIG	1.0	124	1	55
MD	Jarosik	CHE	1.0	116	2	67
MD	Gerrard	LIV	6.0	309	22	2
MD	Steven Davis	AST	2.5	153	13	28
ST	Henry	ARS	8.0	343	53	1
ST	D Bent	CHA	3.0	199	10	9

Dream Team 2006 winner Chris Marshall (whose side is listed in the table above, along with the Dream Team team of the year) had the top three bargains of the season in his team, with Jimmy Bullard, Jiri Jarosik and Hayden Mullins. He also had the top three points scorers in Thierry Henry, Steven Gerrard and John Terry and four of the top five if you also throw in Jamie Carragher. That is a very strong backbone to build the remainder of a Fantasy Football-winning side around.

DREAM TEAM WINNER 2005						
Pos	Player	Club	£m	Total	BR	PR
GK	Friedel	BLA	2.0	139	3	43
DF	Terry	CHE	6.0	368	7	1
DF	El Karkouri	CHA	1.5	114	1	75
DF	Hreidarsson	CHA	2.0	90	27	115
DF	Cole	ARS	4.5	153	76	27
MD	Okocha	BOL	3.0	126	39	55
MD	T Cahill	EVE	2.5	150	8	30
MD	Lampard	CHE	6.5	342	10	2
ST	Defoe	TOT	4.0	201	14	6
ST	Crouch	SOT	2.0	87	34	119
ST	Rooney	EVE	5.5	181	82	15

Pos	Player	Club	£m	Total	BR	PR
GK	Friedel	BLA	2.0	139	3	43
DF	Terry	CHE	6.0	368	7	1
DF	El Karkouri	CHA	1.5	114	1	75
DF	Todd	BLA	2.0	147	2	32
DF	Carragher	LIV	4.0	198	17	8
MD	Scholes	MAN	5.0	202	46	5
MD	T Cahill	EVE	2.5	150	8	30
MD	Lampard	CHE	6.5	342	10	2
MD	Gravesen	EVE	2.5	122	20	63
ST	Defoe	TOT	4.0	201	14	6
ST	A Johnson	CPA	4.0	175	32	19

The same applied in 2005, with our Dream Team winner Gary Utting having five of the top-ten bargain players in the game (El Karkouri, Friedel, Terry, Cahill and Lampard). He also had three of the top-ten points-scorers in Terry (first with 368 points), Lampard (second with 342 points) and Jermain Defoe (sixth with 201). Note that the Chelsea pair of Terry and Lampard finished very high in both categories that season. The more players you pick in your squad who can double up like that, the more chance you have of winning the game. Note also, though, that Terry and Lampard were priced at £6 million and £6.5 million, respectively. You have had to pay top dollar for them both in recent years, with both being available at £8 million in 2006–07.

Pulling all this together, the table below takes a look at the Dream Team of the Year from the four years from 2004 to

2007. This shows the number of players in the perfect team who ranked in the top ten and top 20 of the bargains category and the top ten and top 20 of the biggest points-scorers.

	Bargain		High score			
WINNING INGREDIENTS						
Year	Top 10	Top 20	Top 10	Top 20	Neither	Both
2003–04	5	9	4	6	1	5
2004–05	6	9	5	6	0	4
2005–06	4	6	5	6	0	1
2006–07	4	5	6	9	1	4

The column titled 'Neither' is for players who ranked outside the top 20 in both value-for-money and high-score terms (step forward, Newcastle's Olivier Bernard and goalkeeper David James, who in 2006-07 was listed as a Manchester City player but ultimately ended up at Portsmouth) and the 'Both' column shows the number of players who ranked in the top 20 of both categories, that is a player who scored well and who also provided fantastic value for money. What, hopefully, you will see is that a pattern emerges, which shows that what you are looking for in a perfect team is an almost even split between bargain players and big points-scorers, with the emphasis being slightly more on value for money. To rank among the top-20 bargains, you generally have to score 50 points per million. Some food for thought: to represent true value for money, your £8-million players would have to score 400 points – something that has never been done before.

PRICES OF PLAYERS IN TEAM OF THE YEAR				
£m	2006–07*	2005–06	2004–05	2003–04
1.0	0	2	0	0
1.5	0	1	1	0
2.0	1	0	2	1
2.5	0	1	2	2
3.0	1	2	0	4
3.5	1	0	0	0
4.0	2	1	3	1
4.5	2	1	0	1
5.0	1	0	1	1
5.5	1	1	0	0
6.0	1	1	1	0
6.5	0	0	1	0
7.0	0	0	0	0
7.5	0	0	0	1
8.0	1	1	0	0

*=budget increased from £40million to £50million in 2006-07

For those who like their numbers, the preceding table shows the price breakdown of the players in our Dream Team 'dream team' over the past three years. So, in 2005–06, for example, we had one top-priced £8-million player (Thierry Henry), a couple slightly cheaper (Steven Gerrard at £6 million and Rio Ferdinand at £5.5 million), all the way down to two players at just £1 million. Note the spread of prices across the board and the fact that these winners are not loaded up with the top-priced stars with a couple of bargains thrown in to make up the numbers.

PRICES OF PLAYERS IN WINNER'S TEAMS			
£m	2006–07*	2005–06	2004–05	2003–04
1.0	0	3	0	0
1.5	0	1	1	0
2.0	0	1	3	3
2.5	1	0	1	3
3.0	0	2	1	1
3.5	2	0	0	0
4.0	2	0	1	1
4.5	2	0	1	1
5.0	2	0	0	0
5.5	1	1	1	0
6.0	0	1	1	0
6.5	0	0	1	0
7.0	0	0	0	0
7.5	0	0	0	2
8.0	1	2	0	0

*=budget increased from £40million to £50million in 2006-07

The table shows the difference in make-up between the winning manager's team and the perfect XI he could have chosen earlier. Winning managers have tended to go for more of the top-priced players and look for their bargains right at the bottom end of the market. This is probably because it is easier to tell which players are going to do particularly well in Dream Team, and, even though they will be accordingly priced as the most expensive, it is good to know you should have some near-guaranteed points in the bag before trying to sift through the player list to unearth a few nuggets. Remember, though, that the Dream Team budget went up from £40 million to £50 million in 2006–07, giving you the chance either to sneak in another top-priced player or to adjust the price bracket of where you went looking for your bargains.

CHAPTER 17

LET'S GO ON A BARGAIN HUNT

AS WE SAW in the last chapter, if you are to make a real challenge in Dream Team, one of the keys to success is finding the bargain players who are going to perform better than their price tag suggests. Get in your own mind what constitutes a bargain – any player who you believe will score 50 points per million pounds of his valuation in Dream Team, so a £2-million player who scores 100 points, or a £3-million player who nets you 150, or hopefully better.

And it's not just one or two you are after, you are going to have to identify up to half a dozen of these types of players. If you spot a £6-million star who can net you 300 points, then that is an expensive bargain, if there is such a thing. The best players are the ones who provide you with the double whammy net of scoring you big points and still proving value for money. It's similar to Test cricket, where having a world-class all-rounder makes it feel like you have an extra player on your side. Don't be despondent if not all your picks hit that mark. As has been mentioned before, nobody to date has picked the perfect Dream Team. So 40 points per million – such as a £4-million player scoring 160 points – may not be a bargain, but it certainly represents good value for money.

A word of caution, though. Do not expect miracles from your bargain-basement players. They are not going to perform as well as your superstars, but that is why their price is set accordingly low. Set yourself realistic expectations of what they can achieve or you will fall well short of your target. There is no point looking at a player valued at £1 million and saying, 'Well, he's going to get me 300 points for a start.' He won't, because it has never happened in the history of the game. Looking back at the scoring over the past few seasons, the table below gives an indication of what a very good, but not extraordinary, score can be achieved by some of the players with a modest price tag. For example, £1-million Jimmy Bullard scored 124 points in 2006 and, a year earlier, Jermain Defoe, priced at £4 million, netted 201 points.

WHAT TO EXPECT FROM YOUR BARGAINS							
£m	1.0	1.5	2.0	2.5	3.0	3.5	4.0	4.5
Points	120	130	150	160	180	200	200	250

OK, SO WE KNOW WHAT THEY ARE NOW, BUT HOW DO WE FIND THEM?

The problem is that bargains do not stay bargains for long. Unfortunately, those people at Dream Team have read the 'Setting Fantasy Football Player Prices for Dummies' book (actually, come to think of it, because they've been doing it so long they probably wrote it) and if a cheap-priced player does well one year you can rightly assume that his price will rocket the next. But that's part of the fun, using your skill to predict the players who are going to outperform the market. And, if it was easy, everybody would be doing it. Enjoy the bargain hunt. Here are a few factors to get you thinking.

Players changing clubs

In Dream Team, you are only allowed to have a maximum of two players from one club, but you can cheat the system after the player list is published if a star switches to another team, and it can work to your advantage. For instance, Wigan's unsettled full-back Pascal Chimbonda finally made a move to Tottenham in the summer of 2006, but for the purposes of the game he remained a Wigan player, meaning that you could have included another two Spurs players in your Dream Team XI if you had been so inclined. Chimbonda looked a good selection: only those plans were somewhat scuppered when Martin Jol's side suddenly started to look a lot less assured at the back than they had been the previous season. Similarly, Ashley Cole was listed as an Arsenal player in 2005–06, and remained so for Dream Team purposes after his move to Chelsea, so you could have included him and two more players from the reigning champions. Cole, though, was not cheap at £5 million and again largely disappointed, mainly because of injury.

Round pegs in square holes

In your opinion, has Dream Team listed a player in a position that he does not normally play, or in a position from which he has been switched? For instance, Portsmouth's Matthew

Taylor was one of the most attacking left-backs in the country, but when Harry Redknapp stocked up with defenders in the 2006 summer sales he pushed Taylor into a midfield role. Result – because he is down in the game as a defender, Taylor still collected points for the clean sheets that Pompey kept, but he also found himself further forward and in a position to score goals – therefore boosting his points total.

Another such player was Paul Scharner at Wigan, who was listed as a defender but who played many of his games in midfield and is sometimes thrown even further forward in a bid to grab a late goal. Remember, though, it's not just a case of finding people who are listed out of their normal positions and picking them; they still have to represent good value for money, must still be playing regularly and you have to be confident they are going to score goals or else they will earn no more points than if they were playing in defence.

And this phenomenon can work the other way. Chelsea's Michael Essien, listed as a midfielder, had to play much of the 2006–07 season in central defence. He did not get five points for a clean sheet that his Blues team-mates picked up (midfielders only get two) and this also negated his chances of being able to attack and boost his Dream Team total with goals.

Unknowns from newly promoted Championship sides

Players from clubs in their first season after promotion from the Championship tend to be priced lower than their counterparts. The main reason for this is that their teams are predicted to struggle for survival and in all probability will be relegated again at the end of the season. Even if that is the case, it does not mean that everybody is going to perform badly. It is always a worry that promoted sides are going to leak goals, so perhaps steer clear of goalkeepers and defenders and look for a choice signing or two further forward. Look more closely still at promoted sides you believe will hold their own in the Premiership. Watford were always going to struggle in 2006–07, especially when they made it quite clear that investment in new players was going to be kept to a minimum.

The table below shows the positions played by the top-30 bargain-buy players over the past five seasons. Note that most of the value-for-money players came from defenders and midfielders, with 26 of the top-30 bargains in 2005–06 filling one of those two positions. Note also that this sort of scotched the notion that all the promoted clubs always offer rich pickings. Take a look in the column headed 'Prom' and that was certainly the case in 2005–06 when 14 of the top-30 bargains came from the promoted clubs, six from Wigan, who finished tenth, and eight from West Ham, who finished ninth and reached the FA Cup final. Start watching Football League reviews on ITV or Sky come April when it emerges which Championship sides are likely to be promoted. If you unearth a gem that few others notice, it could prove a worthwhile investment of your valuable time.

WHERE HAVE THE BARGAINS BEEN?					
Season	GK	DEF	MID	STR	Prom
2006–07	5	13	7	6	8
2005–06	0	11	15	4	14
2004–05	2	14	11	3	3
2003–04	6	8	7	9	4
2002–03	4	13	6	8	2

Goalkeepers moving on a season's loan

In recent years, it has been a much more common occurrence to see second-choice goalkeepers going out on a season-long loan to another Premiership club. Because there seemed no way in the world they were going to get a game at club No. 1, they are priced at a bargain-basement price around £1.5 million or £2 million. But, if they take over the gloves and become first choice at club No. 2, then their value suddenly looks ridiculously cheap.

There were a couple of instances of this in 2006-07, though neither was totally satisfactory. Liverpool reserve Scott Carson – a back-up goalkeeper for England in the World Cup – went on loan to Charlton as the Reds already boasted Jose Reina and Jerzy Dudek on their staff. Carson played the season and would only have cost you £1 million in Dream Team. The problem was that the former Leeds man moved to a side that was to struggle and therefore conceded a fair number of goals and, for the purposes of the game, Carson was listed as a Liverpool player, so that would have prevented you from picking both Carragher and Gerrard, you would have had to settle for one or the other.

The other low-priced second-choice keeper to go out on loan was Ben Foster to Watford, where he returned for a second season. Even though he was still on Manchester United's books, Foster was listed in the game as a Watford player, so selecting him in your final XI would not have counted against your allocation of up to two players from Sir Alex Ferguson's side. The only problem in Foster's case was that he was joining up with a newly promoted club who were tipped to struggle – and we have already advised you to steer clear of defenders and goalkeepers from sides fresh out of the Championship.

One man to really strike paydirt with a bargain goalkeeper was John Bell. His 2002–03 Dream Team winning line-up included future England international Paul Robinson, who was valued at £2 million but who took over as first choice at Elland Road and netted 169 priceless points, the most by any goalkeeper that season.

Players joining top clubs in the January transfer window
It does not happen very often, but be very aware of players joining the big clubs from a lesser Premiership rival in the January transfer window. Louis Saha scored 15 goals for Fulham in the first half of the 2003–04 season and made a January 2004 switch to Manchester United. For the second half of the season, you had a United striker – on top form – available for just £3 million and counting as a Fulham player. This was a no-brainer – Saha was an absolute snip and finished the season ranked fifth among forwards with 188 points.

Value dropped because of injury
Has a big-money player's value fallen because his points total also fell due to a prolonged period on the sidelines? It's something to look out for. See in the table below how the value of some of Dream Team's better players soars after a good season or two. Frank Lampard and Jamie Carragher each would have set you back just £4 million in 2002–03. Wayne Rooney's value actually went up after the 2003–04 season despite a very modest campaign which had been down on the previous year. But that was because the boy was obviously destined for superstardom and had just signed for Manchester United.

	HOW PLAYER VALUES RISE AND FALL									
Season	2006/7		2005/6		2004/5		2003/4		2002/3	
	Pts	Val	Pts	Val	Pts	Val	Pts	Val	Pts	Val
Carragher	219	6.0	256	5.5	198	4.0	111	4.0	134	4.0
Terry	201	8.0	302	8.0	368	6.0	249	4.0	127	5.0
Gerrard	242	8.0	309	6.0	212	6.5	226	5.0	187	5.0
Lampard	375	8.0	302	8.0	342	6.5	250	4.5	172	4.0
Rooney	263	8.0	252	5.5	181	5.5	103	4.0	117	2.5

Don't risk signing players who have a record of getting injured regularly, hoping that this is the year they will come back to full fitness and enjoy an uninterrupted campaign. Unfortunately, it does not often work out like that. Wait for the player to prove himself again and enjoy an extended run in the first team before starting to convince yourself that his injury woes are over.

There is a difference between that philosophy and picking John Terry for the 2007–08 campaign. Yes, the Chelsea captain had a bad run with injuries in 2006–07, but most of that was related to a back problem and as he had an operation to cure it, there is no reason to think the problem will recur. Add to that the fact that Terry is one of the bravest players in the Premiership, is someone who has a history of playing through the pain barrier and would probably try to turn out on one leg if needed, then this season can go down as a blip. If his price falls, he will represent excellent value, and the same goes for any of the other big hitters whose price tag tumbles.

Michael Owen at Newcastle? That is a difficult one. Owen's season was a write-off due to his injuring a knee at the World Cup, and, although an operation saved his career, he has had more than his fair share of injuries in recent seasons and his road back to full fitness could well be a long one.

Ignorance is bliss

Keep an eye out for new faces who forced their way into Premiership sides towards the back end of the season. Dream Team only adds a handful of players during the two transfer windows in October and February, so any latecomers can fly in under the radar. If they are part of the game the following season, the chances are they could be undervalued because there is no guideline as to how many points they are capable of scoring. Keep your eyes out for new players in March and April and regularly check out their Dream Team ratings in the *Sun* newspaper. Because they are not part of the game, these ratings will not be collated anywhere and you'll have your own exclusive insight into a potential bargain or two come the following season.

Big names moving on create chances for others

Also watch out for players whose chances of first-team football have greatly increased because the team-mate they were competing against has left the club or has suffered a serious injury and is likely to be spending a prolonged period on the sidelines. Ashley Cole moved from Arsenal to Chelsea on the last day of the August transfer window, though it was evident for several weeks prior that he had no future at the Emirates Stadium. That suddenly left Gael Clichy as first-choice at left-back, at a very attractive price of £2.5 million for an Arsenal defender.

	TOP-30 BARGAINS 2006–07					
Rank	**Player**	**Club**	**Pos**	**Value**	**Total**	**PPM**
1	Carson	LIV	GK	1.0	100	100.0
2	Foster	WAT	GK	1.5	110	73.3
3	Drogba	CHE	STR	4.5	310	68.9
4	Lescott	EVE	DEF	2.0	135	67.5
5	Agbonlahor	AST	STR	1.5	97	64.7
6	Ronaldo	MAN	MID	5.0	314	62.8
7	S Harper	NEW	GK	1.0	62	62.0
8	B McCarthy	BLA	STR	3.5	215	61.4
9	Shorey	REA	DEF	2.0	122	61.0
9	S Taylor	NEW	DEF	2.0	122	61.0
11	Bouma	AST	DEF	1.0	57	57.0
12	Berbatov	TOT	STR	4.5	255	56.7
13	Ingimarsson	REA	DEF	2.0	113	56.5
14	DeMerit	WAT	DEF	1.5	81	54.0
15	Lita	REA	STR	2.0	105	52.5
16	Bridge	CHE	DEF	2.5	130	52.0
16	Jagielka	SHU	MID	2.5	126	50.4
18	Essien	CHE	MID	4.5	226	50.2
19	Arteta	EVE	MID	3.5	175	50.0
19	Barry	AST	MID	3.5	175	50.0
21	Doyle	REA	STR	2.5	123	49.2
22	Carsley	EVE	MID	2.0	98	49.0
22	Hahnemann	REA	GK	2.0	98	49.0
22	Mellberg	AST	DEF	2.0	98	49.0
22	Volz	FUL	DEF	1.0	49	49.0
26	Evra	MAN	DEF	2.5	121	48.4
26	Primus	POR	DEF	2.5	121	48.4

28	James	MNC	GK	3.0	145	48.3
29	Bocanegra	FUL	DEF	1.0	48	48.0
30	Scholes	MAN	MID	4.0	190	47.5

Note: Two on-loan goalkeepers topped the list of bargains last season, both playing for clubs that were relegated. Scott Carson spent 2006-07 with Charlton, while Ben Foster was at Watford. Note, though, that while Carson was listed as a Liverpool player, Foster's Dream Team club was Watford and therefore if you were astute enough to pick him he did not count as one of your two permitted Manchester United stars. There are five Reading players in this list and what bargains Didier Drogba, Cristiano Ronaldo and Dimitar Berbatov proved to be. Do not expect any of those three stars to be priced so generously this time around.

TOP-30 BARGAINS 2005–06

Rank	Player	Club	Pos	Value	Total	PPM
1	Bullard	WIG	MID	1.0	124	124.0
2	Jarosik	CHE	MID	1.0	116	116.0
3	Mullins	WHM	DEF	1.0	94	94.0
4	Ridgewell	AST	DEF	1.0	89	89.0
5	Chimbonda	WIG	DEF	1.5	131	87.3
6	Kavanagh	WIG	MID	1.0	83	83.0
7	Benayoun	WHM	MID	1.5	115	76.7
8	Roberts	WIG	STR	2.0	149	74.5
9	Gabbidon	WHM	DEF	1.5	103	68.7
10	D Bent	CHA	STR	3.0	199	66.3
11	MG Pedersen	BLA	MID	2.0	129	64.5
12	Konchesky	WHM	DEF	1.5	96	64.0
13	Simon Davis	AST	MID	2.5	153	61.2
14	Reid	BLA	MID	2.0	122	61.0
15	Harewood	WHM	STR	2.5	150	60.0
16	Nolan	BOL	MID	3.0	174	58.0
16	A Ferdinand	WHM	DEF	1.5	87	58.0
18	Stelios	BOL	MID	3.0	170	56.7
19	Reo-Coker	WHM	MID	2.5	141	56.4
20	N'Gotty	BOL	DEF	3.0	166	55.3
21	O'Neil	POR	MID	2.5	130	52.0
22	Gerrard	LIV	MID	6.0	309	51.5
23	Matt Taylor	POR	DEF	1.5	77	51.3
24	Hyypia	LIV	DEF	4.5	230	51.1
25	Martin Taylor	BIR	DEF	1.0	50	50.0
26	Zamora	WHM	STR	2.0	99	49.5
27	Teale	WIG	MID	1.0	49	49.0

28	B Hughes	CHA	MID	1.5	73	48.7
29=	Arteta	EVE	MID	2.0	96	48.0
29=	Jackson	WIG	DEF	1.0	48	48.0

Note: This was the year that West Ham and Wigan had been newly promoted. Both ducked the recent trend for sides coming out of the Championship to struggle and both had a host of players who finished prominently among the Dream Team bargains of the year. In tenth position was Charlton's Darren Bent, who represented magnificent value at just £3 million for any Dream Team bosses astute enough to have picked up his goal-scoring potential early.

Rank	Name	Club	Pos	Value	Total	PPM
TOP-30 BARGAINS 2004–05						
1	El Karkouri	CHA	DEF	1.5	114	76.0
2	Todd	BLA	DEF	2.0	147	73.5
3	Friedel	BLA	GK	2.0	139	69.5
4	Stubbs	EVE	DEF	2.0	129	64.5
5	Weir	EVE	DEF	2.0	127	63.5
6	J Cole	CHE	MID	3.0	188	62.7
7	Terry	CHE	DEF	6.0	368	61.3
8	T Cahill	EVE	MID	2.5	150	60.0
9	Dunne	MCY	DEF	2.5	134	53.6
10	Lampard	CHE	MID	6.5	342	52.6
11	Neill	BLA	DEF	2.0	104	52.0
11	Francis	NOR	MID	2.0	104	52.0
11	Solano	AST	MID	3.0	156	52.0
14	Cech	CHE	GK	4.0	201	50.3
14	Defoe	TOT	STR	4.0	201	50.3
16	Makelele	CHE	MID	3.0	149	49.7
17	Bent	EVE	STR	2.0	99	49.5
17	Carragher	LIV	DEF	4.0	198	49.5
19	Hibbert	EVE	DEF	2.0	98	49.0
20	Gravesen	EVE	MID	2.5	122	48.8
21	M Hughes	CPA	MID	2.0	97	48.5
22	Earnshaw	WBA	STR	2.5	120	48.0
23	W Brown	MAN	DEF	3.0	140	46.7
24	Routledge	CPA	MID	2.0	92	46.0
24	Distin	MCY	DEF	2.5	115	46.0
26	Zenden	MID	MID	3.5	160	45.7
27	Hreidarsson	CHA	DEF	2.0	90	45.0

27	King	TOT	MID	3.0	135	45.0
29	Kishishev	CHA	DEF	1.5	67	44.7
30	Naybet	TOT	DEF	2.0	89	44.5

Note: Despite their high price-tags, Frank Lampard and John Terry still made it into the top-ten value-for-money signings for Dream Team managers in 2004–05 and any boss having both of those players in his side had already made a very healthy start to their campaign.

Rank	Name	Club	Pos	Value	Total	PPM
TOP-30 BARGAINS 2003–04						
1	Forssell	CHE	STR	2.0	174	87.0
2	Sorensen	AST	GK	1.5	104	69.3
3	Saha	FUL	STR	3.0	188	62.7
4	Terry	CHE	DEF	4.0	249	62.3
5	De Zeeuw	POR	DEF	1.5	92	61.3
6	Angel	AST	STR	3.0	183	61.0
7	Jones	SOU	GK	1.5	90	60.0
8	Cunningham	BIR	DEF	2.0	119	59.5
9	Wright-Phillips	MAN C	MID	2.5	148	59.2
10	Martyn	LEE	GK	2.0	116	58.0
11	Yakubu	POR	STR	3.0	170	56.7
12	Nolan	BOL	MID	2.5	140	56.0
12	Dickov	LEI	STR	2.5	140	56.0
14	Lampard	CHE	MID	4.5	250	55.6
15	Howard	MAN U	GK	2.5	135	54.0
16	Rae	WOL	MID	2.0	107	53.5
17	Henry	ARS	STR	7.5	393	52.4
18	Bridge	CHE	DEF	4.0	206	51.5
19	van der Sar	FUL	GK	3.0	151	50.3
20	Anelka	MAN C	STR	4.5	224	49.8
21	Dodd	SOU	DEF	2.0	98	49.0
22	Malbranque	FUL	MID	3.5	164	46.9
23	S Gerrard	LIV	MID	5.0	226	45.2
24	G Johnson	CHE	DEF	2.5	112	44.8
25	Speed	NEW	MID	3.0	134	44.7
25	Sheringham	POR	STR	3.0	134	44.7
27	Bernard	NEW	DEF	3.0	131	43.7

28	Shearer	NEW	STR	6.0	261	43.5
29	Knight	FUL	DEF	2.5	107	42.8
30	Schwarzer	MID	GK	3.0	124	41.3

Note: John Terry was available at only £4 million and it was no surprise at that price that the Dream Team defensive favourite made it in near the top of our best bargains of 2003–04. And who's that in there at No. 17? Thierry Henry, who represented fantastic value despite his massive £7.5-million prize tag. That's because the Frenchman racked up 393 points, a Dream Team record total.

Rank	Name	Club	Pos	Value	Total	PPM
TOP-30 BARGAINS 2002–03						
1	Barry	AST	DEF	2.0	180	90.0
2	P Robinson	LEE	GK	2.0	169	84.5
3	Schwarzer	MID	GK	1.5	114	76.0
4	Zola	CHE	STR	2.5	180	72.0
5	Beattie	SOU	STR	3.0	204	68.0
6	Geremi	MID	DEF	2.5	160	64.0
7	Okocha	BOL	MID	2.0	124	62.0
8	Euell	CHA	STR	2.5	154	61.6
9	Mellberg	AST	DEF	2.5	150	60.0
10	O'Shea	MAN U	DEF	2.5	149	59.6
11	Parker	CHA	MID	2.0	117	58.5
11	Fernandes	SOU	MID	2.0	117	58.5
13	Gallas	CHE	DEF	3.5	200	57.1
14	Brevett	FUL	DEF	2.0	111	55.5
15	Woodgate	LEE	DEF	3.0	162	54.0
16	Niemi	SOU	GK	2.0	107	53.5
16	Lundekvam	SOU	DEF	2.0	107	53.5
18	Tugay	BLA	MID	2.0	105	52.5
19	Friedel	BLA	GK	3.0	157	52.3
20	Shearer	NEW	STR	5.0	260	52.0
20	M Taylor	BLA	DEF	2.5	130	52.0
22	Henry	ARS	STR	6.5	335	51.5
23	Cunningham	BIR	DEF	2.0	103	51.5
24	v Nistelrooy	MAN U	STR	7.0	359	51.3
25	Moore	WBA	DEF	1.5	76	50.7
26	K Campbell	EVE	STR	2.5	126	50.4
27	Unsworth	EVE	DEF	2.0	99	49.5

28	Scholes	MAN U	MID	4.5	219	48.7
29	Murphy	LIV	MID	4.0	193	48.3
30	M Svensson	SOU	DEF	2.5	117	46.8
30	Rooney	EVE	STR	2.5	117	46.8

Note: For the one and only time in his career, Wayne Rooney was available at a bargain £2.5 million. Rooney, now one of the Premiership's top players, was a teenager at Everton at the time and not a certain starter in his early days at Goodison Park. Still, those prepared to back his talent were to be rewarded for their judgement, as Rooney picked up 117 points.

CHAPTER 18

THE YELLOW PERIL

BECAUSE WE LIKE to encourage fair play and sportsmanship among players in Dream Team (and managers as well, for that matter), Premiership stars lose points for each yellow and red card they collect throughout the season. It's one off for a yellow and minus three in total for a sending-off. With some of the more frequent offenders it deals a double blow, because they lose the points for their misdemeanour, plus they also miss points-scoring opportunities for the time they spend sitting on the sidelines suspended.

If the player has a less-than-exemplary disciplinary record, but still looks like a bargain, then consider picking him anyway. Just factor in how many games you think he will miss on past form and how that is going to affect his points tally. If, after taking that into consideration, you think he represents less value for money, then stay well clear. The bottom line is that, if a player is going to score less than 100 points and if he has disciplinary problems as well, then a fair percentage of his total is going to be eaten away. That is not quite such a worry with more successful players, although, having said that, because they do score more heavily, each game they miss will cost you more points.

Phil Neville, probably trying a little too hard to win over an initially somewhat sceptical Everton support following his transfer from Manchester United, collected ten yellow cards and two red cards in 2005–06 in Premiership matches alone. As well as costing him 16 Dream Team points, his bans meant he missed another five Premiership games through suspension.

Neville actually scored 83 points in 39 games that season, a little over two points per game. So it would not have been unreasonable to expect him to earn around ten points from the five games he missed. Add that ten on to the 16 points he was actually penalised for the cards he collected and he could have had another 26 points had he behaved impeccably and not received a single yellow card all season. Neville's 83 points would suddenly have become 109 and would have looked a much more respectable total.

It is worth looking at how the Football Association's disciplinary system works, because it is not always easily understood and knowing how many games a recently red-carded player is likely to miss can make a difference to your decision to pick him up at transfer-window time.

BOOKINGS

The FA operates a totting-up procedure so a player is in trouble as he passes thresholds of five, ten and 15 yellow cards by certain stages of the season. Note that some only apply up to a specific time during the season, after which the threat of suspension is lifted.

Five yellow cards = one-match ban starting on the seventh day after the player receives his fifth booking.

Note that this only applies if they are accumulated between the start of the season and the end of February. If the player collects his fifth yellow after that, he escapes punishment.

Ten yellows = two-match ban starting on the seventh day after the tenth booking.

These must be accumulated between the start of season and the second Sunday in April for a ban to apply.

15 yellows = three-match ban starting on the seventh day after the 15th booking.

15 yellow cards is an unusually high number and the qualifying period for bans to apply is the whole season.

SENDINGS-OFF

A red card for two bookable offences = immediate one-game ban.

Note, though, that neither of the bookings counts towards the player's total for the season. But, if a player is booked and then receives a *straight red card* later in the game for a separate offence, the yellow card *does* count against his disciplinary record.

A red card for a professional foul or deliberate hand ball to prevent a goal = immediate one-match ban.

A red card for offensive or insulting behaviour = immediate two-match ban.

A red card for violent conduct or serious foul play = immediate three-match ban.

If a player is sent off for the second time in the same season, he is given the appropriate ban plus an extra game. So, if a player is dismissed for the second time in a particular season for insulting behaviour, he collects a three-game ban in total, two as the standard punishment and an extra game for a second offence.

Note: These rules apply to Premiership, FA Cup and Carling Cup matches only. There is a separate disciplinary procedure for European games. Here players are generally banned for the next game after a sending-off (though UEFA can increase this punishment for more serious offences). It's a one-game ban after a third yellow card of the competition and an additional game after reaching five, seven and nine cautions and so on.

Players appearing frequently in the Dream Team disciplinary list over the past few years include Lucas Neill, El-Hadji Diouf, Gareth Barry, Tim Cahill, Gavin McCann, Robbie Savage, Kevin Davies, Joey Barton, Ivan Campo and Scott Parker. But a complete list of those to lose most Dream Team points through bookings and sendings-off in Premiership matches over the past two years can be found in the statistics section later in this book.

CHAPTER 19

EUR ON TO A WINNER WITH EXTRA GAMES

BRITAIN MIGHT HAVE joined the Common Market, as it was called back then, in 1973, but Dream Team did not embrace Europe until 2000-01. From that season onwards, British teams playing in Champions League and UEFA Cup matches have earned points, just as they do in Premiership and domestic cup competitions. How much of a difference does it make to your players? Potentially, if they do well and progress to the latter stages, a massive one.

Generally, the top four teams in the Premiership at the end of the season go into the Champions League. The champions and runners-up automatically qualify for the group stages, while the third- and fourth-placed teams must confirm their places by winning a two-legged tie against a side you'd expect them to beat. These qualifying games do not count for Dream Team, but it's then game on from the group stages onwards.

Should a team lose in this qualifying round they are placed in the UEFA Cup. Each of the eight groups consists of four teams and each plays the other three, home and away, with the top two progressing to the knockout stages. The third-placed team in the group is put into the UEFA Cup and the bottom side is eliminated altogether. In the last 16, the group winners are drawn against the group runners-up, though clubs from the same country (or who qualified from the same group) cannot play each other until the next round, the quarter-finals, when it is a free-for-all. With six group games, and three rounds of two-legged knockout matches before a one-off final, teams could play 13 games. Potentially, it is even better in the UEFA Cup, with a maximum of 15 games on offer.

Generally, there are three places awarded to English clubs in this competition, which go to the FA Cup winner, the League Cup winner and the side that finished fifth in the league, though the cup places can instead by handed to teams finishing lower than fifth if the League Cup winner has already qualified for Europe via another route. Sides can also sneak into the UEFA Cup if they win a pre-qualifying tournament called the Intertoto Cup, or if they are lucky enough to be picked out of a hat as one of the winners of a Fair Play League, though the odds of the latter occurring are slim.

English clubs in the UEFA Cup play a two-legged first-round tie, with the winners progressing to the group stages, with five teams in each of the eight groups. The top three from each group go through, with the group winners being drawn against third-placed finishing teams who cannot be from the same group or country. The eight group runners-up are paired with the sides demoted from the Champions

League. Two-legged rounds of the last 32, 16, the quarter-finals and semi-finals, along with a single match in the final means a maximum of 15 games are on offer to a club making it all the way through to the final.

EXTRA GAMES FOR TEAMS IN EUROPE			
Champions League		**UEFA Cup**	
Stage	**Matches**	**Stage**	**Matches**
Group	6	Rnd 1	2
Last 16	2	Group	4
Q/F	2	Last 32	2
S/F	2	Last 16	2
Final	1	Q/F	2
Max total	**13**	S/F	2
		Final	1
		Max total	**15**

With leading Dream Team players averaging upwards of six points a game, this could represent a lucrative European bonus of 90 points or more. From the first transfer window onwards, it is important that you get as many players in your side from teams competing in Europe. See chapter 11, 'Transfers: A Window of Opportunity', for a fuller explanation.

The table below shows how European campaigns helped boost the points tally of defenders in 2005–06. And this only relates to the points earned from clean sheets and lost for goals conceded; there are points for good marks and goals on top. Arsenal, you may recall, lost to Barcelona in the final of the Champions League and Middlesbrough took a beating by

Seville. But the Gunners' defenders kept a whopping ten clean sheets on their way to Paris, meaning 49 extra points (the only time they conceded more than one goal was in the final). Boro's defenders added 29 more points to their total, actually doing far better in their 15 matches in Europe than they managed in the 38 games they played in the Premiership.

	Prem	Europe	Total
Chelsea	96	24	120
Manchester United	76	14	90
Liverpool	101	24	125
Arsenal	71	49	120
Middlesbrough	20	29	49
Everton	41	1	42
Bolton	57	9	66

CHAPTER 20

THE CUP THAT CHEERS

OBVIOUSLY, HOW WELL your players are performing in the Premiership goes a long way to determining whether your Dream Team side falls into the 'high-flier' or 'flop' category. But, since way back in 1997–98, performances in the FA Cup have swelled players' points totals and can make the difference between a very good side and a champion. May becomes a very tense month for managers in the running for a shot at the top prize, a whopping £125,000.

In 2005–06, Steven Gerrard broke West Ham hearts and single-handedly won the FA Cup for Liverpool with a Star Man display to end all Star Man displays. The England international scored two goals and his man-of-the-match performance thrilled Scousers up and down the land, though few of those would have had as much riding on it as Chris Marshall.

The trainee accountant from Huddersfield had gone into the final game trailing rival Jim Munsey, but the 18 points Stevie G earned that day allowed Marshall's Galpharm

Dream XI to take the Dream Team title by a single point, leaving Munsey having to settle for second place and a cheque for £50,000.

Liverpool manager Rafa Benitez had learned his lesson from the year before as he put out a weakened side against Burnley and saw his side crash out to a humiliating own-goal in the third round at Turf Moor. Although the FA Cup is not the coveted prize it once was, bosses of most clubs do tend to take it seriously and field a full-strength side.

The Carling Cup, however, is a different story, where the managers of some of the top clubs treat the competition as an inconvenience or a training exercise. Just because Arsenal, say, get to the final, it does not necessarily mean big points for Thierry Henry, who seldom plays and did not feature at all in the club's run to the 2007 final where they succumbed to Chelsea. Having said that, it gives one or two of the club's lesser lights the chance to shine.

Benitez put out a weakened Liverpool side in the Carling Cup against Arsenal in January 2007 and it cost him spectacularly as his side were ripped apart by Arsenal's precocious youngsters. The Gunners famously won that quarter-final clash 6–3 with the man nicknamed 'The Beast', Julio Baptista, scoring four and grabbing 33 points for himself in the process, having managed just five in the whole of the season up to that point.

Manchester United manager Sir Alex Ferguson has viewed the Carling Cup as a chance to get an early-season trophy in the bag to quieten supporters or members of the board uneasy with Chelsea's emergence as a threat to the Red Devils' previous stranglehold on the Premiership. Fergie generally plays one or two of his younger players and his second-choice goalkeeper along with a sprinkling of established stars.

And Jose Mourinho's Blues have been the one side out of the Big Four who regularly put out the nearest to what could be termed a full-strength side. Frank Lampard, for instance, played in every match of Chelsea's run to their 2007 Carling Cup success, albeit with some of those appearances coming as a substitute.

There are a maximum of seven games in the Carling Cup for Premiership sides entering in the second round. That total is six for teams playing in Europe, because they do not enter until the third round.

Excluding replays, teams reaching the final of the FA Cup have to play six matches to get to the showpiece final, meaning a maximum of 13 games for a club reaching both domestic cup finals against just two for a side exiting both at the first hurdle.

In reality, though, the domestic cup competitions are a welcome bonus and you should not select your Dream Team side around them. The only possible exception is in the second transfer window in February. If you are considering bringing one of two players in and you cannot make up your mind which, if one is playing for a side that is still in the FA Cup and has an easy-looking draw in the next round (in other words they are at home and have not been drawn against Arsenal, Liverpool, Chelsea or Manchester United) then it makes sense, all other things being equal, to plump for the man who has some cup games to look forward to.

CHAPTER 21

FINAL FANTASY XI: THE CONCLUSION

OK, SO WHAT have we learned? Listed below is a summary of the major points we have covered in the preceding chapters.

1. If you are serious about winning, then make sure you do your homework. Read pre-season match reports on club websites so you get an idea of who is in favour and who is not. If you try unofficial websites as well it will give you a fan's perspective of how new signings are settling in. It is also vital to keep tabs on players picking up injuries before the start of the campaign and on new signings. Swotting up on who were the useful players from the promoted sides is not a bad idea, either.

2. Make a mental shortlist of players you were impressed with or you missed out on from the previous season who you think will have a major impact in the following campaign. Similarly, pick out players who came into the Premiership later in the season and did well but who were not listed in the Dream Team game (you may be

surprised when you look back, there will be quite a few)
and players whose totals will have suffered because they
were out with injury.

3. Be careful with injuries, though. Steer clear of players
who have a history of spending much of their team on
the treatment table. You need your stars to be performing
and you need to be realistic in your expectations. If a
player has missed much of the past four seasons with
injury, can you honestly predict that he will play every
game this time around? Unlikely ... very unlikely.

4. When the first Dream Team player list comes out in early
July, scour the list for potential bargains.

5. Are there any players listed out of position, and who will
end up playing in a more attacking position, which you
think should benefit their scores?

6. Value for money is the name of the game. Remember, we
are looking for players in any position who are going to
score 50 points for each million of the price tag assigned
to them in Dream Team. So a £2-million player who is
going to score 100 points is good value, as is a £3-million
player earning 150 points and so on.

It is unrealistic to expect your superstar players to reach
50 points per million of their value. There were six top-
priced players in 2006–07, all at £8 million, which would
have meant they needed to reach 400 points to represent
a bargain. That target is extremely improbable and has
never been hit (Thierry Henry came the closest in
2003–04 with 393), so cut your stars a little slack and,
instead of setting them the 50-points-per-million target,

pick the big-name players who you feel are going to represent the best value. If they are all priced the same, then they are the players who are going to score the most points, but sometimes even the values of superstars can drop if they have suffered a disappointing season. The year after, they can represent incredible value and that can be the time to pick them up and cash in.

In recent seasons, there have been more bargains among defenders and midfielders than among goalkeepers or strikers, and you can unearth the odd nugget or two from the promoted sides, though give their keepers and defenders a particularly wide berth, because they tend to leak goals.

7. Pick a goalkeeper from a solid team, but not necessarily the top sides because you are only allowed two stars from one club and keepers are normally outscored by defenders, midfielders and strikers.

8. Defenders from the Big Four generally score best because these sides leak fewer goals and keep more clean sheets. But because they are expensive you will have to strike a balance and identify bargains from lesser teams as well if you want to succeed.

Look to double up on two defenders or a goalkeeper and a defender from a defensively solid team who you think will keep plenty of clean sheets.

9. Defensive midfielders are not penalised as badly in Dream Team as in other Fantasy Football games, but in most cases they are probably best avoided and you should find better value elsewhere.

10. It does not matter really which formation you employ. Both 4-4-2 or 4-3-3 work out roughly equal, so make your choice as to which you opt for on which player provides the better value out of a fourth midfielder or a third striker. Very often this will be the midfielder.

11. Do not plough all your money into goalscorers, but spread it around the team so you have a good balance. You will need all your players to contribute rather than having a couple of players to carry the rest.

12 Enter your team as late as possible (ideally the day before) so you pick up any last-minute injury or transfer news.

13 If you have dreams of winning through the Golden Gamble, you probably shouldn't enter later than after the first week of fixtures. It is still worth having a crack at the Golden Gamble after that because there are still some tasty weekly and monthly prizes on offer.

14 You would be silly not to enter a Mini-League as they represent great fun and offer another way of winning a prize at no extra cost.

15. Don't be disappointed if your team does not start out quite as you had hoped. Console yourself that no winning manager thus far has picked the perfect side and that even they have could have done better in terms of points scored in the opening weeks of the campaign. Even if you have got off to a dodgy start, you can use the transfer windows wisely – you only get two of them – and can be back in the game. Look to ditch players who are no longer in the Premiership, who are out of the first-team picture or who are on the long-term injury list before you look at the players who are not performing. Do not make a knee-jerk reaction and jettison your established stars who have made a quiet start and will in all probability come good for someone who has made a fast start to the season but who may not maintain that pace for the whole campaign. You know the cliché about class being permanent and form only temporary? It could have been written with Dream Team managers in mind.

16. When making your transfer moves, remember to look at the overall picture. If you are making three changes, predict how many points the trio in total is going to score for your team and see if there are better threesomes out there. Sometimes bringing in three mid-price players can be a sounder move than signing one superstar and two cheap duffers because you have run out of money.

17. Consider a player's disciplinary record, but do not live or die by it, unless it is particularly bad.

18. Be aware that there is an extra scoring criterion this year, with points also being awarded for the *News of the World*'s team of the day. It should not affect your strategy unduly but do not dismiss it out of hand and keep an eye on whether particular players are benefiting as a result of these new ratings.

19. The domestic cup competitions can make a difference to your score, but it is European football that provides the greatest boost to your total, so look to have as many players in Champions League or UEFA Cup action as you can, particularly after the first transfer window.

CHAPTER 22

STATISTICALLY SPEAKING: 2006–07 DREAM TEAM STANDINGS

– GOALKEEPERS –

Name	Club	Value	P1	P2	TOT	PPM
Friedel	BLA	4.5	30	72	159	35.3
Reina	LIV	5.0	11	76	150	30.0
Cech	CHE	5.5	31	19	146	26.5
James	MCY	3.0	39	66	145	48.3
P Robinson	TOT	4.0	28	66	129	32.3
Van der Sar	MAN	5.0	28	56	125	25.0
Howard	EVE	2.5	18	62	113	45.2
B Foster	WAT	1.5	5	55	110	73.3
Jaaskelainen	BOL	4.5	41	56	110	24.4
Carson	LIV	1.0	24	46	100	100.0
Hahnemann	REA	2.0	20	29	98	49.0
Sorensen	AST	3.0	35	20	90	30.0
Lehmann	ARS	5.0	20	42	69	13.8
Kenny	SHE	1.5	16	42	68	45.3
R Green	WHM	2.0	0	28	65	32.5
S Harper	NEW	1.0	12	35	62	62.0

Name	Club	Value	P1	P2	TOT	PPM
Kirkland	WIG	2.5	15	37	59	23.6
Niemi	FUL	3.5	9	26	59	16.9
Given	NEW	3.5	11	29	58	16.6
Schwarzer	MID	3.0	5	39	54	18.0
Cudicini	CHE	2.0	4	34	43	21.5
Filan	WIG	2.0	0	0	31	15.5
Isaksson	MCY	2.5	0	-2	30	12.0
Almunia	ARS	1.0	0	15	25	25.0
Myhre	CHA	2.0	5	5	10	5.0
Carroll	WHM	2.5	-1	2	4	1.6
Kiely	POR	2.5	3	0	3	1.2
Andersen	CHA	1.0	0	0	0	0.0
Ashdown	POR	1.0	0	0	0	0.0
R Wright	EVE	1.0	0	-2	-2	-2.0
Warner	FUL	1.0	0	-2	-2	-2.0

– DEFENDERS –

Name	Club	Value	P1	P2	TOT	PPM
Carragher	LIV	6.0	23	118	219	36.5
Carvalho	CHE	4.5	30	98	211	46.9
Terry	CHE	8.0	38	70	201	25.1
Agger	LIV	4.0	39	85	189	47.3
R Ferdinand	MAN	6.0	40	77	189	31.5
Toure	ARS	5.5	27	105	178	32.4
Vidic	MAN	4.0	16	83	152	38.0
Finnan	LIV	4.0	19	87	147	36.8
Dawson	TOT	4.0	35	83	143	35.8
O'Shea	MAN	4.0	23	59	142	35.5
Lescott	EVE	2.0	23	65	135	67.5
Bridge	CHE	2.5	26	48	135	54.0
Dunne	MCY	3.0	27	77	135	45.0
Matt Taylor	POR	3.0	30	66	128	42.7
G Neville	MAN	4.5	23	68	126	28.0
Yobo	EVE	3.0	23	50	125	41.7
Distin	MCY	3.0	20	60	124	41.3

Name	Club	Value	P1	P2	TOT	PPM
S Campbell	POR	3.0	40	57	124	41.3
Steven Taylor	NEW	2.0	1	81	122	61.0
Shorey	REA	2.0	20	50	122	61.0
Woodgate	MID	3.0	17	60	122	40.7
Evra	MAN	2.5	26	52	121	48.4
Primus	POR	2.5	41	58	121	48.4
Ingimarsson	REA	2.0	32	42	113	56.5
Ashley Cole	ARS	5.0	15	51	112	22.4
Gallas	CHE	5.5	40	38	107	19.5
Mellberg	AST	2.0	36	24	98	49.0
Ferreira	CHE	4.0	19	29	98	24.5
Chimbonda	WIG	3.5	20	60	95	27.1
Stubbs	EVE	2.0	0	35	92	46.0
Hyypia	LIV	4.5	3	53	92	20.4
M Richards	MCY	3.5	28	59	90	25.7
Khizanishvili	BLA	2.5	18	39	89	35.6
L Young	CHA	2.5	14	25	86	34.4
Clichy	ARS	2.5	0	52	85	34.0
Eboue	ARS	3.0	34	45	85	28.3
Meite	BOL	2.5	35	33	82	32.8
DeMerit	WAT	1.5	9	48	81	54.0
Pogatetz	MID	2.0	9	51	81	40.5
Djourou	ARS	2.5	10	50	75	30.0
Neill	BLA	3.5	19	26	75	21.4
Arca	MID	2.5	-2	42	74	29.6
El Karkouri	CHA	2.0	3	38	71	35.5
L King	TOT	4.0	20	43	71	17.8
Baines	WIG	2.5	8	38	66	26.4
W Brown	MAN	4.5	13	24	66	14.7
Warnock	LIV	2.5	4	18	65	26.0
Scharner	WIG	2.5	18	34	65	26.0
A Taylor	MID	3.0	1	48	65	21.7
Heinze	MAN	4.5	12	14	63	14.0
Ben Haim	BOL	4.0	28	23	61	15.3
Silvestre	MAN	4.0	16	33	61	15.3

Name	Club	Value	P1	P2	TOT	PPM
Hunt	BOL	1.5	22	36	60	40.0
Bouma	AST	1.0	0	18	57	57.0
C Davis	SHE	2.0	9	34	57	28.5
Aurelio	LIV	2.0	17	29	56	28.0
Murty	REA	2.0	15	25	56	28.0
Sonko	REA	2.0	20	35	55	27.5
Assou-Ekotto	TOT	2.0	16	40	55	27.5
G Johnson	POR	2.0	28	13	54	27.0
Ridgewell	AST	3.0	29	20	54	18.0
Mullins	WHM	2.5	2	45	53	21.2
Ooijer	BLA	3.0	16	37	53	17.7
Boulahrouz	CHE	4.0	12	35	52	13.0
Stefanovic	POR	2.0	31	8	51	25.5
M Laursen	AST	1.5	16	5	50	33.3
Jackson	WIG	2.0	1	6	50	25.0
Volz	FUL	1.0	3	56	49	49.0
Bocanegra	FUL	1.0	5	19	48	48.0
Mackay	WAT	1.5	6	30	48	32.0
De Zeeuw	WIG	3.0	16	23	48	16.0
Nelsen	BLA	4.0	0	3	48	12.0
Trabelsi	MCY	2.5	0	39	45	18.0
A Ferdinand	WHM	3.0	0	20	44	14.7
Bramble	NEW	2.5	0	28	42	16.8
James Collins	WHM	2.0	-2	-1	41	20.5
Queudrue	FUL	3.0	8	33	41	13.7
Morgan	SHE	1.5	8	18	40	26.7
Ramage	NEW	2.0	10	31	40	20.0
Hreidarsson	CHA	3.0	-6	23	40	13.3
Boyce	WIG	2.0	8	8	37	18.5
G Cahill	AST	1.5	0	25	36	24.0
Carr	NEW	2.0	11	14	31	15.5
M Gray	BLA	2.5	6	25	31	12.4
Knight	FUL	2.0	5	20	30	15.0
Lee Young Pyo	TOT	2.0	11	5	30	15.0
Senderos	ARS	4.5	0	18	29	6.4

Name	Club	Value	P1	P2	TOT	PPM
Rosenior	FUL	1.5	5	15	28	18.7
Leigertwood	SHE	1.5	1	27	27	18.0
Lauren	ARS	3.0	0	10	26	8.7
A Davies	MID	3.0	7	22	26	8.7
Gabbidon	WHM	3.0	4	22	26	8.7
Jordan	MCY	2.0	11	14	24	12.0
Huth	MID	3.0	0	26	23	7.7
Doyley	WAT	1.5	6	5	21	14.0
Ryan Taylor	WIG	1.5	0	-6	20	13.3
A Gardner	TOT	2.0	0	14	20	10.0
Spector	WHM	2.0	1	8	20	10.0
Sun Jihai	MCY	2.0	0	0	19	9.5
Hibbert	EVE	2.5	4	-1	19	7.6
Weir	EVE	2.5	5	14	19	7.6
Powell	WAT	1.5	1	3	17	11.3
Nuno Valente	EVE	2.5	3	14	17	6.8
Unsworth	SHE	1.5	5	-9	16	10.7
A Hughes	AST	2.0	10	-1	16	8.0
Babayaro	NEW	2.0	5	3	16	8.0
Hall	WIG	2.0	7	9	16	8.0
Todd	BLA	2.5	-3	17	15	6.0
Paletta	LIV	3.5	0	7	14	4.0
De La Cruz	AST	2.0	3	0	13	6.5
Stalteri	TOT	3.0	0	12	12	4.0
Bromby	SHE	1.5	-1	12	9	6.0
Parnaby	MID	3.5	-2	8	8	2.3
Traore	LIV	2.5	-1	3	7	2.8
Berner	BLA	2.0	0	0	5	2.5
Samuel	AST	1.0	-1	2	1	1.0
Cygan	ARS	2.0	0	0	0	0.0
Delaney	AST	2.0	0	0	0	0.0
Jaidi	BOL	2.5	0	0	0	0.0
J O'Brien	BOL	1.5	0	0	0	0.0
Rehman	FUL	2.0	0	0	0	0.0
Mears	WHM	1.5	0	0	0	0.0

Name	Club	Value	P1	P2	TOT	PPM
A O'Brien	POR	2.0	0	-1	-1	-0.5
Ehiogu	MID	3.0	0	-2	-2	-0.7
Sorondo	CHA	2.0	-2	0	-2	-1.0
Sodje	REA	1.5	-1	-1	-2	-1.3
Riggott	MID	4.0	-3	2	-3	-0.8
Pantsil	WHM	2.5	2	-6	-4	-1.6
J Fortune	CHA	1.5	1	-3	-4	-2.7
Konchesky	WHM	2.5	1	2	-5	-2.0
Sommeil	SHE	2.0	0	-5	-5	-2.5
Carlisle	WAT	1.5	0	0	-5	-3.3

– MIDFIELDERS –

Name	Club	Value	P1	P2	TOT	PPM
Lampard	CHE	8.0	55	202	375	46.9
Ronaldo	MAN	5.0	57	143	314	62.8
Gerrard	LIV	8.0	27	134	242	30.3
Essien	CHE	4.5	58	102	231	51.3
Scholes	MAN	4.0	21	97	192	48.0
Barry	AST	3.5	42	73	175	50.0
Arteta	EVE	3.5	29	80	175	50.0
Giggs	MAN	4.0	38	54	165	41.3
Fabregas	ARS	5.0	16	78	161	32.2
Barton	MCY	4.0	26	71	148	37.0
Rosicky	ARS	4.5	27	62	148	32.9
Bentley	BLA	3.0	29	69	142	47.3
Gamst Pedersen	BLA	4.0	21	79	142	35.5
Gilberto	ARS	5.0	24	82	142	28.4
Jagielka	SHE	2.5	27	63	126	50.4
Carrick	MAN	5.0	13	44	125	25.0
Jenas	TOT	3.0	38	33	123	41.0
Xabi Alonso	LIV	5.0	18	68	123	24.6
Speed	BOL	3.0	30	43	115	38.3
Milner	NEW	2.5	4	91	113	45.2
Lennon	TOT	4.0	5	74	113	28.3
Sidwell	REA	2.5	30	51	110	44.0

Name	Club	Value	P1	P2	TOT	PPM
S W-Phillips	CHE	3.0	7	32	108	36.0
Ballack	CHE	8.0	21	50	107	13.4
Makelele	CHE	4.5	16	57	104	23.1
Robben	CHE	5.0	9	62	104	20.8
Dyer	NEW	3.0	0	70	102	34.0
Pennant	LIV	4.0	14	40	99	24.8
Parker	NEW	4.0	39	36	99	24.8
Carsley	EVE	2.0	18	40	98	49.0
P Neville	EVE	3.0	20	41	98	32.7
Tugay	BLA	2.5	24	45	97	38.8
Campo	BOL	2.0	49	34	95	47.5
Butt	NEW	2.0	4	66	95	47.5
Osman	EVE	3.5	11	59	94	26.9
Harper	REA	2.5	13	49	88	35.2
Zokora	TOT	3.0	25	17	86	28.7
T Cahill	EVE	4.5	47	34	86	19.1
Riise	LIV	4.0	9	35	84	21.0
Nolan	BOL	4.5	37	32	84	18.7
Downing	MID	3.5	17	46	83	23.7
Savage	BLA	3.5	25	56	81	23.1
McCulloch	WIG	2.5	13	41	79	31.6
Sibierski	MCY	2.0	12	51	78	39.0
Francis	WAT	2.0	14	34	76	38.0
McCann	AST	3.0	15	53	75	25.0
D Fletcher	MAN	3.0	16	27	74	24.7
Solano	NEW	4.0	0	47	73	18.3
Hleb	ARS	4.5	22	41	73	16.2
Benjani	POR	2.5	23	27	72	28.8
Seol Ki Hyeon	REA	2.5	35	18	69	27.6
Petrov	AST	3.0	10	34	69	23.0
Malbranque	FUL	4.0	0	43	68	17.0
Little	REA	2.0	7	42	64	32.0
Ireland	MCY	1.5	4	36	63	42.0
Emerton	BLA	2.0	20	21	62	31.0
Mendes	POR	2.5	17	29	62	24.8

Name	Club	Value	P1	P2	TOT	PPM
Mikel	CHE	3.0	10	25	62	20.7
Gonzalez	LIV	4.5	17	33	62	13.8
Emre	NEW	4.0	16	33	61	15.3
M Brown	FUL	2.0	2	28	59	29.5
Mahon	WAT	2.0	5	30	59	29.5
Gunnarsson	REA	2.0	7	15	58	29.0
Cattermole	MID	3.0	8	39	58	19.3
Boateng	MID	3.5	-5	29	57	16.3
Park Ji Sung	MAN	4.0	7	10	57	14.3
Reo-Coker	WHM	4.0	5	28	56	14.0
Tonge	SHE	2.0	6	21	55	27.5
Benayoun	WHM	3.5	3	33	54	15.4
Simon Davies	EVE	1.5	3	19	52	34.7
Holland	CHA	2.0	11	22	52	26.0
Landzaat	WIG	2.5	10	20	52	20.8
Flamini	ARS	3.5	5	36	51	14.6
O'Neil	POR	3.5	15	23	51	14.6
Abdoulaye Faye	BOL	2.5	7	36	49	19.6
Ambrose	CHA	2.0	10	15	47	23.5
Sean Davis	POR	2.0	15	22	45	22.5
Richardson	MAN	2.5	0	15	45	18.0
Beasley	MCY	2.5	0	20	44	17.6
Duff	NEW	4.0	21	16	44	11.0
Morrison	MID	2.5	16	28	43	17.2
Thomas	CHA	2.0	0	11	42	21.0
Geremi	CHE	2.0	2	32	42	21.0
Kilbane	EVE	2.0	4	24	42	21.0
Tainio	TOT	2.0	10	18	42	21.0
A Reid	TOT	2.0	2	39	41	20.5
Danny Murphy	TOT	2.5	20	21	41	16.4
McFadden	EVE	2.5	0	27	40	16.0
Sissoko	LIV	4.5	11	14	40	8.9
Rommedahl	CHA	2.0	8	18	38	19.0
Amdy Faye	NEW	2.5	10	23	38	15.2
Mascherano	WHM	3.5	3	-1	38	10.9

Name	Club	Value	P1	P2	TOT	PPM
Zenden	LIV	4.0	2	16	38	9.5
Ljungberg	ARS	3.5	6	13	37	10.6
Berger	AST	2.0	0	5	35	17.5
Mokoena	BLA	2.5	3	11	35	14.0
J Cole	CHE	5.5	1	17	34	6.2
C Jensen	FUL	1.0	0	33	33	33.0
D Dunn	BLA	2.0	0	0	33	16.5
B Hughes	CHA	2.0	2	30	32	16.0
Valencia	WIG	1.5	0	13	31	20.7
Montgomery	SHE	2.0	0	19	31	15.5
A Quinn	SHE	2.0	17	11	30	15.0
Routledge	TOT	2.0	6	24	30	15.0
Steven Davis	AST	4.0	15	13	30	7.5
Idan Tal	BOL	1.5	6	18	27	18.0
N'Zogbia	NEW	3.5	2	20	26	7.4
Reyna	MCY	2.0	3	22	25	12.5
R Hughes	POR	2.0	4	2	24	12.0
Davids	TOT	3.0	15	8	23	7.7
Stelios	BOL	4.5	7	14	23	5.1
Bullard	FUL	4.0	22	0	22	5.5
Diaby	ARS	3.0	0	-1	21	7.0
Bowyer	WHM	3.0	11	9	21	7.0
Kishishev	CHA	2.0	6	14	20	10.0
Etherington	WHM	2.5	2	9	20	8.0
Sinclair	MCY	2.0	9	6	17	8.5
Teale	WIG	2.0	3	14	17	8.5
Rochemback	MID	2.5	0	4	17	6.8
D Thompson	POR	2.5	11	6	17	6.8
Q Fortune	BOL	2.5	13	2	15	6.0
Diop	FUL	3.0	4	2	14	4.7
Hamann	MCY	3.0	4	3	13	4.3
van der Meyde	EVE	2.0	0	8	10	5.0
Spring	WAT	2.0	5	3	8	4.0
Li Tie	SHE	2.5	5	0	5	2.0
Peter	BLA	3.0	0	3	5	1.7

Name	Club	Value	P1	P2	TOT	PPM
Dabo	MCY	3.0	-2	8	5	1.7
Kewell	LIV	4.0	0	0	5	1.3
Smertin	FUL	2.0	0	0	2	1.0
Ifill	SHE	2.5	2	0	2	0.8
Kavanagh	WIG	2.5	2	0	2	0.8
S Reid	BLA	4.0	0	0	0	0.0
Bolanos	CHA	2.0	0	0	0	0.0
S Elliott	FUL	2.0	0	0	0	0.0
Legwinski	FUL	1.5	0	0	0	0.0
C Fletcher	WHM	1.5	0	0	0	0.0
Hendrie	AST	1.0	-1	0	-1	-1.0

– STRIKERS –

Name	Club	Value	P1	P2	TOT	PPM
Drogba	CHE	4.5	68	150	318	70.7
Rooney	MAN	8.0	18	142	263	32.9
Berbatov	TOT	4.5	11	125	255	56.7
McCarthy	BLA	3.5	48	92	215	61.4
Robbie Keane	TOT	4.5	16	61	188	41.8
Viduka	MID	4.0	10	78	185	46.3
Kuyt	LIV	4.0	28	90	171	42.8
Defoe	TOT	3.5	11	111	158	45.1
Martins	NEW	3.5	26	58	146	41.7
Andy Johnson	EVE	4.5	55	46	138	30.7
D Bent	CHA	4.0	42	49	136	34.0
Crouch	LIV	4.0	25	60	135	33.8
Shevchenko	CHE	6.0	17	50	134	22.3
Doyle	REA	2.5	27	64	123	49.2
Adebayor	ARS	3.0	16	69	122	40.7
Saha	MAN	5.0	45	55	113	22.6
Henry	ARS	8.0	29	74	113	14.1
Yakubu	MID	4.5	13	71	111	24.7
McBride	FUL	3.5	19	75	110	31.4
Lita	REA	2.0	21	63	105	52.5
Anelka	BOL	4.0	5	66	102	25.5

Name	Club	Value	P1	P2	TOT	PPM
Tevez	WHM	5.0	3	14	98	19.6
Agbonlahor	AST	1.5	0	53	97	64.7
Kevin Davies	BOL	3.0	10	40	97	32.3
Heskey	WIG	3.0	16	48	93	31.0
A Young	WAT	2.0	27	45	91	45.5
Van Persie	ARS	4.0	13	75	88	22.0
Bellamy	LIV	4.5	6	54	85	18.9
Solskjaer	MAN	2.0	26	37	80	40.0
Zamora	WHM	2.5	36	2	79	31.6
Kanu	POR	3.0	10	47	76	25.3
Kalou	CHE	3.5	6	24	76	21.7
Diouf	BOL	2.0	9	58	75	37.5
Baptista	ARS	5.0	0	50	74	14.8
Hulse	SHE	2.5	19	29	64	25.6
Angel	AST	2.0	39	23	62	31.0
Fowler	LIV	3.5	13	29	54	15.4
Henri Camara	WIG	2.5	7	48	53	21.2
Roberts	BLA	4.0	6	3	52	13.0
Carew	AST	2.0	0	0	50	25.0
Luis Garcia	LIV	4.0	10	40	50	12.5
Samaras	MCY	2.5	23	26	49	19.6
Radzinski	FUL	2.0	2	35	42	21.0
Mido	TOT	4.5	1	37	41	9.1
Walcott	ARS	2.5	11	21	40	16.0
Andy Cole	MCY	4.0	0	40	39	9.8
Hasselbaink	CHA	5.0	7	28	37	7.4
Vassell	MCY	3.0	0	26	36	12.0
L Moore	AST	2.5	19	0	35	14.0
Webber	SHE	2.5	6	29	35	14.0
M King	WAT	2.5	19	0	35	14.0
Kitson	REA	2.5	8	4	33	13.2
D Henderson	WAT	2.0	0	4	32	16.0
Helguson	FUL	3.0	17	7	32	10.7
Harewood	WHM	3.5	-2	23	29	8.3
Ameobi	NEW	3.5	24	5	28	8.0

Name	Club	Value	P1	P2	TOT	PPM
M Bent	CHA	2.0	0	24	27	13.5
Sheringham	WHM	1.5	2	22	24	16.0
LuaLua	POR	3.0	8	8	24	8.0
A Smith	MAN	4.0	0	0	22	5.5
Boa Morte	FUL	3.0	-1	10	19	6.3
Baros	AST	2.5	0	18	18	7.2
Carlton Cole	WHM	2.0	6	11	17	8.5
Beattie	EVE	4.0	9	7	15	3.8
John	FUL	3.0	6	8	14	4.7
Corradi	MCY	3.0	-4	13	13	4.3
Larsson	MAN	4.5	0	0	11	2.4
H Pedersen	BOL	1.0	0	10	10	10.0
Todorov	POR	2.0	9	0	9	4.5
Maccarone	MID	2.5	0	9	9	3.6
Akinbiyi	SHE	2.0	0	8	8	4.0
Convey	REA	2.5	0	8	8	3.2
Jeffers	BLA	2.0	2	5	7	3.5
Kabba	SHE	2.0	0	-1	5	2.5
Dickov	MCY	2.5	2	3	4	1.6
Luque	NEW	3.0	-1	5	4	1.3
Johansson	WIG	2.0	0	3	3	1.5
Vaz Te	BOL	2.5	0	3	3	1.2
Montella	FUL	3.0	0	0	2	0.7
Reyes	ARS	4.0	0	0	0	0.0
Phillips	AST	3.0	0	0	0	0.0
Kuqi	BLA	2.5	0	0	0	0.0
Borgetti	BOL	2.0	0	0	0	0.0
Crespo	CHE	4.5	0	0	0	0.0
Shipperley	SHE	2.0	0	0	0	0.0
Ashton	WHM	3.5	0	0	0	0.0
Connolly	WIG	2.0	0	0	0	0.0

TOP-TEN GOALKEEPERS BY SEASON

– TOP-TEN GOALKEEPERS 2006–07 –

Rk	Player	Club	£m	Tot
1	Friedel	BLA	4.5	159
2	Reina	LIV	5.0	150
3	Cech	CHE	5.5	146
4	James	MNC	3.0	145
5	P Robinson	TOT	4.0	129
6	van der Sar	MAN	5.0	125
7	Howard	EVE	2.5	113
8	Jaaskelainen	BOL	4.5	110
9	Foster	WAT	1.5	110
10	Carson	LIV	1.0	100

– TOP-TEN GOALKEEPERS 2005–06 –

Rk	Player	Club	£m	Tot
1	Lehmann	ARS	4.0	188
2	van der Sar	MAN	4.5	185
3	Reina	LIV	4.0	181
4	Cech	CHE	5.5	149
5	P Robinson	TOT	4.0	147
6	Friedel	BLA	3.5	146
7	Jaaskelainen	BOL	3.0	140
8	Given	NEW	3.5	136
9	Schwarzer	MID	3.5	125
10	Maik Taylor	BIR	3.0	98

– TOP-TEN GOALKEEPERS 2004–05 –

Rk	Player	Club	£m	Tot
1	Cech	CHE	4.0	201
2	P Robinson	TOT	3.5	146
3	Friedel	BLA	2.0	139
4	Carroll	MAN	3.0	127
5	Schwarzer	MID	3.5	123
6	Lehmann	ARS	4.5	122
7	Given	NEW	4.5	118
8	Kiely	CHA	3.0	114
9	James	MCY	3.5	107
10	Martyn	EVE	3.0	106

– TOP-TEN GOALKEEPERS 2003–04 –

Rk	Player	Club	£m	Tot
1	Given	NEW	4.0	164
2	Lehmann	ARS	4.0	153
3	van der Sar	FUL	3.0	151
4	Cudicini	CHE	4.5	142
5	Howard	MAN	2.5	136
6	Schwarzer	MID	3.0	119
7	Dudek	LIV	4.5	116
8	Martyn	LEE	2.0	111
9	M Taylor	FUL	3.0	110
10	Niemi	SOU	3.0	104

– TOP-TEN GOALKEEPERS 2002–03 –

Rk	Player	Club	£m	Tot
1	P Robinson	LEE	2.0	169
2	Dudek	LIV	4.5	167
3	Friedel	BLA	3.0	157
4	Cudicini	CHE	4.0	125
5	Seaman	ARS	3.5	121
6	Barthez	MAN	4.5	117
7	Schwarzer	MID	1.5	114
8	Given	NEW	3.5	112
9	Niemi	SOU	2.0	107
10	Kiely	CHA	3.0	105

– TOP-TEN GOALKEEPERS 2001–02 –

Rk	Player	Club	£m	Tot
1	Dudek	LIV	4.5	230
2	Cudicini	CHE	3.5	196
3	Martyn	LEE	4.5	191
4	Given	NEW	2.5	159
5	van der Sar	FUL	3.5	143
6	Friedel	BLA	3.0	131
7	Barthez	MAN	4.5	127
8	Kiely	CHA	3.0	114
9	James	WES	3.0	102
10	Crossley	MID	1.5	101

TOP-20 GOALKEEPERS: CUMULATIVE

TOP-20 DREAM TEAM GOALKEEPERS OF THE LAST FIVE YEARS								
Rank	Player	Club	06–07	05–06	04–05	03–04	02–03	Total	Avg.
1	Friedel	BLA	159	146	139	52	157	**653**	130.6
2	P Robinson	TOT	129	147	146	35	169	**626**	125.2
3	van der Sar	MAN	125	185	81	151	79	**621**	124.2
4	Given	NEW	58	136	118	164	112	**588**	117.6
5	Schwarzer	MID	54	125	123	119	114	**535**	107.0
6	Lehmann	ARS	69	188	122	153		**532**	133.0
7	Cech	CHE	146	149	201			**496**	165.3
8	Jaaskelainen	BOL	110	140	101	67	64	**482**	96.4
9	James	MCY*	145	91	107	39	68	**450**	90.0
10	Sorensen	AST	90	83	76	99	40	**388**	77.6
11	Cudicini	CHE	43	24	47	142	125	**381**	76.2
12	Kiely	POR*	3	25	114	101	105	**348**	69.6
13	Niemi	FUL*	59	10	66	104	107	**346**	69.2
14	Howard	EVE*	113	16	78	136		**343**	85.8
15	Reina	LIV	150	181				**331**	165.5
16	Carroll	WHM*	4	31	127	43	41	**246**	49.2
17	Green	WHM*	65		79			**144**	72.0
18	R Wright	EVE*	-2	22		0	101	**121**	30.3
19	B Foster	WAT*	110					**110**	110.0
20	Carson	LIV*	100					**100**	100.0

(* alongside club name = played for more than one club, played on loan at another club or was subsequently transferred to a side different from that which he was originally listed for)

TOP-TEN DEFENDERS BY SEASON

– TOP-TEN DEFENDERS 2006–07 –

Rk	Player	Club	£m	Tot
1	Carragher	LIV	6.0	219
2	Carvalho	CHE	4.5	211
3	Terry	CHE	8.0	201
4	Agger	LIV	4.0	189
4	R Ferdinand	MAN	6.0	189
6	Toure	ARS	5.5	178
7	Vidic	MAN	4.0	152
8	Finnan	LIV	4.0	147
9	M Dawson	TOT	4.0	143
10	O'Shea	MAN	4.0	142

– TOP-TEN DEFENDERS 2005–06 –

Rk	Player	Club	£m	Tot
1	Terry	CHE	8.0	302
2	Carragher	LIV	5.5	256
3	Hyypia	LIV	4.5	230
4	R Ferdinand	MAN	5.5	213
5	Toure	ARS	4.5	197
6	Finnan	LIV	4.0	186
7	Gallas	CHE	5.0	184
8	N'Gotty	BOL	3.0	166
9	O'Shea	MAN	4.5	157
10	Riggott	MID	3.5	154

– TOP-TEN DEFENDERS 2004–05 –

Rk	Player	Club	£m	Tot
1	Terry	CHE	6.0	368
2	Carragher	LIV	4.0	198
3	Gallas	CHE	5.0	197
4	R Ferdinand	MAN	6.0	195
5	Ferreira	CHE	5.0	167
6	Heinze	MAN	4.5	165
7	Ashley Cole	ARS	4.5	153
8	Toure	ARS	4.0	153
9	Todd	BLA	2.0	147
10	Silvestre	MAN	5.0	146

– TOP-TEN DEFENDERS 2003–04 –

Rk	Player	Club	£m	Tot
1	Terry	CHE	4.0	249
2	Bridge	CHE	4.0	206
3	Gallas	CHE	5.0	180
4	Campbell	ARS	5.0	179
5	Hyypia	LIV	6.0	173
6	G Neville	MAN	4.5	163
7	Silvestre	MAN	4.0	154
8	A Cole	ARS	4.5	151
9	Barry	AST	4.5	149
10	O'Shea	MAN	5.0	138

– TOP-TEN DEFENDERS 2002–03–

Rk	Player	Club	£m	Tot
1	Hyypia	LIV	6.0	244
2	Gallas	CHE	3.5	200
3	Barry	AST	2.0	180
4	Campbell	ARS	6.0	178
5	Woodgate	LEE	3.0	162
6	Geremi	MID	2.5	160
7	Silvestre	MAN	3.5	152
8	Mellberg	AST	2.5	150
9	O'Shea	MAN	2.5	149
10	Southgate	MID	4.0	138

– TOP-TEN DEFENDERS 2001–02 –

Rk	Player	Club	£m	Tot
1	Hyypia	LIV	6.0	279
2	Henchoz	LIV	4.5	258
3	Terry	CHE	2.5	214
4	R Ferdinand	LEE	5.5	198
5	Campbell	ARS	5.5	192
6	Carragher	LIV	4.5	190
7	Southgate	MID	4.0	188
8	Weir	EVE	2.5	167
9	Harte	LEE	4.5	160
10	Finnan	FUL	2.5	153

TOP-50 DEFENDERS: CUMULATIVE

Rank	Player	Club	06–07	05–06	04–05	03–04	02–03	Total	Avg.
	**TOP-50 DREAM TEAM DEFENDERS OF THE LAST FIVE YEARS**								

Rank	Player	Club	06–07	05–06	04–05	03–04	02–03	Total	Avg.
1	Terry	CHE	201	302	368	249	127	**1247**	249.4
2	Carragher	LIV	219	256	198	111	134	**918**	183.6
3	Hyypia	LIV	92	230	134	178	244	**878**	175.6
4	Gallas	ARS*	107	184	197	180	200	**868**	173.6
5	Ferdinand, R	MAN*	189	213	195	121	130	**848**	169.6
6	O'Shea	MAN	142	157	145	137	149	**730**	146.0
7	Campbell	POR*	124	108	82	179	178	**671**	134.2
8	Neville, G	MAN	126	126	118	163	136	**669**	133.8
9	Silvestre	MAN	61	128	146	153	152	**640**	128.0
10	Toure	ARS	178	197	153	98*	11*	**637**	127.4
11	Finnan	LIV*	147	186	121	73	99	**626**	125.2
12	Cole, A	CHE*	112	51	153	151	130	**597**	119.4
13	Bridge	CHE*	135	19	104	206	119	**583**	116.6
14	Mellberg	AST	98	53	73	137	150	**511**	102.2
15	Carvalho	CHE	211	132	140			**483**	161.0
16	Dunne	MCY	135	62	134	86	60	**477**	95.4
17	Brown, W	MAN	66	115	140	58	95	**474**	94.8
18	Lauren	ARS*	26	87	142	99	118	**472**	94.4
19	Queudrue	FUL*	41	110	125	108	81	**465**	93.0
20	Distin	MCY	124	64	115	78	69	**450**	90.0
21	Woodgate	MID*	122		0	135	162	**419**	104.8
22	Yobo	EVE	125	72	40	89	69	**395**	79.0
23	King	TOT	71	106	135*	49	22	**383**	76.6
24	Ferreira	CHE	98	107	167			**372**	124.0
25	Stubbs	EVE*	92		129	56	95	**372**	93.0
26	De Zeeuw	WIG*	48	110	92	92		**342**	85.5
27	Riggott	MID	-3	154	107	63	15	**336**	67.2
28	Hreidarsson	CHA	40	116	90	83		**329**	82.3
29	Bramble	NEW	42	94	54	96	36	**322**	64.4
30	Neill	BLA	75	114	104	23		**316**	79.0

31	Hughes, A	AST*	16	60	51	94	93	**314**	62.8
32	Taylor, Matt	POR	128	77	26	76		**307**	76.8
33	Young	CHA	86	96	65		33	**280**	70.0
34	Todd	BLA	15	73	147	21	22	**278**	55.6
35	Carr	NEW*	31	41	100	41	45	**258**	51.6
36	Johnson, G	POR*	54	15	75	112		**256**	64.0
37	Primus	POR	121	15	58	58		**252**	63.0
38	Heinze	MAN	63	23	165			**251**	83.7
39	O'Brien	POR*	-1	33	51	99	62	**244**	48.8
40	Knight	FUL	30	25	77	107		**239**	59.8
41	Hibbert	EVE	19	61	98	58		**236**	59.0
42	Delaney	AST	0	54	65	66	50	**235**	47.0
43	Chimbonda	WIG*	95	131				**226**	113.0
44	Unsworth	SHU*	16		47	41	99	**203**	50.8
45	Gardner	TOT	20	49	67	67		**203**	50.8
46	Stefanovic	WBA	51	38	51	59		**199**	49.8
47	El Karkouri	CHA	71	12	114			**197**	65.7
48	Agger	LIV	189					**189**	189.0
49	Babayaro	NEW*	16	60	43	38.0	28.0	**185**	37.0
50	Nelsen	BLA	48	136				**184**	92.0

(* alongside club name = played for more than one club, played on loan at another club or was subsequently transferred to a side different from that he was originally listed for)

(* alongside season points score = was listed in Dream Team in a different playing position that particular season from the one which he was listed in the game for 2006-07)

TOP-TEN MIDFIELDERS BY SEASON

– TOP-TEN MIDFIELDERS 2006–07 –

Rk	Player	Club	£m	Tot
1	Lampard	CHE	8.0	375
2	Ronaldo	MAN	5.0	314
3	Gerrard	LIV	8.0	242
4	Essien	CHE	4.5	231
5	Scholes	MAN	4.0	192
6	Barry	AST	3.5	175
7	Arteta	EVE	3.5	175
8	Giggs	MAN	4.0	165
9	Fabregas	ARS	5.0	161
10	Rosicky	ARS	4.5	148
10	Barton	MNC	4.0	148

– TOP-TEN MIDFIELDERS 2005–06 –

Rk	Player	Club	£m	Tot
1	Gerrard	LIV	6.0	309
2	Lampard	CHE	8.0	257
3	Nolan	BOL	3.0	174
4	J Cole	CHE	5.5	171
5	Stelios	BOL	3.0	170
6	Xabi Alonso	LIV	5.0	166
7	Steven Davis	AST	2.5	153
8	Pires	ARS	5.0	150
9	Ronaldo	MAN	5.5	147
10	Reo-Coker	WHM	2.5	141

– TOP-TEN MIDFIELDERS 2004–05 –

Rk	Player	Club	£m	Tot
1	Lampard	CHE	6.5	342
2	Gerrard	LIV	6.5	212
3	Scholes	MAN	5.0	202
4	S W-Phillips	MCY	4.5	195
5	J Cole	CHE	3.0	188
6	Vieira	ARS	4.5	185
7	Ljungberg	ARS	4.5	183
8	Duff	CHE	4.5	181
9	Pires	ARS	5.5	180
10	Ronaldo	MAN	5.0	179

– TOP-TEN MIDFIELDERS 2003–04 –

Rk	Player	Club	£m	Tot
1	Lampard	CHE	4.5	250
2	Gerrard	LIV	5.0	226
3	Pires	ARS	5.0	196
4	Scholes	MAN	5.0	172
5	Malbranque	FUL	3.5	159
6	Giggs	MAN	4.5	152
7	S W-Phillips	MCY	2.5	148
8	Nolan	BOL	2.5	135
9	Speed	NEW	3.0	129
10	Robert	NEW	3.5	128

– TOP-TEN MIDFIELDERS 2002–03 –

Rk	Player	Club	£m	Tot
1	Scholes	MAN	4.5	219
2	Murphy	LIV	4.0	193
3	Gerrard	LIV	5.0	187
4	Giggs	MAN	4.5	181
5	Kewell	LEE	4.5	180
6	Lampard	CHE	4.0	172
7	Pires	ARS	5.0	161
8	Malbranque	FUL	3.5	159
9	Duff	BLA	4.5	145
10	Beckham	MAN	6.0	139

– TOP-TEN MIDFIELDERS 2001–02 –

Rk	Player	Club	£m	Tot
1	Ljungberg	ARS	3.5	196
2	Pires	ARS	3.5	185
3	Beckham	MAN	4.5	171
4	Anderton	TOT	2.5	154
5	Duff	BLA	3.0	153
6	Giggs	MAN	4.5	153
7	Malbranque	FUL	2.5	152
8	Riise	LIV	2.5	151
9	Dunn	BLA	2.5	148
10	Roy Keane	MAN	3.5	146

TOP-50 MIDFIELDERS: CUMULATIVE

TOP-50 DREAM TEAM MIDFIELDERS OF THE LAST FIVE YEARS

Rank	Player	Club	06–07	05–06	04–05	03–04	02–03	Total	Avg.
1	Lampard	CHE	375	257	342	250	172	1396	279.2
2	Gerrard	LIV	242	309	212	226	187	1176	235.2
3	Scholes	MAN	192	81	202	177	219	871	174.2
4	Giggs	MAN	165	127	154	152	181	779	155.8
5	Ronaldo	MAN	314	147	179	90*		730	182.5
6	Barry	AST	175	107	102	154*	180*	718	143.6
7	Malbranque	TOT*	68	127	103	164	159	621	124.2
8	Speed	BOL*	115	122	120	134	103	594	118.8
9	Duff	NEW*	44	80	181	88	145	538	107.6
10	J Cole	CHE*	34	171	188	45	99	537	107.4
11	S W Phillips	CHE*	108	48	195	148	36*	535	107.0
12	Murphy	TOT*	41	94	132	69	193	529	105.8
13	Nolan	BOL	84	174	96	140*	33	527	105.4
14	Riise	LIV	84	111	145	79*	105	524	104.8
15	Jenas	TOT*	123	94	124	70	110	521	104.2
16	Ljungberg	ARS	37	74	183	113	112	519	103.8
17	P Neville	EVE*	98	83	59	131*	110*	481	96.2
18	Kewell	LIV*	5	119	48	107	180	459	91.8
19	Solano	NEW*	73	92	156	31	106	458	91.6
20	Gilberto	ARS	142	130	38	64	79	453	90.6
21	Parker	NEW*	99	99	24	112	117	451	90.2
22	Dyer	NEW	102	25	115	70	134	446	89.2
23	Savage	BLA*	81	77	94	84	101	437	87.4
24	Xabi Alonso	LIV	123	166	114			403	134.3
25	Fabregas	ARS	161	130	112			403	134.3
26	Makelele	CHE	104	99	149	48		400	100.0
27	Stelios	BOL	23	170	110	77		380	95.0
28	Barton	MCY	148	118	58	54		378	94.5
29	Carrick	MAN*	125	119	74		59	377	94.3
30	Robben	CHE	104	131	136			371	123.7

31	Zenden	LIV*	38	37	160	97	34	**366**	73.2
32	Tugay	BLA	97	78	34	51	105	**365**	73.0
33	Essien	CHE	231	123				**354**	177.0
34	Cahill	EVE	86	117	150			**353**	117.7
35	Boateng	MID	57	121	79	47	46	**350**	70.0
36	Dunn	BLA*	33	59	37	48	133	**310**	62.0
37	Geremi	CHE*	42	36	26	46	160*	**310**	62.0
38	Milner	NEW*	113	93	50	52		**308**	77.0
39	McCann, G	AST*	75	98	56		60	**289**	72.3
40	Emerton	BLA	62	44	107	75		**288**	72.0
41	Hamann	MCY*	13	59	62	53	92	**279**	55.8
42	Pennant	LIV*	99	100		75		**274**	91.3
43	Davis, Sean	POR*	45	31	13	88	96	**273**	54.6
44	M G Pedersen	BLA	142	129				**271**	135.5
45	Arteta	EVE	175	96				**271**	135.5
46	Campo	BOL	95	50	36	77		**258**	64.5
47	Jensen, C	FUL*	33	40	13	79	93	**258**	51.6
48	Simon Davies	EVE*	52	47	35	34	84	**252**	50.4
49	Butt	NEW*	95	43	54	21	37	**250**	50.0
50	Berger	AST*	35	3	119	76	8	**241**	48.2

(* alongside club name = played for more than one club, played on loan at another club or was subsequently transferred to a side different from that which he was originally listed for)

(* alongside season points score = was listed in Dream Team in a different playing position that particular season from the one for which he was listed in the game for 2006-07)

TOP-TEN STRIKERS BY SEASON

– TOP-TEN STRIKERS 2006–07 –

Rk	Player	Club	£m	Tot
1	Drogba	CHE	4.5	318
2	Rooney	MAN	8.0	263
3	Berbatov	TOT	4.5	255
4	B McCarthy	BLA	3.5	215
5	Robbie Keane	TOT	4.5	188
6	Viduka	MID	4.0	185
7	Kuyt	LIV	4.0	171
8	Defoe	TOT	3.5	158
9	Martins	NEW	3.5	146
10	A Johnson	EVE	4.5	138

– TOP-TEN STRIKERS 2005–06 –

Rk	Player	Club	£m	Tot
1	Henry	ARS	8.0	343
2	Rooney	MAN	5.5	252
3	D Bent	CHA	3.0	199
4	van Nistelrooy	MAN	7.0	183
5	Yakubu	MID	4.5	168
6	Robbie Keane	TOT	4.0	165
7	Hasselbaink	MID	5.0	162
8	Bellamy	BLA	4.0	154
9	Harewood	WHM	2.5	150
10	Roberts	WIG	2.0	149

T

– TOP-TEN STRIKERS 2004–05 –

Rk	Player	Club	£m	Tot
1	Henry	ARS	8.0	279
2	Defoe	TOT	4.0	201
3	Rooney	EVE	5.5	181
4	A Johnson	CPA	4.0	175
5	Hasselbaink	MID	5.5	166
6	Shearer	NEW	5.0	157
7	Gudjohnsen	CHE	4.5	151
8	Yakubu	POR	4.5	139
9	Robbie Keane	TOT	4.5	139
10	Drogba	CHE	7.0	130

– TOP-TEN STRIKERS 2003–04 –

Rk	Player	Club	£m	Tot
1	Henry	ARS	7.5	393
2	Shearer	NEW	6.0	261
3	van Nistelrooy	MAN	7.5	248
4	Anelka	MCY	4.5	224
5	Angel	AST	3.0	183
6	Saha	FUL	3.0	183
7	Forssell	CHE	2.0	174
8	R Keane	TOT	4.5	173
9	Owen	LIV	6.5	172
10	Yakubu	POR	3.0	170

STATISTICALLY SPEAKING: 2006–07 DREAM TEAM STANDINGS

– TOP-TEN STRIKERS 2002–03 –

Rk	Player	Club	£m	Tot
1	van Nistelrooy	MAN	7.0	359
2	Henry	ARS	6.5	335
3	Owen	LIV	6.5	265
4	Shearer	NEW	5.0	260
5	Viduka	LEE	5.0	217
6	Beattie	SOU	3.0	204
7	Zola	CHE	2.5	180
8	Anelka	MCY	4.0	169
9	Smith	LEE	4.5	168
10	Euell	CHA	2.5	154

– TOP-TEN STRIKERS 2001–02 –

Rk	Player	Club	£m	Tot
1	van Nistelrooy	MAN	6.0	329
2	Henry	ARS	5.5	293
3	Shearer	NEW	3.5	262
4	Hasselbaink	CHE	6.0	260
5	Jansen	BLA	3.5	221
6	Solskjaer	MAN	3.5	209
7	Gudjohnsen	CHE	3.5	207
8	Owen	LIV	6.0	193
9	Wiltord	ARS	3.5	166
10	Viduka	LEE	5.0	165

TOP-40 STRIKERS: CUMULATIVE

Rank	Player	Club	06–07	05–06	04–05	03–04	02–03	Total	Avg.
		TOP-40 DREAM TEAM STRIKERS OF THE LAST FIVE YEARS							
1	Henry	ARS	113	343	279	393	335	**1463**	292.6
2	Rooney	MAN*	263	252	181	103	117	**916**	183.2
3	Keane, Robbie	TOT*	188	165	139	178	145	**815**	163.0
4	Viduka	MID*	185	144	66	106	217	**718**	143.6
5	Hasselbaink	CHA*	37	162	166	139	113	**617**	123.4
6	Defoe	TOT*	158	99	201		140	**598**	149.5
7	Yakubu	MID*	111	168	139	170		**588**	147.0
8	Bellamy	LIV*	85	154	101	102	138	**580**	116.0
9	Drogba	CHE	318	115	130			**563**	187.7
10	Anelka	BOL*	102		67	224	169	**562**	140.5
11	Saha	MAN*	113	142	25	188	61	**529**	105.8
12	Beattie	EVE*	15	110	32	167	204	**528**	105.6
13	Owen	NEW*		67	0	172	265	**504**	126.0
14	Cole, Andrew	MCY*	39	108	95	115	138	**495**	99.0
15	Heskey	WIG*	93	42	125	126	101	**487**	97.4
16	Smith, A	MAN*	22	49	78	152	168	**469**	93.8
17	Boa Morte	FUL*	19	80	115	99	93	**406**	81.2
18	Crouch	LIV*	135	111	87	38	5	**376**	75.2
19	Vassell	MCY*	36	78	24	104	130	**372**	74.4
20	Radzinski	FUL*	42	32	83	83	132	**372**	74.4
21	Fowler	LIV*	54	87	104	79	48	**372**	74.4
22	Davies, K	BOL	97	97	104	48	19	**365**	73.0
23	Sheringham	WHM*	24	79		134	99	**336**	84.0
24	Angel	AST	62	18	56	183	17	**336**	67.2
25	Bent, D	CHA	136	199				**335**	167.5

26	Johnson, A	EVE*	138		175			**313**	156.5
27	Ameobi	NEW	28	77	55	87	65	**312**	62.4
28	Dickov	MCY*	4	42	123	140		**309**	77.3
29	Van Persie	ARS	88	110	90			**288**	96.0
30	McBride	FUL	110	97	72		0	**279**	69.8
31	Kanu	POR*	76	67	40	33	62	**278**	55.6
32	LuaLua	POR*	24	86	82	54	30	**276**	55.2
33	John, C	FUL	14	86	42	31	99	**272**	54.4
34	Luis Garcia	LIV	50	77	141*			**268**	89.3
35	Berbatov	TOT	255					**255**	255.0
36	Solskjaer	MAN	80		0	15	133	**228**	57.0
37	McCarthy	BLA	215					**215**	215.0
38	Diouf	BOL*	75	44		9	70	**198**	49.5
39	Zamora	WHM*	79	99		10		**188**	62.7
40	Pedersen, H	BOL	10	23	77	72		**182**	45.5

(* alongside club name = played for more than one club, played on loan at another club or was subsequently transferred to a side different from that which he was originally listed for)

(* alongside season points score = was listed in Dream Team in a different playing position that particular season from the one for which he was listed in the game for 2006-07)

BEST OF THE BEST, TOP-TEN PLAYERS OVERALL PER SEASON IN ANY POSITION

– TOP-TEN OVERALL 2006-07 –

Rk	Player	Club	Pos	£m	Tot
1	Lampard	CHE	M	8.0	375
2	Drogba	CHE	S	4.5	318
3	Ronaldo	MAN	M	5.0	314
4	Rooney	MAN	S	8.0	263
5	Berbatov	TOT	S	4.5	255
6	Gerrard	LIV	M	8.0	242
7	Essien	CHE	M	4.5	231
8	Carragher	LIV	D	6.0	219
9	B McCarthy	BLA	S	3.5	215
10	Carvalho	CHE	D	4.5	211

– TOP-TEN OVERALL 2005-06 –

Rk	Player	Club	Pos	£m	Tot
1	Henry	ARS	S	8.0	343
2	Gerrard	LIV	M	6.0	309
3	Terry	CHE	D	8.0	302
4	Lampard	CHE	M	8.0	257
5	Carragher	LIV	D	5.5	256
6	Rooney	MAN	S	5.5	252
7	Hyypia	LIV	D	4.5	230
8	R Ferdinand	MAN	D	5.5	213
9	D Bent	CHA	S	3.0	199
10	Toure	ARS	D	4.5	197

– TOP-TEN OVERALL 2004-05 –

Rk	Player	Club	Pos	£m	Tot
1	Terry	CHE	D	6.0	368
2	Lampard	CHE	M	6.5	342
3	Henry	ARS	S	8.0	279
4	Gerrard	LIV	M	6.5	212
5	Scholes	MAN	M	5.0	202
6	Cech	CHE	G	4.0	201
7	Defoe	TOT	S	4.0	201
8	Carragher	LIV	D	4.0	198
9	Gallas	CHE	D	5.0	197
10	S W-Phillips	MCY	M	4.5	195
10	R Ferdinand	MAN	D	6.0	195

– TOP-TEN OVERALL 2003-04 –

Rk	Player	Club	Pos	£m	Tot
1	Henry	ARS	S	7.5	393
2	Shearer	NEW	S	6.0	261
3	Lampard	CHE	M	4.5	250
4	Terry	CHE	D	4.0	249
5	van Nistelrooy	MAN	S	7.5	248
6	S Gerrard	LIV	M	5.0	226
7	Anelka	MCY	S	4.5	224
8	Bridge	CHE	D	4.0	206
9	Pires	ARS	M	5.0	196
10	Angel	AST	S	3.0	183

– TOP-TEN OVERALL 2002-03 –

Rk	Player	Club	Pos	£m	Tot
1	van Nistelrooy	MAN	S	7.0	359
2	Henry	ARS	S	6.5	335
3	Owen	LIV	S	6.5	265
4	Shearer	NEW	S	5.0	260
5	Hyypia	LIV	D	6.0	244
6	Scholes	MAN	M	4.5	219
7	Viduka	LEE	S	5.0	217
8	Beattie	SOU	S	3.0	204
9	Gallas	CHE	D	3.5	200
10	Murphy	LIV	M	4.0	193

– TOP-TEN OVERALL 2001-02 –

Rk	Player	Club	Pos	£m	Tot
1	van Nistelrooy	MAN	S	6.0	329
2	Henry	ARS	S	5.5	293
3	Hyypia	LIV	D	6.0	279
4	Shearer	NEW	S	3.5	262
5	Hasselbaink	CHE	S	6.0	260
6	Henchoz	LIV	D	4.5	258
7	Dudek	LIV	G	4.5	230
8	Jansen	BLA	S	3.5	221
9	Terry	CHE	D	2.5	214
10	Solskjaer	MAN	S	3.5	209

LEADING PREMIERSHIP GOALSCORERS

– PREM TOP-SCORERS 2006–07 –

Player	Club	Goals
Drogba	CHE	20
McCarthy	BLA	18
Ronaldo	MANU	17
Viduka	MID	14
Rooney	MANU	14
D Bent	CHA	13
Doyle	REA	13
Berbatov	TOT	12
Kuyt	LIV	12
Yakubu	MID	12
Keane	TOT	11
Zamora	WHM	11
Anelka	BOL	11
Martins	NEW	11
Johnson	EVE	11
Lampard	CHE	11
Van Persie	ARS	11
Defoe	TOT	10
Gilberto	ARS	10
Kanu	POR	10
Henry	ARS	10
Agbonlahor	AST	9
Arteta	EVE	9
Crouch	LIV	9
Heskey	WIG	9
McBride	FUL	9

– PREM TOP-SCORERS 2005–06 –

Player	Club	Goals
Henry	ARS	27
van Nistelrooy	MANU	21
D Bent	CHA	18
R Keane	TOT	16
Lampard	CHE	16
Rooney	MANU	16
Harewood	WHM	14
Bellamy	BLA	13
Yakubu	MID	13
H Camara	WIG	12
Drogba	CHE	12
John	FUL	11
Mido	TOT	11
Gerrard	LIV	10
Shearer	NEW	10
Hasselbaink	MID	10
Crespo	CHE	10
McBride	FUL	10
Beattie	EVE	10
Cisse	LIV	9
Defoe	TOT	9
Ronaldo	MANU	9
Ameobi	NEW	9
Stelios	BOL	9
Nolan	BOL	9
MG Pedersen	BLA	9
A Cole	MANC	9

– PREM TOP-SCORERS 2004–05 –

Player	Club	Goals
Henry	ARS	25
A Johnson	CPA	21
Pires	ARS	14
Lampard	CHE	13
Hasselbaink	MID	13
Yakubu	POR	13
Defoe	TOT	13
A Cole	FUL	12
Gudjohnsen	CHE	12
Crouch	SOT	12
Keane	TOT	12
Cahill	EVE	11
Earnshaw	WBA	11
Rooney	MANU	11
Heskey	BIR	10
S Wright-Phillips	MANC	10
Fowler	MANC	10
Phillips	SOT	10
Drogba	CHE	10
Ljungberg	ARS	10
Reyes	ARS	9
Diouf	BOL	9
Scholes	MANU	9
Dickov	BLA	9
Baros	LIV	9

– PREM TOP-SCORERS 2003–04 –

Player	Club	Goals
Henry	ARS	30
Shearer	NEW	22
van Nistelrooy	MANU	20
Saha	MANU	20
Anelka	MANC	17
Forssell	BIR	17
Yakubu	POR	16
Owen	LIV	16
Angel	AST	16
Keane	TOT	14
Beattie	SOT	14
Pires	ARS	14
Viduka	LEE	13
Phillips	SOT	13
Hasselbaink	CHE	13
Ferdinand	LEI	12
Dickov	LEI	11
A Cole	BLA	11
Euell	CHA	10
Lampard	CHE	10
Crespo	CHE	10
Sheringham	POR	9
Djorkaeff	BOL	9
A Smith	LEE	9
Nemeth	MID	9
Nolan	BOL	9
M Bent	LEI	9
K Davies	BOL	9
Rooney	EVE	9
Boa Morte	FUL	9
Vassell	AST	9
Scholes	MANU	9

DISCIPLINARY TABLES

2006–07 DISCIPLINARY				
Player	Club	Yell	Red	Pts
Campo	BOL	10	1	13
Davies	BOL	10	1	13
Barton	MNC	10	1	13
Reo-Coker	WHM	13	0	13
Nolan	BOL	9	1	12
Helguson	FUL	9	1	12
Neill	WHM	9	1	12
Boateng	MID	5	2	11
Scholes	MAN	8	1	11
Barry	AST	7	1	10
Ballack	CHE	7	1	10
Konchesky	WHM	7	1	10
Diouf	BOL	7	1	10
Brown	FUL	10	0	10
Cattermole	MID	10	0	10
Pogatetz	MID	10	0	10
Thatcher	CHA	6	1	9
Alonso	LIV	9	0	9
Arteta	EVE	9	0	9
Drogba	CHE	9	0	9
Parker	NEW	9	0	9
McCann	AST	9	0	9
Scharner	WIG	9	0	9
Faye	BOL	9	0	9
Corradi	MNC	2	2	8
Bentley	BLA	5	1	8
Mellberg	AST	8	0	8
Baines	WIG	8	0	8
El Karkouri	CHA	8	0	8
Lehmann	ARS	8	0	8

2005–06 DISCIPLINARY				
Player	**Club**	**Yell**	**Red**	**Points**
Neville	EVE	10	2	16
Neill	BLA	11	1	14
Savage	BLA	11	1	14
Breen	SUN	10	1	13
Barton	MNC	10	1	13
Boa Morte	FUL	10	1	13
Davids	TOT	10	1	13
Barry	AST	10	1	13
Dawson	TOT	6	2	12
Sissoko	LIV	9	1	12
Parker	NEW	9	1	12
Ben Haim	BOL	8	1	11
Ronaldo	MAN	8	1	11
Wallwork	WBA	11	0	11
Alonso	LIV	7	1	10
McCulloch	WIG	7	1	10
Caldwell	SUN	7	1	10
Whitehead	SUN	10	0	10
K Davies	BOL	10	0	10
Carvalho	CHE	6	1	9
Mikel Arteta	EVE	6	1	9
McCann	AST	9	0	9
Dunne	MNC	9	0	9
Hughes	POR	8	0	8
Henchoz	WIG	8	0	8
Rooney	MAN	8	0	8
Hibbert	EVE	8	0	8
Young	CHA	8	0	8
Cahill	EVE	8	0	8

DREAM TEAM HALL OF FAME

– TOP-TEN SCORES BY GOALKEEPERS –

Year	Player	Club	£m	Tot
2001/2	Dudek	LIV	4.5	230
2000/1	Westerveld	LIV	4.0	215
2004/5	Cech	CHE	4.0	201
2001/2	Martyn	LEE	4.5	191
2005/6	Lehmann	ARS	4.0	188
2005/6	Van der Sar	MAN	4.5	185
2000/1	Barthez	MAN	4.5	183
2005/6	Reina	LIV	4.0	181
2002/3	P Robinson	LEE	2.0	169
2002/3	Dudek	LIV	4.5	167

– TOP-TEN SCORES BY DEFENDERS –

Year	Player	Club	£m	Tot
2004/5	Terry	CHE	6.0	368
2005/6	Terry	CHE	8.0	302
2000/1	Hyypia	LIV	5.0	293
2001/2	Hyypia	LIV	6.0	279
2001/2	Henchoz	LIV	4.5	258
2005/6	Carragher	LIV	5.5	256
2000/1	Babbel	LIV	3.5	255
2003/4	Terry	CHE	4.0	249
2002/3	Hyypia	LIV	6.0	244
2000/1	R Ferdinand	WHM	2.5	244

– TOP-TEN SCORES BY MIDFIELDERS –

Year	Player	Club	£m	Tot
2006/7	Lampard	CHE	8.0	375
2004/5	Lampard	CHE	6.5	342
2006/7	Ronaldo	MAN	5.0	314
2005/6	Gerrard	LIV	6.0	309
2005/6	Lampard	CHE	8.0	257
2003/4	Lampard	CHE	4.5	250
2006/7	Gerrard	LIV	8.0	242
2006/7	Essien	CHE	4.5	231
2003/4	Gerrard	LIV	5.0	226
2000/1	Bowyer	LEE	2.5	224

– TOP-TEN SCORES BY STRIKERS –

Year	Player	Club	£m	Tot
2003/4	Henry	ARS	7.5	393
2002/3	v Nistelrooy	MAN	7.0	359
2005/6	Henry	ARS	8.0	343
2002/3	Henry	ARS	6.5	335
2001/2	v Nistelrooy	MAN	6.0	329
2006/7	Drogba	CHE	4.5	318
2001/2	Henry	ARS	5.5	293
1999/0	Phillips	SUN	3.5	290
2004/5	Henry	ARS	8.0	279
2002/3	Owen	LIV	6.5	265

CHAPTER 23

THE DREAM TEAM CHAMPIONS

2007: IAN PREEDY

LIVERPOOL FAN IAN Preedy may have been disappointed that the Anfield side were beaten in the Champions League final in Athens, but at least he could watch the game against AC Milan – the last one of the Dream Team season – knowing that he was sitting pretty at the top of the table with a £125,000 windfall certain to be coming his way.

Helped by an increase in the Dream Team player budget from £40 million to £50 million, Preedy, a self-employed plumber from near Banbury in Oxfordshire, set a new points-scoring record of 2,324; his Wot Not To Wear team finishing a handsome 58 points clear of Marios Leontiou and his This Team Cost Me Nothin! side in second place.

'It's a huge amount, a life-changing amount,' Preedy said. 'I enter a team with my partner Sarah, we go into a mini-league and we've always said we would split anything we won. We talked about using it help towards paying off the mortgage, but hopefully I can talk her into perhaps investing it into a flat that we can rent out.'

He added, 'It's been a real rollercoaster year for me.'

Preedy, 37, had been playing Dream Team from the very start and finally hit the jackpot after developing his keys to victory over a number of years. 'My winning formula was looking at where you get your points from and that mainly is goals,' he said. 'I choose my defenders first, looking for attacking defenders, centre-backs who get forward for corners, the John Terry or Nemanja Vidic-type players who can get you five or six goals a season and give your points total a real boost. And if you've got a defender who takes penalties, that is a bonus too.

'Next it's strikers who have got the potential to get 20 goals a season, you need strikers from the best teams.

'I remember Dimitar Berbatov from when he was 19 or so and playing for one of the Sofia teams. I once read that he was transferred to one club for the cost of 20 pairs of football boots, so he's always been someone I look out for, you remember things like that.

'I also saw him playing for Bulgaria five or six years ago and he looked good then, so I knew what he could do.'

– WOT NOT TO WEAR (before first transfer window) –

Pos	Player	Club	Value	Total
GK	Reina	LIV	£5.0m	11
DF	Queudrue	FUL	£3.0m	8
DF	Eboue	ARS	£3.0m	34
DF	Scharner	WIG	£2.5m	18
DF	Toure	ARS	£5.5m	27
MD	Barry	AST	£3.5m	42
MD	Lampard	CHE	£8.0m	55
MD	Ronaldo	MAN	£5.0m	57
ST	Shevchenko	CHE	£6.0m	17
ST	Berbatov	TOT	£4.5m	48
ST	B McCarthy	BLA	£3.5m	11

OUT: Queudrue, Eboue, Shevchenko
IN: Michael Dawson (Tottenham), Daniel Agger (Liverpool) and Didier Drogba (Chelsea)

Preedy made three changes in the first transfer window, jettisoning defenders Emmanuel Eboue and Franck Queudrue and misfiring Chelsea striker Andriy Shevchenko. In their place came Michael Dawson of Tottenham and Liverpool's Daniel Agger, with Chelsea's red-hot Didier Drogba coming in to strengthen the forward line.

Preedy said: 'Eboue was doing okay, but he picked up an injury at the time or the transfers. I checked out several websites and some said he could be out for up to eight weeks, so I decided to make the switch.

'Queudrue and Shevchenko simply were not performing, so

they had to go. Queudrue used to take free-kicks for Middlesbrough and got a few goals, so I though he would be raring to go and determined to prove himself at a new club, though it did not work out like that.'

– WOT NOT TO WEAR (before second transfer window) –

Pos	Player	Club	Value	Total
GK	Reina	LIV	£5.0m	76
DF	Agger	LIV	£4.0m	46
DF	M Dawson	TOT	£4.0m	48
DF	Scharner	WIG	£2.5m	52
DF	Toure	ARS	£5.5m	132
MD	Barry	AST	£3.5m	115
MD	Lampard	CHE	£8.0m	257
MD	Ronaldo	MAN	£5.0m	200
ST	Drogba	CHE	£4.5m	218
ST	Berbatov	TOT	£4.5m	136
ST	B McCarthy	BLA	£3.5m	140

OUT: Scharner
IN: Patrice Evra (Manchester United)

Things were going so well come transfer window No. 2 that Preedy made just one change, replacing Wigan's Paul Scharner, who was injured, with Patrice Evra of Manchester United.

Preedy said, 'I had Scharner in from the start, he filled another important criterion, because I also look at the start of the season for players who are not listed in their natural position.

'He was listed as a defender but actually played more as midfielder and it was like being able to pick an extra midfielder in your side.

'I knew Evra was not going to score many goals, but I only had £2.5 million to spend and he was getting the nod ahead of Gabriel Heinze at Manchester United so seemed like a good pick.'

– WOT NOT TO WEAR (winning team at end of season) –

Pos	Player	Club	Value	Total
GK	Reina	LIV	£5.0m	150
DF	Agger	LIV	£4.0m	150
DF	M Dawson	TOT	£4.0m	108
DF	Evra	MAN	£2.5m	43
DF	Toure	ARS	£5.5m	178
MD	Barry	AST	£3.5m	175
MD	Lampard	CHE	£8.0m	375
MD	Ronaldo	MAN	£5.0m	314
ST	Drogba	CHE	£4.5m	250
ST	Berbatov	TOT	£4.5m	255
ST	B McCarthy	BLA	£3.5m	215

Despite there being six players valued at £8 million in the game (John Terry, Steven Gerrard, Frank Lampard, Michael Ballack, Thierry Henry and Wayne Rooney) Preedy chose just the one: Lampard. Instead he plumped for players in the £3.5 million to £5 million bracket and unearthed some absolute bargains in Drogba, Berbatov, Cristiano Ronaldo and Blackburn's Benni McCarthy.

He said: 'I always thought that Lampard was going to be the top points scorer. I know people were saying he was having a bad season, but he was scoring loads of goals and picking up Star Man awards. But I would have swapped him for someone else at transfer time if they looked like they were going to score more points.

'I think I was around second come the last transfer window, so I printed out all the teams of the other managers around me and worked out the permutations.'

He added, 'I had two Tottenham players in my team, Dawson and Berbatov, because they were in Europe. Dawson played every game, he was a rock and we all know what sort of season Berbatov had. I always think about which sides are in Europe before I pick my team at the start of the season because that means more games, more goals, more points.'

The final top-five leaderboard: 1. Ian Preedy: Wot Not To Wear – 2,324pts; 2. Marios Leontiou: This team cost me nothin! – 2,266pts; 3. Jonathan Proctor: AC Coalbrook – 2,258pts; 4. Lee Ledbrook: Proper Bo!! – 2,245pts; 5. Daniel Helps: The Rusty Rebels – 2,205pts.

2006: CHRIS MARSHALL

Chris Marshall's expertise in the transfer windows was the main reason behind his £125,000 Dream Team success in 2006. The trainee accountant from Huddersfield won the league by just one point in a nail-biting finale – and gave hope to all those thousands of managers who get off to a dodgy start in the world's No. 1 Fantasy Football game.

Marshall had Bradley Wright-Phillips in his original starting line-up and the misfiring Manchester City striker failed to score a single point for the Huddersfield Town fan before he was jettisoned at the earliest opportunity.

He said, 'I was nowhere at the first transfer window, but there is no doubt the moves I made there made the difference for me. That, and a bit of luck, as none of my key players got injured.'

Marshall had a couple of tips for Dream Team hopefuls keen to repeat his success. 'I think it's important you spend big on players that are going to score most heavily like midfielder or strikers, probably midfielders most. I also suggest putting defenders in from the same teams, two from Manchester United, two from Chelsea. That way if the side keeps a clean sheet you are going to double your points.'

Marshall, 23, was true to his word, picking two Chelsea and two West Ham defenders in his title-winning Galpharm Dream XI. This is how his side looked before he made his first changes.

– GALPHARM DREAM XI (before first transfer window) –

Pos	Player	Club	Value	Total
GK	Jussi Jaaskelainen	BOL	£3.0m	34
DF	Asier Del Horno	CHE	£4.0m	48
DF	John Terry	CHE	£8.0m	62
DF	Anton Ferdinand	WHM	£1.5m	32
DF	Danny Gabbidon	WHM	£1.5m	25
MD	Steven Gerrard	LIV	£6.0m	47
MD	Anthony Le Tallec	LIV	£1.5m	14
MD	Morten G Pedersen	BLA	£2.0m	40
ST	Bradley Wright-Phillips	MCY	£1.5m	0
ST	Thierry Henry	ARS	£8.0m	23
ST	Darren Bent	CHA	£3.0m	73

OUT: Wright-Phillips, Le Tallec, Gabbidon
IN: Brian McBride (Fulham), Jimmy Bullard (Wigan) and Hayden Mullins (West Ham)

Understandably, Marshall let Wright-Phillips and Le Tallec go, bringing in Brian McBride, who had 37 points at the time, and in-form Wigan midfielder Jimmy Bullard, who had 18. And he switched West Ham defenders, bringing in Hayden Mullins for Danny Gabbidon to save £500,000 and make sure he was still within the £40-million budget.

McBride netted 53 points for Marshall between the first and second transfer windows, but he made an astute move to ditch the Fulham striker, who was to be plagued by injury and would only go on to score another seven points the rest of the season. Chelsea's Asier Del Horno, who had done well for Marshall up to that point, also got the boot.

– GALPHARM DREAM XI (before second transfer window) –

Pos	Player	Club	Value	Total
GK	Jussi Jaaskelainen	BOL	£3.0m	99
DF	Asier Del Horno	CHE	£4.0m	101
DF	John Terry	CHE	£8.0m	179
DF	Anton Ferdinand	WHM	£1.5m	60
DF	Hayden Mullins	WHM	£1.0m	33
MD	Steven Gerrard	LIV	£6.0m	196
MD	Jimmy Bullard	WIG	£1.0m	51
MD	Morten G Pedersen	BLA	£2.0m	90
ST	Brian McBride	FUL	£2.5m	53
ST	Thierry Henry	ARS	£8.0m	155
ST	Darren Bent	CHA	£3.0m	134

OUT: McBride, Del Horno
IN: Jiri Jarosik (Chelsea), Jamie Carragher (Liverpool)

In their places came Liverpool defender Jamie Carragher, who was piling on the points, and Chelsea's unheralded midfielder Jiri Jarosik, who was on loan at Birmingham and was proving one of the bargains of the season at £1 million.

Jarosik's form dipped a little, but Carragher and Liverpool marched on. Marshall's second transfer window signings brought him 117 points, 73 more than if he had stuck with McBride and Del Horno.

He went on to win the £125,000 jackpot by a point and the money helped him buy his first house. In his words: 'At the end of the day it's just a bit of fun, but the prizes are the biggest in the business.'

Gerrard's two-goal Star Man performance in Liverpool's FA Cup final triumph over West Ham was another key to Marshall's victory.

Marshall explained, 'I thought the FA Cup final was going to turn it against me. When West Ham were winning I thought I'd blown it. But Steven Gerrard getting the Star Man was what won it for me. He had a real blinder and his two goals pretty much sealed it.

'My closest rival, Jim Munsey, had Yossi Benayoun in his side and he was playing really well, too. I knew it would come down to who had the best game out of Benayoun and Gerrard. I'm a Huddersfield fan, but I was screaming for Liverpool that day, that's for sure.

'Fortunately, Gerrard stepped up and did the business. So I owe this prize to him really.'

Marshall's Galpharm Dream XI won the title on 1,987 points while Munsey, from Suffield, Norfolk, picked up the £50,000 runners-up prize.

Our winner added, 'This was only the second time I've entered the *Sun*'s Dream Team competition. Last year I was hopeless and wasn't even in the top 100,000.'

THE DREAM TEAM CHAMPIONS

– GALPHARM DREAM XI (winning team at end of season) –

Pos	Player	Club	Value	Total
GK	Jussi Jaaskelainen	BOL	£3.0m	140
DF	Jamie Carragher	LIV	£5.5m	81
DF	John Terry	CHE	£8.0m	302
DF	Anton Ferdinand	WHM	£1.5m	87
DF	Hayden Mullins	WHM	£1.0m	62
MD	Steven Gerrard	LIV	£6.0m	309
MD	Jimmy Bullard	WIG	£1.0m	106
MD	Morten G Pedersen	BLA	£2.0m	129
MD	Jiri Jarosik	CHE	£1.0m	36
ST	Thierry Henry	ARS	£8.0m	343
ST	Darren Bent	CHA	£3.0m	199

Marshall had three players in his team who all scored over 300 points: Thierry Henry, John Terry and Gerrard. He also had Morten Gamst Pedersen in from the start of the game and the Blackburn midfielder turned out to be one of the bargains of the season. Jussi Jaaskelainen of Bolton was a sound and sensible choice in goal and the transfers did the rest. He was also helped when Manchester United striker Wayne Rooney – who was in the teams of some of his challengers – broke his foot and was ruled out for the rest of the season.

The final top-five leaderboard: 1. Chris Marshall: Galpharm Dream XI – 1,987pts; 2. Jim Munsey: Compositions B Wish White – 1,986pts; 3. A Crawford: Richby Avenue – 1,961pts; 4. Sean Townsend: Inter Mivan – 1,935pts; 5. Patrick Hart: Shamon Ye Bullard – 1,931pts.

2005: GARY UTTING

Gary Utting had one of the most stress-free final weeks of the season in Dream Team history when he landed the top prize in 2005.

The run-in to the end of the season can be an absolute nightmare for managers with the biggest prize in Fantasy Football on the line, particularly as the prize money could all boil down to one booking over the course of the season. But there were no such fears for the 24-year-old storeman from Basingstoke, who romped to the £125,000 first prize.

His Super Furry Animals line-up managed 1,971 points and finished **79 points** clear of Aaron Blackwell from Newhaven, East Sussex, in second place. Katherine Waldock of Sandy, Beds, was another eight points further back in third place.

Victory for Utting capped a remarkable week for the Liverpool fan, as the Reds also completed a miracle comeback to beat AC Milan on penalties and win the Champions League final in Istanbul.

Gary admitted, 'I keep having to pinch myself. I've never had a week like this before. I can't believe it... I was four, the same age as Steven Gerrard, when we last won the European Cup. I invited a few mates around to watch the final on TV – but the drinks were on me.'

Even with such a comfortable winning margin, Gary still had to make use of the transfer windows, dumping West Brom's Darren Moore, who had managed just four points in the first window, along with Manchester United's Alan Smith.

He brought in two low-cost Charlton defenders who were performing well that season, Talal El Karkouri and Hermann

Hreidarsson, though the really smart move was to add Southampton's Peter Crouch and Wayne Rooney of Everton in the second window, going with form players whose performance gave him the cushion going into the last few months of the season.

Runner-up Aaron had Manchester United's Wes Brown to thank for keeping a clean sheet in the FA Cup final with Arsenal, which was the difference between £50,000 for second and £10,000 for third.

Gary Utting's Super Furry Animals team for 2005 was: Friedel (Blackburn); Ashley Cole (Arsenal), Terry (Chelsea), El Karkouri, Hreidarsson (both Charlton); T Cahill (Everton), Lampard (Chelsea), Okocha (Bolton); Defoe (Spurs), Crouch (Southampton), Rooney (Everton).

The final top-five leaderboard: 1. G Utting of Basingstoke: The Super Furry Animals – 1,971pts; 2. Aaron Blackwell of Newhaven: Twxi – 1,892pts; 3. Katherine Waldock of Sandy: Barry's Boys – 1,887pts; 4. James Phillips of Worcester Park: Jim Bob Junior FC – 1,870pts; 5. Derek Tam of London: Attis A3 – 1,868pts.

2004: MICHAEL BAYLISS

Chelsea fan Michael Bayliss turned into a Red Van Man for the day to land the Dream Team title and £100,000 in 2004.

Michael's team, called Mick's Blobby Army, went into the FA Cup final trailing Sara James's team, Sara's Calm and Collective, by 12 points and he needed Manchester United striker Ruud van Nistelrooy to score big against Millwall. The flying

Dutchman did just that, with his FA Cup double and a rating of seven points giving Michael victory by just a single point.

After watching United's 3–0 win on TV, Michael said, 'It must be the first time a Manchester United player has done a Chelsea fan a favour. I knew I was close to winning the competition – but even finishing second would have been a great boost. I didn't cheer when van Nistelrooy scored from the penalty spot and I didn't cheer when he scored his second because I was convinced it was offside but, when the second goal stood, I gave the Ruud boy a big cheer. That was something, coming from a man who has followed the Blues all his life!'

Michael even had time to spare a thought for runner-up Sara, who just missed out on making a little history of her own. He admitted, 'I feel sorry for Sara – but, don't forget, it is a competition and a point is a point, but I hope she can go one better and become the first woman to win the SunSport Dream Team – I can tell her, it's a fabulous feeling to be crowned the winner.'

Sara, who worked on the shop floor at a Stoke paper mill, looked on the bright side. She said, 'Michael led for most of the season and probably deserved to win more than I did. I've still picked up 30 grand – nearly three years' wages for me.'

The backbone of Michael's side was made up of his Stamford Bridge heroes – with big points-earners like centre-half John Terry and free-scoring midfielder Frank Lampard leading the way. He also splashed out big at the start of the season on Arsenal striker Thierry Henry, who took a huge chunk out of his transfer budget.

Michael, who lives near Didcot, Oxon, added, 'This was only the second time I've entered the competition and it couldn't have gone better for me. Back in October, I was 52 points behind the leader and when I checked my points total in December I was up to fifth. Then, around Christmastime, I received a nice present when I went top – and picked up a cheque for £2,000. I stayed top until a couple of weeks to go, when Sara overtook me. But I wouldn't have been too disappointed as the second-place prize money of £30,000 is still a tidy sum.'

Michael was definitely a man with a plan. He added, 'I tried to pick a team with as many players as possible playing in Europe as that gives them a lot of extra games and earns them more points.'

But he also revealed that he almost blew it big time, by ditching Shaun Wright-Phillips. 'My biggest mistake was getting rid of Shaun Wright-Phillips in the second transfer window and bringing in Bruno Cheyrou,' he said. 'He came back and couldn't stop scoring; if I'd have kept him I would have had it won by the end of March and saved myself a lot of grief. I'd just seen Cheyrou get the winner in a league game at Stamford Bridge and thought he looked a good player, but he hardly scored again all season.'

Sara used different criteria for selecting her team. She said, 'I tried my best to be professional, picking players on skill. But I signed some of them up purely because I fancy them! Frank Lampard is gorgeous. But there were three criteria: skills, looks and value for money.'

Michael Bayliss' Mick's Blobby Army team for 2004 was: Howard (Man U), Cunningham (Bham), Dodd (Soton), Terry (Chelsea), Knight (Fulham), Rae (Wolves), Cheyrou (Lpool), Lampard (Chelsea), Saha (Fulham), Henry (Arsenal), van Nistelrooy (Man U).

Sara's Calm and Collective team (with selection criteria) for 2004 was: Howard (Man U, skill), Cunningham (Bham, cheap), M Svensson (Soton, skill), Terry (Chelsea, skill and looks), Charlton (Bolton, cheap), Malbranque (Fulham, skill), Lampard (Chelsea, looks), Giannakopoulos (Bolton, cheap), Saha (Fulham, skill), Henry (Arsenal, skill), Shearer (Newcastle, skill).

The final top-five leaderboard: 1. Michael Bayliss: Mick's Blobby Army – 1,907pts; 2. Sara James: Sara's Calm and Collective – 1,906pts; 3. Peter Mullen – 1,890pts; 4. S Stainton – 1,888pts; 5. Duncan Fletcher – 1,883pts.

2003: JOHN BELL

RAF airman John Bell was flying high after winging his way to the £100,000 prize in 2003 and proving there's more than one way to land the Dream Team jackpot.

Bell, from Nottingham, was stationed in the Falklands for much of his title-winning season and couldn't find out how his team was doing because he forgot his PIN. So he won without making a single transfer!

His Taqela John line-up scored a whopping 2,122 points to leave his rivals grounded, pairing the Premiership's top two scorers Ruud van Nistelrooy and Thierry Henry up front to devastating effect. It could have been even better, but in his own words: 'Nicolas Anelka was a bit of a let-down.'

He revealed, 'I'd spent big on the strikers because, although I know they cost the most, they are the most reliable source of points.'

Van Nistelrooy bagged an extra 20 bonus points for finishing as Dream Team's top points-scorer, while Arsenal striker Henry netted 38 goals. Both frontmen were also in the team of second-placed Tim Andrews, who finished five points behind, despite also boasting Alan Shearer up front.

Bell, though, held on despite making no changes and was another manager whose hard work before the season started paid handsome dividends.

He added, 'My main advice would be to study the form in pre-season friendlies – in case there are any bargains or young players coming through. I did that, particularly when I went for Paul Robinson in goal. He began the summer as Leeds' second-choice keeper but, by August, he was ahead of Nigel Martyn. I also thought Gareth Barry and William Gallas could come good – and they did.

'Another idea is to look for goal-scoring midfielders. That's where my gamble with John Arne Riise paid off. He chips in with a few goals for Liverpool, but you never know how many games he's going to get.'

It was only when he got leave from his posting to the Falklands that he found out he might be in with a chance of winning big. He revealed, 'I didn't get home until 7 March and I had no idea what was going on with my team. We get the *Sun* in the Falklands, but it's always four or five days late.

'I had a month's leave when I returned and it was only at the end of March that I noticed I was in with a shout.

Ignorance has been a blessing because I would have been a bag of nerves in the run-in.'

But John held his nerve to claim first prize and became the most popular man on his Norfolk airbase when Page Three girls Nikkala and Joanne came to present him with his winner's cheque.

John Bell's Taqela John team for 2003 was: Robinson (Leeds), Barry (A Villa), Gallas (Chelsea), Woodgate (Leeds/Newcastle), Geremi (Middlesbrough), Okocha (Bolton), Malbranque (Fulham), Riise (Liverpool), Henry (Arsenal), Anelka (Man City), van Nistelrooy (Man Utd).

2002: CHRISTOPHER HARTLEY

Christopher Hartley avoided a nightmare treble by winning the £100,000 Dream Team top prize in 2002.

Chelsea-mad Chris, 42, had seen his beloved Blues lose the FA Cup final to Arsenal and also suffered a cup final defeat with his own Hull parks team. But the talented fantasy manager carried off the bumper cheque when his Chalk Lane A side held on to secure first place by 17 points from Gerald Franks's Woody's Wonders.

It was a case of sofa, so good for Chris, who worked in a furniture factory. 'It was agony watching Chelsea lose the FA Cup final against Arsenal. Then Chalk Lane, the team I've played with for 20 years, lost in our cup final. I named my Dream Team after Chalk Lane and was worried that they might miss out as well.

'The real Chalk Lane play in the Hull Sunday League and

have not won anything for years. I was hoping the name had not cursed my line-up. We'd probably do a lot better if we could buy Ruud van Nistelrooy, Thierry Henry and Alan Shearer, like I did! Winning the prize is fantastic.'

Chris saw his star-studded team reach the summit in March and then endured a nail-biting six weeks as they just clung on to top spot. But our winner saw his patient approach pay off with a six-figure jackpot after entering every *Sun* Dream Team contest since the World Cup back in 1994.

He added, 'I've always been a keen Dream Team player, but this is the first time I've ever featured at the top of the table. I was in the top ten from the start, but didn't go to the top until the last six weeks. I've hardly stopped worrying about it since.

'This is the first time I have ever bothered with the transfer window. I brought in Graeme Le Saux and Thierry Henry as well as Jon Woodgate, who was a bit of a risk because he had only just come back into the Leeds team. But they all did well for me, as did Alan Shearer, who was a real gamble at the start of the season, but really came back to his best.'

Christopher Hartley's Chalk Lane A team for 2002 was: Given (Newcastle), Le Saux, Terry (Chelsea), Henchoz (Liverpool), Woodgate (Leeds), Malbranque (Fulham), Scholes (Man Utd), Pires (Arsenal), Henry (Arsenal), van Nistelrooy (Man Utd), Shearer (Newcastle).

The final top-five leaderboard: 1. C Hartley (Chalk Lane A) 2,155pts; 2. G Franks (Woody's Wonders) 2,138; 3. P Bysouth (The Wild Bunch) 2,117; 4. M Lawlor (Dots Hamsters) 2,108; 5. Nicola Keeping (Nikki FC) 2,106.

2001: DANNY ROFE

Danny Rofe showed his football-manager dad he also knew a thing or two about picking a team when he became the most famous winner of Dream Team in 2001.

Danny's father Dennis – a former star in his playing days with Leicester and Chelsea – had a spell as Bristol Rovers boss and at the time of his son's triumph was helping Stuart Gray at The Dell following Glenn Hoddle's departure from Southampton.

But it was Rofe Jr who hit the jackpot in a nail-biting finale to the 2001 competition, as his Danny's Dreamers side came up on the rails to snatch the £100,000 first prize from previous leader Errol Julien's Imported line-up on the final day of the season.

It completed an incredible campaign for the one-time Bristol Rovers apprentice, who also won the Dr Martens League Southern Division title with Newport, Isle of Wight.

Danny, who overcame a three-point deficit to finish 12 points clear, said, 'This is just brilliant. What an end to the season. I won the championship, watched Saints beat Arsenal and then worked out I had won the Dream Team. You can't ask for anything more than that.

'I remember telling my dad I had a chance of winning the competition and him saying, "Don't be so silly." Well, I have, so maybe I know a bit more about football than he thought.'

Danny, who has a massive debt to pay to Golden Boot winner Jimmy-Floyd Hasselbaink, had a poor start to the season. Until Hoddle's departure, Rofe Sr was in charge of the reserves and Danny knew all the members of the Saints squad.

He added, 'I did badly before Christmas, but I refused to change my team. One of my best friends is James Beattie, who kept trying to persuade me to put him in my side and dump Marian Pahars. But I think Marian is a great little player and he did really well for me. I am glad I didn't change anyone, though James did get a bit annoyed.

'I am also very glad that I picked Hasselbaink. He was the man who really won it for me and all my mates knew I needed Hasselbaink to score. After the Southampton v Arsenal game, I had 28 text messages telling me he had done!'

It meant a massive change in fortune for Rofe, who could perhaps have been a Dream Team player himself had his hopes of landing a professional contract with Bristol Rovers not been dashed by a serious knee injury.

Danny revealed, 'I was a midfielder and had high hopes of going on to do well. Marcus Stewart was at the club at the time, though he was a couple of years older, and it was obvious he would succeed. Even then I thought he would play in the Premiership.' Therefore, it was no surprise when Ipswich goal-machine Stewart got a place in Danny's winning line-up.

Another crucial member of the victorious side was Leeds star Ian Harte. The Elland Road full-back was out of favour around transfer-window time, but Danny's decision to stand by him was rewarded with a huge surge of vital goals and points in the second half of the season.

Danny's own success on the field simply capped off a season he will never forget. He added, 'We have had a brilliant season and won our league. Winning Dream Team has simply been the icing on the cake.'

Second-placed Errol Julien was not too downhearted after missing out on the first prize, with the £50,000 for runner-up providing a more-than-useful consolation. He said, 'I had never put a team in before, but my brother Eddie persuaded me to. I must admit that he helped me with the team.

'I was in the lead for over two months and I thought I had a chance of winning. Then I faded a bit, but Markus Babbel and Steven Gerrard both did well for me in Europe which saw me through.'

Student Darragh O'Grady thought he was the victim of a wind-up when told he had finished third. He had not made any transfers to his Dodge Rovers side and still pocketed £10,000 after finishing just 23 points behind the winner.

O'Grady confessed, 'I have entered a few times and never done well. In fact, I have always done terribly. I can remember about five of the players. That's it. I had no involvement in the transfer window because the team had gone out of my mind by then.'

Danny Rofe's Danny's Dreamers team for 2001 was: Westerveld (Liverpool), Ferdinand (West Ham), Campbell (Tottenham), Richards (Southampton), Harte (Leeds), Gerrard (Liverpool), Cole (West Ham), Bowyer (Leeds), Stewart (Ipswich), Pahars (Southampton), Hasselbaink (Chelsea).

The final top-five leaderboard: 1. Rofe 1,967 points; 2. Errol Julien (Imported) 1,955; 3. Darragh O'Grady (Dodge Rovers) 1,944; 4. Gary Ferguson (Owen's Allstars) 1,934; 5. Mick Rawding (Blue Blood) 1,929.

2000: TERRY GRIDLEY

Terry Gridley proved that studying the form really does pay off as he became the first person ever to land two big Dream Team prizes back in 2000.

Terry collected £100,000 for finishing top of the pile that season, just four years after claiming third place and scooping another £20,000 and could justifiably lay claim to being the best fantasy league manager in Britain.

The Millwall fan, then 38, from Orpington, Kent, admitted, 'I'm a real anorak when it comes to the Dream Team. It's my hobby really and I spend ages looking at players' form, injuries and pre-season matches.'

His first win enabled him to move house with wife Debbie and buy a white labrador called Sam, after whom he had named his winning team of 2000, the Dog Kennel XI.

Terry's team led from January until the end of the season and finished with a total of 1,676pts, just two points clear of Manchester United fan Andrew Fletcher from Nottingham.

And it was such a close-run thing in the end that he was not even confident enough to go out and celebrate until he got the confirmation he had pipped Andrew to first prize.

Terry said, 'I've been too scared to leave home in case the phone rang and I hadn't won... I was in France for the FA Cup final on a trip to see the battlefields. I booked it four months earlier and didn't expect still to be in the lead. I knew I could be caught, but Paul Merson would have had to get a hat-trick. I rang my wife at 5pm and she told me Chelsea had won 1-0. Even when I got back and checked the ratings, I thought at one stage I had been beaten by a point. My legs gave way, but I hadn't worked it out properly.'

Terry added, 'The key is not picking the very best players from teams like Manchester United, but those who play a lot. And I've six penalty-takers. That helps.'

Terry Gridley's Dog Kennel XI team for 2001 was: Westerveld (Liverpool), Unsworth (Everton), Harte (Leeds), G Kelly (Leeds), Hyypia (Liverpool), Poyet (Chelsea), McAllister (Leeds), Izzet (Leicester), Phillips (Sunderland), Campbell (Everton), Shearer (Newcastle).

Second-placed Andrew's team finished up: Sorensen, Hyypia, Perry, Harte, Elliott, Speed, Lampard, Poyet, Di Canio, Shearer, Phillips.

Every year Dream Team throws up some hard-luck stories and 2000 was no exception, as Raymond Tait was left cursing a change of mind just before he submitted his team.

Raymond, 31, dropped Sunderland hot-shot Kevin Phillips from his side before entering, and paid the price. The programming engineer from Stoke-on-Trent said, 'I changed him for De Bilde. Then I had to drop De Bilde during the transfer window and bring in Di Canio. I'm kicking myself.'

Raymond, a Stoke fan, spent FA Cup final day in London with his wife Justine on a trip to see hit West End show *Whistle Down the Wind*. He added, 'I had the radio on the whole coach trip down. I needed Paul Merson to get a hat-trick, but it wasn't to be.'

Phillips finished as the top-scorer in Dream Team that

season with a whopping 290 points and if Raymond had stuck to his guns he would have won the competition by 91 points. Still, third place and a cheque for £20,000 was some consolation.

His Susikin's United, named after the family dog, finished as:
De Hoey, Elliott, Hyypia, Harte, Ehiogu, Merson, Berger, Poyet, Shearer, Robbie Keane, Di Canio.

1999: TOM MILNE

Tom Milne's £100,000 Dream Team jackpot win could hardly have been better timed when he scooped Fantasy Football's biggest prize back in 1999.

Tom's TM3 team romped home 22 points clear of nearest rival Gerry Matthews, thanks largely to the 29 goals netted by Manchester United hitman Dwight Yorke. And after finishing top of the league he revealed that he had less than 20 quid to his name!

He said, 'I went to the pub on Wednesday night to watch the Manchester United v Bayern Munich match. I stopped on the way to get some cash out of the machine, but my card wouldn't work. I only had £12.03 in my account to get me through the next few days. At least I'll be able to borrow a few bob on the back of winning the Dream Team.'

Milne, 31, promised pals at the Plough Inn, Clapham, free drinks all night to celebrate his windfall. The Arsenal fan, from East Dulwich, also promised to buy a new kit for the pub's football team, in which he played.

He said, 'At the moment we play in a battered old kit

that is similar to the Gunners, but it has definitely seen better days.'

And added, 'I was very happy before, but winning this prize means I can now do a lot of things I always wanted but which seemed out of reach.'

While most people would have plans for a dream break abroad or a flash car, Milne's No. 1 wish showed why he was born to be a winner – what he really wanted was a job with his favourite newspaper, the *Sun*.

He said, 'I would love to be a sports reporter. The *Sun* is *the* paper for football, the one everyone reads.

'Yeah, I may buy my family a holiday home in the sunshine, but working for *SunSport* would be my top priority.'

West Ham striker Ian Wright presented Milne with his cheque and a bottle of bubbly – hours after being hit with a £17,500 misconduct fine by the FA. Former Arsenal hero Wrighty, a *SunSport* columnist at the time, joked, 'Perhaps Tom could lend me a few quid and help me out because I'm a bit skint myself at the moment.'

Wright, 35, added, 'The West Ham boys all follow the Dream Team closely and fans are always telling me to score more because I'm in their team.'

Postman Graham Brooks's team Brooks Borough took third place, 21 points adrift of Gerry's All Stars, managed by Gerry Matthews.

The £20,000 prize for finishing third just about made up for what had been an almost unbearable end to the campaign for the Arsenal fan from Maidstone. He said, 'The season grew so tense I could not go to Highbury because I was so nervous about the other results. I even gave up overtime at work because it was impossible to concentrate if there was a midweek game on. My work-mates all deserve a drink because I've been such a pain recently.'

Tom Milne's TM3 team for 1999 was: Walker (Tottenham), Dixon (Arsenal), Keown (Arsenal), Ferrer (Chelsea), G Neville (Man United), Carbone (Sheffield Wednesday), Bowyer (Leeds), Lampard (West Ham), Yorke (Aston Villa, now Man United), Kewell (Leeds), Zola (Chelsea).
The final top-five leaderboard: 1. TM3 (Tom Milne) 1,657 points; 2. Gerry's All Stars (Gerry Matthews) 1,633; 3. Brooks Borough (Graham Brooks) 1,612; 4. PSE (Paul Foster) 1,595; 5. Slashers (Rob Hamblin) 1,583.

1998: CHRIS HOWIS

Chris Howis and his mates at Tesco landed an incredible Dream Team supermarket sweep in 1998.

Stock controller Howis beat off competition from more than 400,000 other managers to land our terrific £100,000 first prize. And, amazingly, a team representing the supermarket giant also scooped the special £25,000 prize awarded to the best works side.

Howis was whisked to England's training camp at Bisham Abbey, Bucks, to meet Glenn Hoddle's heroes who were preparing for a clash with Saudi Arabia. There, he collected a cheque presented to him by David Beckham and Graeme Le Saux.

And our winner could not believe his eyes as Alan Shearer,

manager Hoddle, David Seaman, Steve McManaman and Michael Owen all lined up to congratulate him.

That was the best possible present for the Leeds fan, who had only celebrated his 36th birthday a day earlier. He said. 'This is incredible – amazing. What a way to celebrate your birthday. I'll never forget this.'

The first to shake his hand was Leeds keeper Nigel Martyn, who also figured in Howis's winning side. Chris' All Stars certainly lived up to their name, clocking up 1,211 points to finish a mammoth 96 points ahead of the side in second.

Martyn grinned: 'It's good to see he had a Leeds shirt on to get his prize. I am glad I could help him.'

Howis collected the prize with his brother Trevor, also a Tesco stock controller. He certainly has his Leeds team to thank after picking Martyn, Lee Bowyer and Jimmy-Floyd Hasselbaink.

Another key to his success was his decision to include the Arsenal trio of Tony Adams, Patrick Vieira and Dennis Bergkamp – along with Barnsley's Neil Redfearn, a big Dream Team points-scorer that season.

But he revealed, 'I didn't even make any changes on transfer-deadline day. Even when Tony Adams and Lee Bowyer weren't playing, I didn't see the point in switching.'

Howis worked at a store in Mansfield, which was served by a distribution depot in Middlewich, Cheshire. And that is where works winners Nicky Steele and Ian Hadley spent their days as forklift-truck drivers.

Hadley, 34, from Winsford, said, 'It is incredible. We deliver every day down to Mansfield and we will all end up in the staff newspaper. Tesco have won the lot.'

Steele's team, called Tic Tac Toe, pipped long-time leaders Philerians of Derby by just one point with a total of 1,063. But he said, 'At Christmas we gave up. We were doing well and then we just disappeared from the top. Then, suddenly, we were second with just two weeks to go. A lot of that is down to Marc Overmars doing so well in the FA Cup. I've won the double Double.'

Chris Howis's Chris' All Stars team for 1998 was: Martyn (Leeds), Hendry (Blackburn), Adams (Arsenal), Ehiogu (Aston Villa), Elliott (Leicester), Redfearn (Barnsley), Bowyer (Leeds), Batty (Newcastle), Vieira (Arsenal), Bergkamp (Arsenal), Hasselbaink (Leeds).

Winning works team: De Goey (Chelsea), Hendry (Blackburn), Leboeuf (Chelsea), Keown (Arsenal), Elliott (Leicester), Overmars (Arsenal), Redfearn (Barnsley), Di Canio (Sheffield Wednesday), Thompson (Barnsley), Hartson (West Ham), Cole (Manchester United).

The final top-five leaderboard: 1. C Howis (Chris' All Stars) 1,211 points; 2. L Rich (Lemons) 1,115; 3. P Chambers (BSB Phil Chambers) 1,112; 4. P Smythe (Sunderland Flappers) 1,109; 5. P Robinson (The Baby Squad) 1,104.

1997: STEVE WELLMAN

Steve Wellman almost missed out on claiming the £100,000 in 1997 – because the Dream Team winner lost his PIN!

The Season Four champion explained, 'I wrote my number on the front of a file and, when I left my old job, I forgot about it and threw it in the bin. I had to go back after I had already cleared out my desk and search through the litter.'

Wellman, girlfriend Alison and some of their friends were thrown out of their local pub in Dorchester on the day of his triumph in football's No. 1 fantasy game for being too rowdy.

When he heard Ian Wright had scored a second goal in Arsenal's 3–1 win at Derby, Gunners fan Steve, 27, knew he was in the big money. Out came the champagne and the celebrations got noisier and noisier.

Steve said, 'We had been working it out in the pub in between a few pints. I knew the second-placed player's team, so I was sitting down working out who was getting so-and-so points and who was not. I was pretty sure I had won, but then this guy walks into the pub and says Wrighty has got a second goal. I thought he was joking. We switched on the Teletext in the pub and there it was. We went a bit mad. I bought a couple of bottles of champagne, it got a bit noisy and the landlord threw us out! It didn't stop us; we just moved on to another pub and carried on. It's fantastic. I've never won anything like this before in my life.'

Steve collected his winnings from BBC TV commentator John Motson and *Sun* Page Three girl Jo Guest and revealed that the £100,000 cheque was equivalent to what he would earn in six years in his job as a civil engineer.

He also won his Fantasy Football competition at work that year, but did the decent thing. Steve said, 'The winner at work got £100. But, seeing as I've won this one, we've made the second-placed player the winner – otherwise I'd get accused of being greedy.'

Steve used the transfer window to drop Nottingham Forest trio Dean Saunders, Stuart Pearce and Mark Crossley. He added, 'I picked the three Forest players for my side because I thought they were going to do well. But it soon became pretty clear I'd have to change them. Saunders had a nightmare year and didn't get anywhere near the amount of goals he was expected to. It's a good job they changed the rules and allowed you to transfer three players instead of two, otherwise I'd have been stuck with one of them right to the end.

'As soon as I brought in Gianfranco Zola, Steve Staunton and Nigel Martyn, I shot into the top ten. I hadn't taken much notice of the tables before that.

'This was the third year I've entered and I did nothing the previous two years. But when I went top I started following it all really closely. I realised I was in with a good chance.'

As well as Wright, who was his top points-scorer, Steve's stars were midfielders David Beckham, Robbie Earle and Paul Merson, until he was injured.

Steve said, 'I went for goal-scoring midfielders like Earle and Beckham when I picked the team – and both of them scored more than 100 points for me. I could have gone for one big striker like Alan Shearer, but what happens if he gets injured?

'Don't ask me what the secret is – it's just down to a bit of luck.'

Steve Wellman's R and All FC team for 1997 was: Martyn (Leeds), Staunton (Aston Villa), Keown (Arsenal), Ehiogu (Aston Villa), Wright (Aston Villa), Merson (Arsenal), Beckham

(Man United), Earle (Wimbledon), Zola (Chelsea), Wright (Arsenal), Dublin (Coventry).

The final top-five leaderboard: 1. R & All FC (Steve Wellman) 863 points; 2. Arsenal Reserves (Kevin Sweeney) 848; 3. Mystery Team (Mystery Caller) 842; 4. Sam's Strollers (JP Atherley) 835; 5. Taghill Allstar (David Barks) 827.

1996: RICHARD TRUNDLE

Richard Trundle put his fan loyalties to one side to land the Dream Team crown in 1996. Spurs fan Trundle picked two Arsenal players, Lee Dixon and Paul Merson, to help him on his way to victory. His Mavericks FC team romped away with the first prize and he called into the *SunSport* office to collect his cheque from soccer boss Dave Bassett.

Richard, a 22-year-old motor mechanic, could hardly believe his triumph. He said, 'I'm still speechless. I nearly fainted when I heard I had won. I went as white as a sheet and nearly dropped the telephone. I haven't come down from Cloud Nine since.

'I just cannot comprehend that amount of money. It would take me ten years to earn this. It hasn't sunk in yet. It's a kick-start to life.'

Richard, from St Leonards in Sussex, was in pole position for nine weeks and took a comfortable 22-point lead into the final day of the season. He finished 13 points ahead. But he admits he spent that Sunday glued to the radio. He said, 'It was a nightmare. I sent my fiancée Rebecca out of the room and just sat there listening to the radio with the Teletext on.'

Richard, who had read the *Sun* every day for six years,

added, 'I carried a mobile phone for a couple of days, expecting to hear I had won. When I didn't hear anything, at first I thought I had blown it. To make it worse, all the family kept ringing to ask if I had won.

'I never imagined I would win when I picked the team at the start of the season. I've never entered before and only had the one go.

'I chose Ian Walker because I am a Spurs fan and, as a goalkeeper, he is my idol. Gary Mabbutt has always been consistent at the back and Spurs kept a lot of clean sheets. Ruud Gullit is just a superstar. He only cost me £2.5 million and did so well.

'Even though I'm a Spurs fan I had to have a couple of Arsenal players. Lee Dixon has helped the Gunners keep a number of clean sheets and Paul Merson was a bargain buy because he hadn't played much last season, but came good.

'I have always admired Andrei Kanchelskis and, as for Steve McManaman, he is young and always wants to do well. Les Ferdinand did well at QPR and I thought he would be even better at Newcastle.'

Richard threw out Tony Yeboah from Leeds during the transfer window – replacing him with Villa's Dwight Yorke. He said, 'Yeboah played well last season and I thought this would carry on. He started off well but began to fade. The African Nations Cup was coming up so I swapped him. It proved to be a good move.'

He also dumped Clive Wilson for Steve Howey. Richard said, 'I only had £1 million left. Spurs started to let in goals and Newcastle had kept a clean sheet so I brought in Howey.

Then he got injured. In the end, though, I had picked up enough points to cushion the blow.'

Richard added, 'The only bad thing about Sunday was that Spurs did not make it into Europe and Arsenal did.'

Richard's team notched up 978 points, Bobby Richardson's Mystery Team 965 and Tel's Best, chosen by Terry Gridley, 961.

Richard Trundle's Mavericks FC team from 1996 was: Walker (Spurs), Howey (Newcastle), Gullit (Chelsea), Dixon (Arsenal), Mabbutt (Spurs), Kanchelskis (Everton), Merson (Arsenal), McManaman (Liverpool), McAllister (Leeds), Yorke (Aston Villa), Ferdinand (Newcastle). Transfers out: Yeboah (Leeds), Clive Wilson (Tottenham).

1995: CHRIS MAPLE

Chris Maple says winning Dream Team in 1995 changed his life. Maple, from Salisbury, banked £100,000 following the exploits of his Devils United team and immediately bought a car and a new house.

The first thing Manchester United nut Chris did was splash out on a Ford Sierra. But he still had enough cash left over to marry girlfriend Vanessa and get a new house as well.

Chris, a computer buyer for the Ministry of Defence at the time of his win, said, 'When I won the contest I was living at home with my parents. Now I am married with my own home. We were able to pay £70,000 in cash for a house. Without the prize we would have had to get a cheaper place and have a mortgage. Winning the competition changed our life completely.'

He added, 'It was quite strange at first after I won the cash. I was a minor celebrity around town. People who didn't really know me would come up and chat about my amazing win. I felt quite relaxed about it all – everyone else was getting excited.

'The Dream Team keeps you interested in all the games throughout the season. Every Saturday I checked through all the Premiership results to see how my players were doing. I eventually won by 120 points. I have taken part in the *Sun* Dream Team every year since, but my teams have all flopped.'

Chris Maple's Chris' Devils team from 1995 was: Miller (Middlesbrough), Dixon (Arsenal), Pearson (Sheffield Wednesday), Hendry (Blackburn), McGrath (Aston Villa), Redknapp (Liverpool), Barnes (Liverpool), McAllister (Leeds), Fox (Newcastle), Klinsmann (Tottenham) and Wright (Arsenal).

1994: ANDY GRINTER

Carpet fitter Andy Grinter floored the opposition and staked his place in the Dream Team Hall of Fame when he became the game's first winner back in May 1994.

Grinter's team, Andy's Lions 36, finished two points clear of runner-up John Sproule, with Newcastle's 41-goal hitman Andy Cole helping him to finish top of the league with 250 points.

Andy, from Sutton, came to London to collect the cash from Cole's club manager, Kevin Keegan. He shared his winnings with pal Darren Coles. The pair actually collected £106,666.66p after a second team they entered won joint third place.

Andy had been in front for the best part of a month, but he was a bag of nerves in the run-in and was sure the chasing pack was going to catch him.

On collecting his cash, the relieved Millwall fan said, 'I've not had a proper night's sleep for some time. The tension got worse and worse. People I've never met have been coming up and shaking my hand and wishing me luck.'

The first thing he planned to splash out on: getting girlfriend Tina a new dress for a friend's wedding, having earlier been too skint to buy it.

Andy Grinter's Andy's Lions 36 team from 1994 was: Sealey (Man Utd), Lydersen (Arsenal), Bjornebye (Liverpool), Piechnik (Liverpool), Busst (Coventry), McAllister (Leeds), Palmer (Sheff Wed), Batty (Blackburn), Earle (Wimbledon), Sutton (Norwich) and Cole (Newcastle).

CHAPTER 24

MORE TOP TIPS TO GET YOUR TEAM IN TIP-TOP SHAPE

IN THE LAST chapter, we looked at some specific tips relating to Dream Team and many of those can be applied to other Fantasy Football games as well. If you are considering casting your fantasy net far and wide, here are a few additional pointers which should help before you take the plunge. After that, we'll take a look in more detail at some of the games on offer, how to play them and what you can expect to win.

KNOW THE GAME YOU ARE PLAYING INSIDE OUT

Don't be caught out by the rules. Before you choose your side, in whatever format of Fantasy Football, you should ask yourself the following questions as a bare minimum: is it a squad-based game or do you just pick 11 players like Dream Team? How many players are you allowed from each Premiership team? What formations are allowed? How many transfer windows are there and when are they, or do you get a certain amount of changes to make whenever you please throughout the season? What is the scoring system? For instance, Dream Team does not give players points for setting up goals for others, but many games reward assists. This can – and will – greatly affect the make-up of your team.

WHAT ARE THE SECRETS TO WINNING?

Most of the Fantasy Football games are similar, but each has its own points-scoring idiosyncrasies, all of which you should take into account. If you are thinking about entering a game for the first time, a good place to start for an idea of how it works (after reading this book) is to have a look at who were the top-ten or top-20 points-scorers from the previous season and how they accumulated their points. This will give you a quick appreciation of where you should spend biggest when constructing your team. It usually turns out you should invest in strikers, but not always.

FOCUS

Don't spread your concentration too thinly. To be in with a chance of winning you cannot afford to take your eye off the ball, so don't play more games than you can handle or you will end up losing interest and doing poorly in all of them.

Work out how much time you will have to spend on each game and whether you are prepared to invest that commitment. One of the beauties of Dream Team, for instance, is that it does not take too much of your spare time on a daily basis to make a success of it. You study the form in pre-season, draw up your player shortlist, study the player value list to work out who the bargains are, and check they are not injured. Then you pick your team before the start of the season and really do not have to do anything other than follow the football until the first transfer window in mid-October. Once you have studied the form again and made your second set of up to three changes come the start of February, that's it, you are done for the season. Everything else is out of your control and you just have to sit back and hope that you have made the right choices and that your players are going to perform to the levels you expect and turn you into a rich man or woman.

There are many Fantasy Football games out there, however, that make you work harder for your money. Some games allow 25 transfers a season, others 50, some allow a specified amount per month and others let you choose a squad which you can change before every set of games.

COMPARE GAME V GAME FOR PRICE DIFFERENCES

Just because a player seems exorbitantly priced in one Fantasy Football game does not mean he will be across the board. Check out the prices of players in three or four fantasy games before the start of the season and look for discrepancies. Take a look at the table below: it shows six of the leading Premiership strikers and how their price ranked among four of the leading Fantasy Football games ahead of the 2006–07 season. So Andriy Shevchenko, for instance, was the second most expensive striker in Fantasy Premier Manager (FPM) and Fantasy League and third most expensive in the *Telegraph* and the *Sun*'s Dream Team.

COMPARE GAMES TO FIND PLAYER VALUE			
	TFF	FPM	FL	DT
Henry	1	1	1	1=
Rooney	2	3	3	1=
Shevchenko	3	2	2	3
Owen	4	5	5	N/A
Bent	5	6	22=	17=
Drogba	6	4	4	8=

TFF = Telegraph; FPM = Fantasy Premiership Manager; FL = Fantasy League; DT = Dream Team

No real differences there. But, if you check out Didier Drogba, he was the fourth most expensive in FPM and Fantasy League, but only the eighth most expensive in Dream Team, where he was ranked at a very modest £4.5 million along with nine other players. The numbers are even more glaring for Charlton's Darren Bent, who was fifth and sixth most expensive in two games, but only equal 22nd and equal 17th in the others. Yes, he still has to go out and put the points on the board (as it turned out, Bent was injured for much of the season), but it still gives you a pointer as to whether a player is over- or under-priced in the particular game you are thinking of playing.

VARIETY IS THE SPICE OF LIFE
If you decide to get serious and play several Fantasy Football games, then maximise your chances by not picking the same player in every game, especially the ones that do not allow

substitutions or transfers. Accepted, there is a core of players who are always going to do well at Fantasy Football, but if you pick Thierry Henry in all your teams and he then picks up an injury that rules him out for the season, that could scupper several of your sides at once. It's OK if you have transfers to bail you out, but think of adding a little more variety to the games where you are stuck with the same side from the beginning of the season to the end. Spread the risk a bit, as you would if investing in the Stock Market.

NEED ANY ASSISTANCE?

Dream Team does not reward the players who create goals, only the scorers, but many games do award points for assists. Set-pieces are a good source of these, so it is worth knowing who takes free-kicks and corners, as well as penalties. These were the likely dead-ball specialists for Premiership sides and Championship contenders in 2006-07. Note that some of these players will have moved on to pastures new in the summer, such as Robbie Fowler, whose contract was not renewed at Liverpool. This opens up opportunities for other players, so study pre-season friendly form closely for sides where there appears to be competition for taking set-pieces.

FREE-KICKS

Club	Takers
Arsenal	Henry, van Persie
Aston Villa	Petrov, Barry
Blackburn	Pedersen, Tugay
Birmingham	McSheffrey
Bolton	Speed, Nolan
Chelsea	Lampard
Derby	Oakley, Jones, Barnes
Everton	Arteta
Fulham	Bullard, Queudrue
Liverpool	Gerrard, Riise
Man City	Barton
Man Utd	Ronaldo, Giggs
Middlesbrough	Downing, Rochemback
Newcastle	Solano, Emre, Milner
Portsmouth	Taylor, Mendes, Lua Lua
Reading	Lita, Long
Sunderland	Whitehead, Edwards
Tottenham	Jenas, Berbatov
West Ham	Tevez, Benayoun
Wigan	Taylor, Baines

CORNERS

Club	Takers
Arsenal	Fabregas, Henry
Aston Villa	Barry, Petrov
Blackburn	Pedersen, Bentley
Birmingham	Larsson, McSheffrey
Bolton	Campo, Speed, Diouf
Chelsea	Lampard, Robben
Derby	Oakley, Johnson
Everton	Arteta
Fulham	Simon Davies
Liverpool	Gerrard, Pennant
Man City	Barton
Man Utd	Ronaldo, Giggs
Middlesbrough	Downing
Newcastle	Solano, Milner
Portsmouth	Taylor, Kranjcar
Reading	Hunt, Shorey
Sunderland	Edwards, Murphy, Stokes
Tottenham	Jenas
West Ham	Tevez
Wigan	Taylor

PENALTIES

Club	Takers
Arsenal	Henry, Gilberto
Aston Villa	Barry
Birmingham	McSheffrey
Blackburn	McCarthy
Bolton	Speed
Chelsea	Lampard
Derby	Howard
Everton	Arteta
Fulham	Bullard, Helguson, Montella
Liverpool	Alonso, Fowler
Man City	Barton
Man Utd	Saha, Ronaldo
Middlesbrough	Yakubu
Newcastle	Solano, Ameobi, Martins
Portsmouth	Taylor, LuaLua
Reading	Doyle
Sunderland	Connolly
Tottenham	Defoe, Keane
West Ham	Harewood
Wigan	Camara, Baines

BE PATIENT

If one of your star players has not amassed as many points as you would expect, do not have a knee-jerk reaction and ditch him for someone who is unproven but on a hot streak. If your player has the pedigree and a proven points-scoring record in Dream Team, the odds are that, if he is fit, he will come good again. Thierry Henry had 23 points by the time the first transfer window opened in 2005–06 and ended up with 343! If, on the other hand, you took an expensive gamble on a foreign star new to the Premiership, you should consider making a move earlier if your gut feeling has not turned out to be true.

Birmingham striker Stern John started the 2002–03 season on fire and his 77 Dream Team points come the first transfer window that year were five more than Henry and also better than any other player in the game. But did we really expect him to continue scoring in the same vein throughout the season? John managed 22 more points during the rest of the campaign and did not even break the century barrier, while Henry ended up with 335. Congratulations if you were smart enough to pick John before the start of the season and ride his success before ditching him come the first transfer window. There were many – yours truly included – who brought him in after the horse had bolted and who were made to regret that move. It is important knowing who to pick, but also when to pick them. No one is able to maintain the same level of performance throughout an entire season and with the lesser-known players in particular, it is just as important knowing when to offload them as it is knowing when to bring them into your team.

BE ON THE BALL

If you are going to play seriously, you simply must keep on top of the latest football news: who is in form, who is out of favour, who is injured and who is strongly being linked with a transfer. If you are interested in playing Fantasy Football, you are probably a footie nut anyway, so this may not be too much of a hardship. But be aware you may be grabbed by the Fantasy Football bug and could kiss goodbye to much of your spare time if you are not careful.

BE IN POSITION

Just like with Dream Team, whichever game you are playing, study the player lists carefully. Sometimes you will find players who are listed as defenders in the fantasy games who are actually midfielders, or midfielders who play further forward. This can score you extra points over the course of a season, but, in a squad-based game, you may find on looking at the team news that one of your players is given a key role for that match only, like a full-back being asked to play wide in midfield, which can give you an extra one-off chance of points through assists. It can work in reverse as well. When Chelsea were hit by an injury crisis during the 2006–07 season, midfielder Michael Essien was often employed as a central defender, greatly reducing his points-scoring potential. A quick check of the team news before each Chelsea game would have told you where Essien was likely to be playing and whether or not there was someone in your squad better placed to score points on that particular day.

SUMMER BURNOUT

Every other year the Premiership season follows a major tournament, either the World Cup or the European

Championships. That often means the top players get little rest during the summer and enter the Premiership season jaded. If you think that is the case, consider waiting and bringing them in during the first transfer window. Thierry Henry, for instance, was a notoriously slow starter and usually gathered momentum before going goal crazy in the second half of the season.

CHEATING THE SYSTEM

Many games limit the number of players you are allowed from one Premiership club, but with a bit of forward planning you can get a third player in from one of the top teams. It was common knowledge that Ashley Cole was going to leave Arsenal in the summer of 2006 and join the league's stingiest defence at Stamford Bridge. But for the purposes of many fantasy games he would remain an Arsenal player for the rest of the season and you could still pick up two more Chelsea stars, giving a total of three from the champions of the past two seasons.

Another good example was Wigan's unsettled defender Pascal Chimbonda, who had been linked with UEFA Cup participants Tottenham throughout the summer. Again, though, study the rules carefully, because there are some subtle differences that could make all the difference. If you play the official Fantasy League game, for example, you have to be quick to take advantage. Players here are changed to their new team within hours of their move, though if you nipped in and got Chimbonda, say, while he was a Wigan player, he remained that way in your side until you transferred him out, despite scoring points all the while in a Tottenham shirt.

THE SCALES OF JUSTICE

Balance is crucial to any successful Fantasy Football team. Work out which positions will score the most points, but also take the price into account as well and look for value for money. Consider using the points-per-million criteria we used earlier to make judgements on potential bargains. Spend more heavily on areas of the team where you are going to earn most points, but not to the extent where you end up having to fill the last few places with cheap players who you know in your heart-of-hearts to be poor choices and players who are not going to perform.

TRANSFER TIMING

Some games do not have transfer windows but allow you to make a certain number of switches during the season whenever you choose. If you are playing such a game and you find one of your players is out for the season, do not switch him until you really need to make the change immediately prior to the next match. There is nothing more frustrating than bringing someone in four days before he is next in action and then finding out he has been hurt in training and is now sidelined. It is a waste of your precious transfers.

FOR SQUAD-BASED GAMES ONLY

Some Fantasy Football games allow managers to pick a squad

of 16 or so players and rotate them in or out on a daily basis. The key to doing well here, in addition to selecting a good squad in the first place, is to take advantage of the fixture schedule. At busy times of the year, particularly around Christmas, there can be two or even three games in a week and it is vital that you draw yourself up a fixture list so you can work out how best you can exploit these points-scoring opportunities. If you are considering making transfers, look for opportunities where you can offload a player immediately after he has played a match and bring someone else in to play the following day. Do not waste your transfers, but, if you have not been hit hard by injuries or loss of form, it can be a way of picking up extra points and should be used especially when you have a chance of collecting a monthly prize.

Generally speaking, strikers get twice as many goals as they do assists, while midfielders grab around 30 per cent more assists than they do goals. Centre-backs score slightly more goals than full-backs, but the wide defenders get around double the assists of their central defensive colleagues.

If you have a squad of players, there are occasions when all your players are in action at the same time and you have no choice but to sit some of them out. If such a clash arises, the smart thing to do before making your decision is to check out the teams half an hour before the match. One of your strikers may only be starting on the bench; his team might be playing a defensive formation away from home, meaning he may only get limited chances in front of goal. In squad-based games, it is sometimes smarter not to play a defender, particularly when they are away from home and almost always against Manchester United, Chelsea, Liverpool or Arsenal.

The statistics in the table below were gleaned from studying all the Premiership results over the 2004–05 and 2005–06 seasons. There is one set of data for the Big Four teams and another for the remaining 16 Premiership sides.

ATTACK AND DEFENCE: THE BIG FOUR

Clean sheets kept	Home	57%
	Away	37%
Clean sheets kept against	Home	54%
other Big Four teams	Away	25%
Goals conceded per game against	Home	0.54
other 16 sides	Away	0.86
Goals conceded per game against	Home	0.88
other Big Four teams	Away	1.33

ATTACK AND DEFENCE: THE REST

Clean sheets kept	Home	38%
	Away	15%
Clean sheets kept against Big Four	Home	24%
	Away	8%
Goals conceded per game against	Home	1.05
other 16 sides	Away	1.45
Goals conceded per game against	Home	1.61
the Big Four	Away	2.23

What does this tell you if you are playing a squad-based Fantasy Football game?

- If you have defenders from the Big Four sides, play them home and away. Even away from home at a title rival, they should come out slightly ahead over the course of a season.

- Do not play defenders from any of the other 16 Premiership clubs against Big Four teams home or away.

- And think carefully about playing them away from home against anyone at all. In Fantasy League scoring, for instance, they will generally tend to come out just worse than zero points, not allowing for any goals or assists they might get, so it is probably best only to play them away at sides with poor scoring records or who are missing their leading marksman.

CHAPTER 25

OTHER FANTASY FOOTBALL GAMES

GUARDIAN/FANTASY LEAGUE™ CLASSIC

Website: http://guardian.fantasyleague.com

How the game works

You are given a budget of £75 million to pick a squad of 16 Premiership players before the start of the season. Your team must conform to one of four formations: 4-4-2 = one goalkeeper, four defenders, four midfielders and two strikers; 4-5-1 = one goalkeeper, four defenders, five midfielders and one striker; 5-3-2 = one goalkeeper, five defenders, three midfielders and two strikers; 5-4-1 = one goalkeeper, five defenders, four midfielders and one striker. You may select a maximum of two players from the same Premiership club.

What will it cost me?

It costs £10 per team for the standard package. Gold packages cost £20 and silver packages £15. These give you access to more features such as a weekly team report, the weekly Insider newsletter emailed to you, live scoring, entry to extra competitions and the chance to win more prize money. There is a fiver off entry to all three tiers of the game after Christmas where you can still enter manager-of-the-month competitions and also take part in the February–May mini-season.

What can I win?

The top prize is £5,000 and there is a prize fund of £75,000.

2006–07 PRIZE FUND
Overall
1st: £5,000
2nd: £500
3rd–10th: £50
11th–50th: £25

Monthly
1st: £600 (gold); £400 (silver); £200 standard
2nd: £300 (gold); £200 (silver); £100 standard
3rd: £150 (gold); £100 (silver); £50 standard

Champions League winner: £3,000 plus trip for two to the Champions League final; prizes down to the last 16.
UEFA Cup winner: £2,000 plus trip for two to the UEFA Cup final; prizes down to last 16.
Intertoto Cup winner: £1,500 plus trip for two to the Intertoto Cup final; prizes down to last 16.
Safety Zone winner: £1,000 plus trip for two to top Premiership match; prizes down to 20th.

Relegation winner: £750 plus trip for two to top Championship match; prizes down to 20th.

Gold & Silver Championship:

1st: £3,000 (gold); £2,000 (silver)

2nd: £1,000 (gold); £500 (silver)

Feb–May Mini-Season winner: £1,000

FA Cup winner: £500

Age limit

18 and over.

Mini-Leagues

Yes, and no limit on size of league.

Which games count?

Premiership only; players do not score points in cup competitions.

HOW YOUR PLAYERS SCORE POINTS	POINTS
Goal	3
Assist	2
Appearance (minimum of 45 minutes played, goalkeepers and defenders only)	1
Clean sheet (minimum of 75 minutes played, goalkeepers and defenders only)	2
Each goal conceded (goalkeepers and defenders only)	-1

So, if a defender plays 80 minutes and his side does not concede a goal, he gets three points, one for the appearance and an extra two for the clean sheet.

Assists

There can be two assists for one goal, if the final touch does not 'significantly alter the speed or direction of the ball'. So, if a corner got the lightest of flick-ons by a player at the near-post and was headed in by a player at the far post, both the corner-taker and the player who provided the flick-on would register an assist.

Assists are also awarded to players who earn penalties – which are successfully converted – if they are fouled or if their shot beats the goalkeeper and would have gone in but was then handballed by a defender.

If a player has his penalty saved but converts the rebound, the original assist stands.

If a player has his penalty saved and someone else converts the rebound, the penalty-taker gets the assist.

A player cannot be credited with scoring and for an assist for the same goal: he just gets three points.

And if a player earns a free-kick that is scored from directly, no assist is awarded.

Goalkeepers/Defenders

Unlike in Dream Team, goalkeepers and defenders only lose points for goals their side concedes while they are actually on the pitch, the only exception being if their side lets in any goals after they are sent off.

Transfers

Unlimited changes are allowed before the start of the season. Once the Premiership season kicks off, managers can make a total of 25 transfers in the season, with no more than five in any single week.

Game notes

You can enter a Mini-League with your friends and work-mates, but either way there is the element of competition because, whether in a Mini-League or not, each manager also gets his side put into a 20-team Premier League with 19 other teams entered by strangers. Come mid-November, their position in that division dictates the extra competition they are entered into for the remainder of the season, with each competition carrying its own extra prize.

1st–4th: Teams go into the Champions League. They are put into a four-team group, playing a match a week against the three other teams, with the winner being the team that scores the most points during the Premiership matches over the week. With three points for a win and one for a draw, the top team in the group advances to the knockout stages, and carries on playing until he either loses a match or wins the competition.

5th–8th: Teams go into the UEFA Cup. Run along exactly the same lines as the Champions League, with a four-team group followed by a knockout stage for group winners.

9th–12th: Teams go into the Intertoto Cup. Again, as with the Champions League and the UEFA Cup, managers compete in a four-team group followed by a knockout stage for group winners.

13th–16th: Teams finishing in what the game organisers call the Safety Zone are put into one big league. For purposes of this competition only, their points are reset to zero (it does not affect your position in your Mini-League). Teams accumulate points week by week from then on as in the normal game until the penultimate week of the season. The top 100 advance to the final stage where points go back to zero again and there are prizes for the sides finishing in the top 20 for points scored in the final week of the season only.

17th–20th: Teams finishing in the Relegation Zone are also put into one big league of their own. As with the Safety Zone above, teams start from zero and score as many points as they can until the week before the end of the season when the top 100 battle it out for prizes with the winner ultimately being the team that gains the most points over the final week of the season.

One of the many excellent innovations on the Fantasy League is the Supersubs facility, which allows busy managers to set up their squad changes two, four, six, eight or ten days in advance. This also stops messing around between games on the same day to rest a player when his game is over and bring someone else in who is playing later in the day. The Supersubs option takes care of all this for you.

So what's the secret?

I will come clean here: don't ask me! Some Fantasy League veterans at work invited me to enter their Mini-League for the first time in 2006 and it was a chastening experience, taking some three months just to extricate myself from the bottom of the table.

Rookie mistakes include making alterations to your squad and forgetting to press the 'Save Changes' button, which means that your substitutions are not processed. And, even if a player is in your 16-man squad, if he is not in your starting XI at kick-off time then he will not score points for you.

The prolific Frank Lampard and Cristiano Ronaldo aside, it is strikers who score big in this game and where the bulk of your budget should be ploughed. Goals and assists are key, so look for attacking midfielders, central defenders who go up for corners and full-backs who like to raid down the wings and who are good crossers of the ball. Penalty-takers and free-kick-takers can give your team an added boost, and corner-takers can provide much-needed assists. You may not be able to afford all defenders from the Big Four sides by the time you have shelled out on attackers and midfielders, but your backline should still be from defensively solid teams in the top half of the table.

And don't mind-numbingly play all your players in every game. If one of your defenders is making the trip to Old Trafford, unless he is playing for another of the big guns the odds of him keeping a clean sheet are remote, so keep him on the bench.

It is up to you how you divide your 16-man squad. But you

can only ever start with two strikers, so it is certainly not worth buying more than three, especially as they are the most expensive players in the game. Defenders do not score all that well and you should pick stoppers who play for the top echelon sides. But before you think about picking only two full-backs remember that means both will have to play even when they go to Anfield, Old Trafford or Stamford Bridge. An extra full-back means you could choose to sit one out for the difficult games where you are likely to concede goals and lose points.

Make use of the 'Supersubs' button, it is excellent and stops you having to be at your computer every minute of the day on Saturday making changes as one game finishes and the next one kicks off.

Sometimes you will find that all your players have identical kick-off times, so you will not be able to manipulate your side and must make the decision on who has to sit it out. Check the late team news when the sides are announced and, if no one is a late drop-out, think about ditching players who are up against the sides near the top of the table and remember that players generally score better at home than they do away.

Our verdict

The *Guardian*'s site has many similarities to the official Fantasy League game. It is cleverly packaged and is a game in its own right. But people entering from the *Guardian*'s Fantasy League game or the official Fantasy League site are, in fact, playing against each other and the top of one league is also the top of the other, with everyone playing for the one prize.

Speaking of prizes, the actual money on offer is pretty

skinny when you compare it to what is up for grabs elsewhere, and the fact that entry is also the most expensive. But counterbalance that with the Fantasy League's level of customer service, which is among the best out there, because the game runs smoothly and there are rarely any headaches with the well-designed and easily navigable website. There are regular email reports telling you how your side is doing and the website gives you tips on the players to look out for and an in-depth injury and suspension list so you can keep tabs on whether your players are likely to be playing, watching from the sidelines or going shopping with the missus.

The game also maintains interest on many levels because your team can compete in two different leagues at the same time, one with your friends and work-mates and the other with 19 total strangers. There are European Cup competitions, a separate FA Cup competition and a prize for who does best over the second half of the season, so there is never any excuse to get bored or give up. Very cleverly thought out and the benchmark for all the other games.

TELEGRAPH **FANTASY FOOTBALL (TFF)**
Website: http://tfft.gfm.co.uk or
www.telegraph.co.uk/fantasygames

How the game works
You are given a budget of £50 million to pick a team of 11 Premiership players before the start of the season. Your team must conform to one of two formations: 4-4-2 = four defenders, four midfielders and two strikers; or 4-3-3 = four

defenders, four midfielders and three strikers. There is no limit to the number of players you can select from any one Premiership side. This is the game that is promoted each week inside the newspaper, and is not to be confused with the more complex web-only game TFFO (*Telegraph* Fantasy Football Online).

Is there a lucky dip facility?
No.

What will it cost me?
£6 per team or three for £15.

What can I win?
The top prize is £50,000 and a total cash prize fund of more than £100,000 with monthly and weekly prizes plus cash for the best Super League and other special prizes.

2006–07 PRIZE FUND
Overall
1st: £50,000
2nd: £5,000
3rd: £2,500

Some of the other major prizes include:
Manager of the month: £1,000
Manager of the week: £250
Manager whose team scores most goals: £2,500
Manager with best starting XI (regardless of later transfers): £2,500

Top-scoring Super League: £5,000
Best-performing Super League chairman: £2,500

Age limit
18 and over.

Mini-Leagues
Yes, but they need to have a minimum of five teams to qualify for prizes. League chairman are additionally entered into another league with a £2,500 prize to the winner.

Which games count?
Premiership and FA Cup games involving Premiership sides.

HOW YOUR PLAYERS SCORE POINTS	POINTS
Goal (including FA Cup penalty shootouts)	5
Assist (see 'Key contributions' below)	3
Man of the match	3
Starting appearance	2
Substitute appearance	1
Sending-off	-5
Booking	-2
Own goal	-3
Penalty miss (including FA Cup penalty shootouts)	-5
Penalty save (including FA Cup shootouts, but goalkeepers must touch ball)	5
Clean sheet by goalkeepers and defenders playing 90 minutes	4
Clean sheet by goalkeepers and defenders playing less than 90 minutes	2
Goal conceded by goalkeeper and defenders while on the pitch	-1

Key contributions

What the *Telegraph* calls a 'key contribution' we know as an assist, but with the odd wrinkle or two. Short passes to players who then score wonder goals, either with 35-yard blockbusters or Maradona-style dribbles, do not count as key contributions. Players being fouled for penalties (which are subsequently scored) count as an assist, but only if the player fouled is in possession of the ball, so getting pushed in the back at a corner going up to contest a header would not be deemed a key contribution.

Transfers

Unlimited changes are allowed up to two days before the start of the season. Teams are then given 30 transfers to use throughout the campaign, but can use no more than four in any week, which runs from Tuesday to Monday. A password for Internet transfers or a telephone number for phone transfers was published in the newspaper each Wednesday during the season.

So what's the secret?

There are no hidden catches here. Your chosen 11 must all be regular starters for their clubs, with goals and assists for your forwards and midfielders and clean sheets for your defenders and goalkeeper getting the job done. Note that there is no limit on the number of players from any one club, so you can pick defenders from the top clubs and still be able to get in Frank Lampard and Steven Gerrard (if your budget allows). Use your transfers wisely early on, but, if you are lucky enough to avoid injuries, make strategic switches later in the season if you spot a run of games for a particular club coming up which looks likely to result in a goal frenzy for their strikers and/or a string of clean sheets at the back. Although strikers generally tended to score slightly more heavily than midfielders, there was not all that much to choose between the top-ranked players in each position. What was noticeable was that Thierry Henry, Wayne Rooney and Didier Drogba would have set you back £9 million, £8 million and £7 million, respectively, while Steven Gerrard, Frank Lampard and Cristiano Ronaldo only cost £5 million, £4.7 million and £4.4 million. Little doubt there, then, where the value was and picking an extra midfielder instead of a striker would leave you much more money to invest in a solid defence.

Our verdict

The website is excellent and is as good as there is out there among the Fantasy Football games available in the UK. It has all the player statistics you could want, a game-by-game log of how they are performing and a Value for Money index to see which of your squad has been performing and who has been slacking, both over the whole season and the last six weeks so you can make informed decisions at a glance or by studying the numbers more extensively yourself. If you enter as a group of friends in a Super League, the chairman will get an updated Super League table emailed to him every week. The game is also among the best at adding new players who come into the Premiership.

TELEGRAPH TFFO SQUAD MANAGER

Website: http://tffo.gfm.co.uk

How the game works

You are given a budget of £80 million to pick a squad of 18 Premiership players. The squad must comprise two goalkeepers, three full-backs, three centre-backs, six midfielders and four strikers.

For each set of games, managers just pick a starting team of 11 from their squad and must play a standard 4-4-2 formation, which consists of one goalkeeper, two full-backs, two centre-backs, four midfielder and two strikers.

There is no limit to the number of players you may select from any one club and you are allowed to make unlimited substitutions, so if your players appear in the early game on a Saturday you can ship them out and bring in some fresh legs for the matches later that afternoon, after you've checked out the team news, of course.

There is also a very handy 'Timed Team Changes' facility – very much like Fantasy League's Supersubs innovation – which lets managers with less time on their hands make their changes up to seven days in advance.

Is there a lucky dip facility?

No.

What will it cost me?

£10 per team or three for £25.

What can I win?

The top prize in 2006–07 was £20,000, with a total cash prize fund of more than £25,000. Prizes only went down to third overall, with £100 on offer to the weekly winner.

2006–07 PRIZE FUND

Overall

1st: £20,000

2nd: £2,000

3rd: £1,000

Ties are split by most goals and then key contributions (assists, to you and me). If still deadlocked after all that, those clever people at the *Telegraph* must have known Steve McClaren was going to struggle, because the ultimate tiebreaker was to write a job advertisement for the next manager of the England football team, in not more than 50 words.

Weekly

1st: £100 (points scored from Tuesday to Monday).

Age limit

18 and over.

Mini-Leagues

Yes, with a minimum of five teams in a league, but no prizes. A free trophy is awarded to the chairman of every league with 20 or more teams registered before the competition begins.

Which games count?

Premiership and FA Cup games involving Premiership sides.

HOW YOUR PLAYERS SCORE POINTS	POINTS
Goal	5
Assist (see 'Key contributions' below)	3
Starting appearance	2
Substitute appearance	1
Sending-off	-5
Booking	-2
Own goal	-2
Penalty miss	-2
Penalty save by goalkeepers (must touch the ball)	4
Clean sheet by goalkeepers and defenders playing 90 minutes	4
Clean sheet by goalkeepers and defenders playing less than 90 minutes	2
Goal conceded by goalkeeper and defenders while on the pitch	-1

Picking a captain

For each round of games, you must nominate a captain from your 11-man team and he will score double points.

Key contributions

For a detailed description of what constitutes a 'Key contribution', see the preceding guide to the *Telegraph* Fantasy Football (TFF) game.

Transfers

Unlimited changes are allowed up to two days before the
start of the season. Teams are then given 12 transfers to use
throughout the season and a bonus of three more at the end
of December, making a total of 15. You can use those changes
right up until just before kick-off.

Game notes

There are only 15 transfers allowed for the whole season, so
most of these will be used to bring in replacements if any of
your stars get injured, or if a new player is added to the game
that you simply must have. Use the Timed Team Changes
facility to swap your players in and out and maximise your
potential for points-scoring. Remember, also, that teams
playing in Europe (particularly the UEFA Cup) often have the
following weekend's Premiership match switched to a
Sunday, giving you extra chances to boost your score as your
players will not all be in action at the same time. The scoring
is very similar to the *Telegraph* Fantasy Football game the
newspaper pushes heavily, but there are subtle differences.
For instance, no points are awarded to the man of the match
in this game.

Our verdict

This game is for the *serious* football and Fantasy Football fan.
With a squad of 18 to keep happy, you are continually
working out who to bring in and who to leave out and, as
with the *Guardian* game, it is important to work out when
you should play your defenders and when it is best to leave

them on the bench so they do not concede a hatful. As with the main *Telegraph* Fantasy Football game, the website is excellent with all the player statistics you could want, a game-by-game log of how they are performing and a Value for Money index to see who of your squad has been meeting expectations and who has been slacking, both over the whole season and the previous six weeks.

METRO
Website: http://fantasyfootball.metro.co.uk/

How the game works
You are given a budget of £55 million to pick a team of 11 Premiership players before the start of the season. Your team must conform to one of two formations: 4-4-2 = one goalkeeper, four defenders, four midfielders and two forwards; or 5-3-2 = one goalkeeper, five defenders, three midfielders and two forwards. You may only choose a maximum of only *three* players from any one club. If you are lazy, there is a lucky dip facility for the computer to pick your team, but you may well do better on your own and it will certainly be more fun.

What will it cost me?
The game is free to enter and you can put in a team at any stage of the season and still be in with a chance of winning one of the smaller prizes.

What can I win?
The top prize in 2006–07 was £15,000 and there was a prize fund of £40,000.

2006–07 PRIZE FUND
Overall
1st: £15,000
2nd: £5,000
3rd: £2,500
4th: £1,000
5th: £750

Monthly
1st: £1,000
2nd: £500
3rd: £250

Age limit
18 and over.

Mini-Leagues
Yes, and no limit on size of league.

Which games count?
Premiership only; players do not score points in cup competitions.

HOW YOUR PLAYERS SCORE POINTS	POINTS
Goal	3
Assist	2
Appearance (minimum of 45 minutes played, goalkeepers and defenders only)	1
Clean sheet (minimum of 75 minutes played, goalkeepers and defenders only)	2
Each goal conceded (goalkeepers and defenders only)	-1

So, if a defender plays 80 minutes and his side does not concede a goal, he gets three points, one for the appearance and an extra two for the clean sheet.

Assists

For a detailed description of what constitutes an assist, please refer back to the first game in this section entitled *Guardian*/Fantasy League Classic.

Goalkeepers/Defenders

Unlike in Dream Team, goalkeepers and defenders only lose points for goals their side concedes while they are actually on the pitch, the only exception being if their side lets in any goals after they are sent off.

Transfers

Unlimited changes are allowed before the start of the season. Once the Premiership season kicks off, managers can make a total of 50 transfers in the season with no more than three in any single week, though they cannot be made while games are being played and have to be made in certain 'windows' each week. After all transfers, teams must remain within the £55-million budget and the 4-4-2 or 5-3-2 formations.

So what's the secret?

The *Metro* game is powered by the Fantasy League people, so the general tips are similar to those found in the 'So what's the secret?' heading of the *Guardian*/Fantasy League Classic section.

Because transfers can only be made at certain times of the week (in a window when no games are taking place), there is no benefit to be gained from one-match tactical substitutions where you get rid of a striker after he has played on the Saturday and bring in a replacement who will feature on the Sunday. Instead, look ahead to the fixture schedule for blocks of games where teams have a run of matches against sides in the bottom third of the table, particularly at home where they tend to score more goals. This can be particularly handy when you are looking for the edge to land a monthly prize.

Our verdict

Free to enter, a £15,000 first prize and a functional website, you cannot really go wrong. If you are new to fantasy gaming, the *Metro* game should be at or near the top of your list. If you only want to dip your toe in the water in your first season of management it is ideal. You can just leave your team to see how they get on or get heavily involved and with 50 transfers at your disposal throughout the season, it will not be long before you are hooked and looking at your options for who to bring in up front as a replacement for a misfiring striker.

THE TIMES FANTASY GAME

Website: www.timesfantasyfootball.co.uk/

How the game works

You are given a budget of £55 million to pick a team of 11 Premiership players and a manager before the start of the season.

You can pick up to four players from a single Premiership club. Your manager's club does not count in that allocation. If your manager leaves mid-season to take charge of another side, his club is considered to be the one he was at when the manager list was produced. So, if Alan Pardew moves from West Ham to Charlton mid-season, he would continue to score points for West Ham wins and not for his new side.

Your team must at all times conform to one of four formations: 4-4-2 = one goalkeeper, four defenders, four midfielders and two strikers; 4-3-3 = one goalkeeper, four defenders, three midfielders and three strikers; 3-4-3 = one goalkeeper, three defenders, four midfielders and three strikers; 3-5-2 = one goalkeeper, three defenders, five midfielders and two strikers.

Once your team is submitted, it automatically gains entry to two different leagues, the Lite League and the Pro League. The Lite League is for busy people who cannot be fussed with chopping and changing. The 11 players picked at the start of the season remain your side for the remainder of the campaign. So if someone gets injured or gets loaned out to a side in the Championship, well, tough.

The Pro League allows you to make up to four transfers a week and switch your formations as often as you like, as long as you keep within the game rules of the £55-million budget and four players per club.

What will it cost me?
£5 per team to enter, transfers are free.

What can I win?
The top prize in each game in 2006–07 was £30,000 and there was a prize fund of £58,500 for the Pro game and £41,500 for the Lite game.

2006–07 PRIZE FUND (FOR PRO AND LITE GAMES)
1st: £30,000
2nd: £5,000
3rd: £2,500
4th: £1,000
5th: £600
6th: £500
7th: £400
8th: £300
9th: £200
10th: £50
Last (wooden spoon): £200

The tie-breaker for teams finishing level on points was

whichever team had scored the most points in April, the last full month of the season. With ties for the wooden spoon, the award goes to the team with the fewest points in April. Entrants can only win one prize at the end of the season, so if your teams finish first and second you just get the winner's prize worth £30,000.

£250 weekly prize in Pro game only for the side moving most places up the table.

£750 for top of the table in both Pro and Lite at mid-season, generally near end of December.

£5,000 top prize for best performing Super League (minimum of ten teams, Pro League only), £2,250 for second and £1,000 for third.

Age limit
16 and over.

Mini-Leagues
Yes, maximum size 2,500 teams, ten or more teams to qualify for a prize.

Which games count?
Premiership, FA Cup, League Cup, Champions League and UEFA Cup.

HOW YOUR PLAYERS SCORE POINTS	POINTS
Goal	4
Hat-trick bonus	5
Starting appearance	2
Substitute appearance	1
Sending-off	-3
Booking	-1
Penalty save by goalkeepers	2
Clean sheet (first half only) goalkeepers or defenders must play minimum of 25 minutes	2
Clean sheet (match) goalkeeper or defender must play minimum of 60 minutes	4
Goal conceded by goalkeeper and defenders while on the pitch	-1
Player is named Barclays Premiership player of the month	5
Midfielder/Striker plays in game won	2*
Midfielder/Striker plays in game drawn	1*
Manager's team wins home game	3*
Manager's team draws home game	1*
Manager's team wins away game	6*
Manager's team draws away game	2*
Manager named Barclays Manager of the Month	5

* – points for win and draw bonuses for players and managers are doubled in Premiership games only if the victory came against a side that was higher in the league table at start of play. Cup games on neutral grounds count as away matches for both sides.

Goalkeepers/Defenders

Unlike in Dream Team, goalkeepers and defenders only lose points for goals their side concedes while they are actually on the pitch.

Transfers

As many changes as you want before the season starts, then up to four are allowed per week. The transfer week runs from Thursday to Thursday apart from the opening week of the season and over Easter. Changes cannot be made while matches are being played and do not take effect for points-scoring purposes until the start of the next transfer week. There is no extra cost for transfers.

There is only one opportunity to boot out your manager, which comes in the 'Manager Transfer Week' at the start of January. This counts as one of your changes for the week.

Lite teams are not allowed any transfers.

Game notes

You can enter a team up to four weeks after the start of the season, but, as you are allowed to make four changes a week with your Pro team, this will really only benefit late entrants in the Lite category of the game.

Note that teams only start scoring the following Saturday after entry, so if you enter after the early kick-off on a Saturday you will miss out on all points available until the following weekend.

So what's the secret?

The game is more heavily weighted in favour of midfielders and attackers; so your team should be too. Most of your money should be spent further forward. Starting appearances, goals, wins and defensive clean sheets are vital scoring components; so first-choice players in successful teams are a no-brainer. With the Pro version of the game, transfers will form a huge part of your strategy. If you study the fixture schedule and plan ahead wisely and methodically, you can earn your side many more chances to gain points. If your player has turned out on a Saturday, you can transfer him out and bring someone else who you think will do well for you on the Sunday.

Our verdict

A solid enough game, with a reasonable prize fund, that offers a variety of team formations and two chances to win. The double points available to midfielders, strikers and managers for games won against sides higher in the table is a novel twist that will make you think twice before selecting your side.

SKY SPORTS FANTASY FOOTBALL CHALLENGE
Website: http://fantasyfootballchallenge.skysports.com

How the game works

You are given a budget of £200 million to pick a team of 11 Premiership players before the start of the season.

Your can choose one of seven formations for your team:

4-4-2, 5-3-2, 4-5-1, 5-4-1, 3-4-3, 4-3-3 and 3-5-2. This relates to defenders, midfielder and strikers, so, for example: 4-4-2 = one goalkeeper, four defenders, four midfielders and two strikers. There is no limit to the number of players you may select from any one club.

Each week you designate one of your players as your captain and he will score double points for your team that week.

At the end of the week, player values decrease or increase depending on how well they have done in the game. For every point they gain, their value increases £50,000, and they lose £50,000 in value for every negative point. Your salary cap increases or decreases accordingly.

So, if your £2-million midfielder scores 20 points, his value at the end of the week increases by 20 points x £50,000 = £1,000,000. He will therefore be worth £3 million instead of £2 million and your salary cap will increase from £200 million to £201 million.

The value of your team fluctuates depending on how your players are performing, but the winner is not the most expensive team at the end of the season, but the one who has the most points.

What will it cost me?

£5 for one team with 20 free transfers per quarter, 80 in total. Blocks of four extra transfers can be bought at a cost of £1.

What can I win?

The top prize in 2006–07 was £60,000 and there was a prize fund of £300,000.

2006–07 PRIZE FUND
Overall competition
1st: £60,000
2nd: £20,000
3rd: £5,000
4th: £3,000
5th: £2,000
6th–10th: £1,000
11th–15th: £500
16th–25th: £250

In addition, there are prizes down to 25th place every quarter, ranging from £5,000 for the winner and £750 for second place down to £20 for between 16th and 25th. There are also weekly prizes (which run from Saturday to Friday) for the top-ten teams, with £1,000 going to the winner and £5 for tenth. Each team is automatically put in a 30-team public league carrying prizes of £50, £25 and £10 for the top three.

Age limit
18 and over.

Mini-Leagues
Yes, and no limit on size of league. These are called private leagues and are different from the 30-team public leagues your team is automatically entered into on joining.

Which games count?

Premiership only; players do not score points in cup competitions.

HOW YOUR PLAYERS SCORE POINTS	POINTS
Goal	10
Match-winning goal	3
Assist	5
Appearance (minimum of 60 minutes)	2
Shot on target and no goal scored	3
Tackle won	2
Interception	1
Free-kick won	1
Cross to team-mate	1
Corner won	1
Caught offside	-1
Free-kicks conceded	-1
Booking	-3
Sending-off	-7
Penalty missed	-5
Own goal	-10

GOALKEEPERS ONLY	
Win	6
Draw	2
Save	2
Penalty save	10
Clean sheet (must play minimum of 60 minutes)	5
Each goal conceded	-3

DEFENDERS ONLY

Clearance	0.5
Clean sheet (must play minimum of 60 minutes)	5
Each goal conceded	-1

Transfers

There are 20 free changes allowed per quarter and, if not used, these will be carried over to the next quarter. After all transfers, teams must remain within their salary cap and keep to one of the seven permitted formations. Teams are locked down for the week, so there is no ditching someone on a Saturday and bringing in another player who is playing the following day. You can make transfers at any time, but they only kick into effect for the next round of games.

So what's the secret?

Timing is everything in this game and of paramount importance after picking a good starting team is your ability to spot when a player is about to hit a hot streak or when your star striker's performance is about to nosedive. If you get it right, you buy players when they are cheap, sell them off near their peak price and go hunting for other bargains. All the while you can plough the profits you make into strengthening your side. Midfielders were the best scoring players in the game, followed by defenders. The top-scoring strikers and goalkeepers came in with around the same points total, but there was far more strength in depth among the forwards, with far more of them recording decent scores than keepers. Busy goalkeepers were better than ones playing behind watertight defences, and Tim Howard of Everton and Reading's Marcus Hahnemann did particularly well, because, even though they did not keep as many clean sheets as the goalies from the big teams, they made so many more saves.

The usual popular Fantasy Football choices – Cristiano Ronaldo (Manchester United), Frank Lampard (Chelsea) and Mikel Arteta (Everton) – all did predictably well in midfield. But also featuring surprisingly high up the table were the likes of Aston Villa's Gavin McCann and Scott Parker of Newcastle, due in no small part to their phenomenal tackle count.

If you're not in with a chance of winning the big prize, it's probably worthwhile stockpiling your transfers for the third and fourth quarter, which may give you a better chance of winning the quarter prize, which is a more-than-handy £5,000.

Our verdict

This is quite an intriguing game and greatly different from the majority of the Fantasy Football offerings out there. The scoring is complicated – down to half a point for a clearance – but if you can cope with that it makes the game well balanced and allows for more scope and skill in choosing players instead of just going for the usual suspects, such as goal-scoring defenders and midfielders. The statistics available on the website are as good as they get, and it is almost worth entering a team just to get your hands on all the stats alone, which are very useful as a reference tool for the other Fantasy Football games.

FANTASY PREMIER LEAGUE

Website: http://fantasy.premierleague.com

How the game works

You are given a budget of £100 million to pick a squad of 15 players before the start of the Premiership season. Choose wisely as you are only allowed to enter one team. Your 15-man squad must be broken down like this: two goalkeepers, five defenders, five midfielders and three forwards. You may only choose a maximum of three players from any one club.

You pick your 11 players for each match day from your squad in any formation you choose as long as you have a goalkeeper, three defenders and a striker.

Pick a captain for each round and if he plays he will score double points.

If any of your selected starting line-up does not play for any reason, the game automatically tries to substitute in one of your four reserves, though this feature is only applied after all the games are over.

Points-scoring categories are pretty standard, with one notable exception: there are three, two and one bonus point on offer to the top three players of each match, as decided by an analyst from the Press Association. Votes are in within an hour of the final whistle.

This is the official fantasy game of the FA Premier League and was run by the same people who operate the UEFA.com game. It also employs the same rules over player values. These change depending on how many people buy and sell individuals, meaning that, if you land a successful player before he gets hot, his value will soar and you will be able to sell him on for a profit and strengthen your squad if you like.

Like the UEFA game, though, you lose half the profit you make on any player sale, and that loss is then rounded up to the nearest £100,000. So, if you buy a player for £5.3 million and sell him for £6 million, you would lose half the £700,000 profit (£350,000, rounded up to £400,000) leaving you with just £300,000 on the deal.

Your team is entered into several leagues, the big overall one, a league for managers from your country, if you are a late starter a league for managers who join the game at the same time as you (an excellent idea) and some other optional leagues, including leagues for people who support the same team and mini-leagues for friends and work-mates.

There is also a Fantasy Cup competition, where entry was automatic for every team taking part in the game before week 18. The draw is random and winning teams progress until just two remain to contest the final. Winners are decided by the highest score from the respective game week.

What will it cost me?
Entry was free in 2006–07.

What can I win?
The overall prize was a VIP trip for two to see their favourite Premiership team in action including two nights' accommodation at a top hotel, all transfers, pre-match hospitality and £250 spending money. The monthly prizes were a replica shirt and two VIP tickets to a pre-selected

Premiership match including match-day hospitality. Be warned, though, among the mouth-watering matches on offer were Blackburn v Portsmouth and Charlton v Wigan.

Age limit
18 or over.

Mini-Leagues
Yes, and no limit on size of league.

HOW YOUR PLAYERS SCORE POINTS	POINTS
Game played, 60 minutes or more	2
Game played, less than 60 minutes	1
Goal scored by goalkeeper or defenders	6
Goal scored by midfielders	5
Goal scored by forwards	4
Assist	3
Clean sheet, goalkeeper or defender (must play at least 60 minutes)	4
Clean sheet, midfielder (must play at least 60 minutes)	1
For every two goals conceded by your goalkeeper or defenders	–1
Bonus points for best three players in a match	3, 2 or 1
Penalty save	5
Penalty miss	–2
Every three saves by your keeper	1
Yellow card	–1
Red card (includes any yellow card points)	–3

Transfers

You may make one change per week, with any additional transfers costing you a four-point deduction from your running total for each change made. Unused transfers do not carry over.

Game notes

There is a weekly Pundit column which covers the week's games with suggestions for players worth taking a look at, and which gives the odd handy hint.

So what's the secret?

Even with a four-point penalty for every transfer made over and above the weekly limit of one, most of the leaders still made them, so in an emergency it is obviously worth getting that player you really need in before a game in which you think they will do well. It is worth noting that if a striker plays and scores a goal that's six points alone, giving you a handy two-point profit on your transaction. Also bear in mind that any transfer-points deductions were not applied to your cup score, so if you're doing rubbish in the league it's worth making bundles of transfers to get your team in shape for the cup rounds.

Again, attacking players are rewarded, but midfielders fared far better than forwards, because they scored five points for a goal as opposed to four for strikers and they also collected a point if their team kept a clean sheet. Midfielders also scored far better than strikers in the bonus points awarded by the Press Association reporters and it was also heartening to see that defenders were also better rewarded than attackers in the man-of-the-match awards, a very refreshing change. And do not forget to take into account assists, with three points for making a goal and four for scoring one for forwards, strikers who create chances for team-mates – like Wayne Rooney at Manchester United and Dimitar Berbatov at Tottenham – also prospered.

Our verdict

With all the money on offer elsewhere, the first prize was not one to get particularly excited about, but the game itself proved very enjoyable. Where this site is a winner is its stats section. You can look at all the leading players by position or on a team-by-team basis. And there is a game-by-game analysis of each individual player which is excellent and worth noting for use with other Fantasy Football games.

CHANNEL 4

Website: http://channel4.fantasyleague.com

How the game works

You are given a budget of £55 million to pick a team of 11 Premiership players before the start of the season.

Your team must be a 4-4-2 formation of one goalkeeper, two full-backs, two centre-backs, four midfielders and two strikers. You can select a maximum of two players from any one Premiership side.

Managers play for monthly prizes and you can enter at any time, because at the end of every month the points totals are reset to zero.

There is also a prize for the top total score from any manager's best three months throughout the season.

This game is run by Fantasy League and used to be very popular on the BBC website. When the Beeb decided to end its association after the 2004–05 season, Channel 4 picked it up.

Lazy managers will be happy to see there is a lucky dip option.

What will it cost me?
The game is free to enter and transfers are free as well.

What can I win?
Generally, tickets to exotic footballing locations: the top prize in 2006–07 was a four-night trip for two to Argentine capital Buenos Aires with tickets to a Boca Juniors home fixture. Second prize was a 26-inch plasma TV and third a PlayStation 3 console.

Top prizes in the monthly competition alternated between two tickets to a Premiership match of the winner's choice and two tickets, plus travel and accommodation, to see either Barcelona or Real Madrid play in Spain. Second prizes each month were a personalised Premiership replica jersey of the winner's choice.

Age limit
None. Under-18 prize-winners must be accompanied by adult on trips won.

Which games count?

Premiership only; players do not score points in cup competitions.

HOW YOUR PLAYERS SCORE POINTS	POINTS
Goal	3
Assist	2
Appearance (minimum of 45 minutes played, goalkeepers and defenders only)	1
Clean sheet (minimum of 75 minutes played, goalkeepers and defenders only)	2
Each goal conceded (goalkeepers and defenders only)	-1

So, if a defender plays 80 minutes and his side does not concede a goal, he gets three points, one for the appearance and an extra two for the clean sheet.

Assists

For a detailed description of what constitutes an assist, please refer back to the first game in this section entitled *Guardian*/Fantasy League Classic.

Goalkeepers/Defenders

Unlike in Dream Team, goalkeepers and defenders only lose points for goals their side concedes while they are actually on the pitch, the only exception being if their side lets in any goals after they are sent off.

Transfers

You are allowed to make up to six changes to your team in any one month. There are unlimited changes between the end of one month and the start of the next.

So what's the secret?

As it runs on the Fantasy Football scoring format, your midfielders and attackers must be scoring heavily with goals and assists. While the occasional goal or assist is more than handy from your defenders, it is clean sheets that gain them the majority of their points, so you should choose a backline featuring sides in the top half of the table with good defensive records. As it is the attacking players who score more heavily, you should invest more of your budget on them. The six transfers a month is the tie-breaker that splits the really good teams and careful studying of the advance fixture list is crucial to success, for instance bringing in strikers who have consecutive home games against weak opposition and whom you think are going to score well. Because each month is a separate season, in effect, you can tinker for the first month or two to get the feel for the game. If it does not work out, no worries, ditch your side and start from scratch the following month.

Our verdict

Another good free game, like the one run by *Metro*. Six monthly transfers, new team each month, manageable amount just about right for someone not wanting Fantasy Football to take over their lives.

Because all the scores are reset at the end of the month, you can enter at any stage and still be in with a chance of winning a prize. Obviously, you need to have played for three months to be in with a chance of winning the overall top prize.

If you are a Fantasy Football novice, it's another option you might want to cut your teeth on before playing any of the more serious offerings where you have to pay an entry fee.

PREMIERSHIP FANTASY MANAGER
Website: http://premier.fantasy-manager.co.uk

How the game works
You are given a budget of £100 million to pick a team of 11 Premiership players and a manager before the start of the season. Your team must conform to one of four formations: 4-4-2 = one goalkeeper, four defenders, four midfielders and two forwards; 4-3-3 = one goalkeeper, four defenders, three midfielders and three forwards; 5-3-2 = one goalkeeper, five defenders, three midfielders and two forwards; or 3-5-2 = one goalkeeper, three defenders, five midfielders and two forwards. There is no limit to the number of players you may select from any one club.

Is there a lucky dip facility?
Yes.

What will it cost me?

That depends, you can enter as either an amateur team or a professional team.

Amateur teams are free and are given one transfer a month. Managers are only allowed to have one amateur team. Professional teams cost £8 per team or three teams for £16, half-price from January. There is no limit on the number of professional teams you can enter. Professional teams get five transfers a month and also get a monthly email about how their team is getting on and the latest Premiership news.

What can I win?

The top prize is £10,000 and a total cash prize fund of £15,000. Prizes only go down to third overall, and there is one monthly winner.

2006–07 PRIZE FUND
Overall
1st: £10,000
2nd: £5,000
3rd: 32-inch flat-screen TV

Monthly
1st: 30GB iPod Video

Age limit

Unspecified in 2006–07 terms and conditions, but presumed to be 18.

Mini-Leagues

Yes, and no limit on size of league.

Which games count?

Premiership only, players do not score points in cup competitions.

HOW YOUR PLAYERS SCORE POINTS	POINTS
Goal scored – goalkeeper	7
Goal scored – defender	5
Goal scored – midfielder	4
Goal scored – striker	3
Goal conceded – goalkeeper	–2
Goal conceded – defender	–1
Clean sheet – goalkeeper	2
Clean sheet – defender	1
Played full game	2
Substituted (on or off)	1
Yellow Card	–3
Red Card	–10
Win (as starter or used substitute)	3
Draw (as starter or used substitute)	1

HOW YOUR MANAGER SCORES POINTS	POINTS
Win	5
Draw	2
Defeat	–2

Points for victories and draws

Note that players also score points for their team's performance, but only if they get on the pitch. If your striker is on the bench and his side wins 7–0, sorry, Mr Shevchenko, but no points. Note also that your manager loses you points if the team he is in charge of in real life loses!

Transfers

Unlimited changes are allowed before the start of the season. From then on, amateur teams get to make one change a month and professional teams get five transfers each month. If amateur teams catch the bug, you can upgrade to a professional team, or, if you own an amateur team and desperately want to make changes at any stage, you can buy what the game calls an 'Emergency Transfer Kit' for £1.50 which will allow you to transfer two extra players. You can buy two of these kits in any one month, giving you a maximum of five changes, the same as a professional team. Note, though, that at no time can transfers be carried over from one month to the next. Come month's end, if you haven't used them, you'll lose them.

So, what's the secret?

With two points for playing 90 minutes and another three if it's on the winning side, you need players who are frequent starters, are rarely substituted and who play for the successful sides. It was noticeable among the midfielders that the likes of Michael Essien (Chelsea), Arsenal's Gilberto Silva and James Harper of Reading all did extremely well, despite none of them being particularly attack-minded. The game was better balanced than most, with strikers and midfielders being roughly equal in their points totals, followed by defenders and managers, who also scored about the same as each other, and finally goalkeepers.

Transfers play a big part in this game and if you want to compete seriously you will have to invest in a professional team, giving five changes a month. Amateur teams are permitted just one swap and that's like trying to win with one arm tied behind your back and your legs lashed together. In most other Fantasy Football games, there is no point changing your side if it is doing well. Here, though, timing is everything and you should be prepared to chop and change often. The upcoming fixture list will play a huge part in your strategy, particularly at the end of the month. If many of your players have played on a Saturday and earned you points, and the following day has some games which are the last of that particular month, it will be worthwhile using some of your transfers to go chasing extra points, particularly if one of the big guns – like free-scoring Manchester United – are at home to one of the whipping boys. But make sure you check the team news before making the switch: it's a waste of time bringing a player in if he's going to be sitting on the bench.

Our verdict

The game is run by the TEAMTALK group, which also includes among its stable of websites the highly informative *Sporting Life* website, as well as the very popular *Football365*. It is an acquired taste and the appearance and site navigation took a bit of getting used to, but overall it is a winner and full of good information once you know where to look. Tables list players by position and by club, and there are even statistics showing the players whom most managers are buying or selling during the season, so you can keep up with the action. Although the player lists are good and better than some, there were some omissions.

YAHOO

Website: http://uk.premiership.fantasysports.yahoo.com

How the game works

You are given a budget of £100 million to pick a team of 11 Premiership players before the start of the season. You may choose between the following five formations: 4-4-2 = one goalkeeper, four defenders, four midfielders and two strikers; 4-3-3 = one goalkeeper, four defenders, four midfielders and three strikers; 3-4-3 = one goalkeeper, three defenders, four midfielders and three strikers; or 3-5-2 = one goalkeeper, three defenders, five midfielders and two strikers. There is no limit to the number of players you can select from any one Premiership side.

Line-ups must be selected by 10.59am on Saturday morning and are then set for the week. Changes can be made during that time, but they do not take effect until the following week.

Players score points for their performances, but their transfer values go up or down depending on how heavily they are scoring, so there is lots of wheeling and dealing to be done in the transfer market.

What will it cost me?
The game is free to enter.

What can I win?
This game was 'just for fun' last year. Winners collected a Blankety Blank chequebook and pen, with a twist. There was no chequebook. And no pen. Just Blankety Blank. But don't fret if you thought all your hard-earned work studying the form was going to be for nothing. In the website's own immortal words: 'You are fighting to end atop the standings so you can have bragging rights over friends, colleagues and game players from across the globe.' Rumours are that winning this competition gave the clever manager the exclusive right to thrust his arms skyward in celebration and utter the word 'Yahoo', hence the name of the game. But keep an eye out, because a company that makes as many millions as Yahoo worldwide has to throw some prize money at this game sometime.

Age limit
None.

Which games count?
Premiership only; players do not score points in cup competitions.

HOW YOUR PLAYERS SCORE POINTS	POINTS
Goal	10
Assist	4
Game-winning goal	2 bonus
Goal from set-piece	3 bonus
Shot on target (but no goal scored)	3
Cross to team-mate	1
Foul won	0.5
Corner won	1
Penalty not converted	-5
Yellow card	-3
Red card	-6
Opposition shot blocked	2
Opposition pass intercepted	0.5
Tackle won	0.5
Goal-saving tackle	2
Foul committed	-0.5
Penalty conceded	-3
Own goal	-3
Clean sheet (defenders only)	4

GOALKEEPERS ONLY	
Game won	4
Game lost	-2
Game drawn	1
Save	2
Penalty kick save	6
Clean sheet	5
Goal allowed	-3

Game notes

The website is not stunningly pretty to look at, but it is functional and has some good tools to help you play the game. Player-performance tables chart how your team and possible transfer targets have been getting on throughout the season and how their price has altered.

This graphical tool provides you with an easy way to follow a given player's performance over the course of the season. For each player, you'll see a unit value chart, a fantasy points-scored chart and a team distribution chart that cover each week of the season. A 'Who's Hot' section lists the players who are currently piling on the points and 'Bargain Hunters' shows which players are offering the best value for money comparing both points scored and price. The 'Player Distribution Table' shows which are proving the most popular players.

With the varied and slightly complex scoring system rewarding everything down to intercepting a pass, it was not just the usual suspects at the top of the player rankings. Goal-scoring and attack-minded defenders seem to do well in this one and by no means do the stoppers from the Big Four dominate as you might expect. Portsmouth's Matthew Taylor and Nicky Shorey of Reading, for instance, featured prominently among the top defenders.

Think carefully about selling your top players expecting to make a profit which you can then plough back into your team. If Didier Drogba starts out at £15 million but his exceptional performances push his price to £30 million, you would think that you would be rewarded for your foresight in picking him in the first place. You only get the original price you paid for a player, in Drogba's case £15 million, but, if after selling him you decided you wanted to buy him straight back again, you would have to pay the new price of £30 million. What it does mean, however, is that, with his transfer fee rising, it becomes increasingly difficult for other managers to buy a player on form. It is a little confusing at first, admittedly, but give it time and you soon pick it up.

So what's the secret?

With ten points for a goal and four for an assist, this game rewards attacking football from all over the pitch. Prolific strikers, attacking midfielders such as Cristiano Ronaldo and Frank Lampard, defenders who score goals like Portsmouth's Matthew Taylor, should all be at or near the top of your shortlist. Despite Charlton's dismal season, Talal El Karkouri was surprisingly among the top defenders, partly because of the number of passes he intercepted, but also due in no small part to the number of shots he had on target and the fact he also contributed goals. Successful crosses are a good attribute to have as well, so attacking full-backs, like Reading's Nicky Shorey, were also a prize asset.

Our verdict

It may have taken a panning for its total lack of anything worth winning, but this game proved very popular last year and attracted loads of entrants. If you are out to make money, then obviously it is a waste of time, but, if you have time on your hands and want to hone your Fantasy Football skills, then it is certainly worth giving it a go. Nothing to win, true, but then again, nothing to lose and if you set up a league with friends or work-mates it is quite different from the other games out there.

The website also has a companion Fantasy Football blog that is regularly updated by Jeremy Spitzberg and Neil Thursman and contains some handy team news and other tips on picking your team. Check it out at: http://uk.sports.yahoo.com/fantasy-football-blog.

UEFA.COM
Websites:
Champions League game:
http://en.uclfantasy.uefa.com/M/home.mc
UEFA Cup game: http://en.ucupfantasy.uefa.com/M/home.mc

How the game works
You are given a budget of £100 million to pick a squad of 15 players before the group stages of the Champions League. Your 15-man squad must be broken down like this: two goalkeepers, five defenders, five midfielders and three forwards. You may only choose a maximum of two players from any one club.

During the group stages, you may make one transfer between each set of games, but any additional switch you make will cost you two points off your total score.

You pick your 11 players (and design your own team strip) for each match day from your squad in any formation you choose as long as you have a goalkeeper.

Pick a captain for each round and if he plays he will score double points.

If any of your selected starting line-up does not play for any reason, the game automatically tries to substitute in one of your four reserves, though this feature is only applied after all the games are over.

After the group stages are over, you choose a new 15-man squad from a revised list of players and may choose up to four players from any one club.

It's all change again after the quarter-finals, with another 15-man squad to be picked and a maximum of six players from one club.

In between rounds that do not feature wholesale chopping and changing, you are allowed to make one transfer, except prior to the final, when it's two.

Confused? If not, you soon will be. A bit like the stock market, player values change depending on how many people buy and sell them after the game has begun. If you make a good choice and more managers jump on the bandwagon, your star's value then increases, meaning if you then decide to sell him at a later stage you will get more for your money.

Only it's not as simple as that. Presumably in a nod to the money that player agents take out of the game, you have to pay a sell-on fee. You lose half the profit you make on any player sale, which is then rounded up to the nearest £100,000.

So, if you buy a player for £4.5 million and sell him for £5 million, you would normally expect to pocket £500,000. Only the fee claws away half your profit (£250,000, which becomes £300,000 when rounded up). That leaves you with a meagre £200,000 for your foresight in the transfer market, meaning you have a total of £4.7 million to bring a new player in.

I don't know how long it takes to get a rocket-science degree, but it's easy to see what boffins working on the European Space Station do in their spare time: they are playing Fantasy Football on uefa.com.

You only get to pick one team, which is probably a blessing, but it gets put in a whole host of leagues, the big overall one, a league for managers from your country, a league for managers who join the game at the same time as you if you are a late starter and some other optional leagues including leagues for people who support the same team and mini-leagues for friends and work-mates.

You can also take on your mates in one-off, head-to-head challenges to prove who knows most about European football.

What will it cost me?
Entry is free.

What can I win?
The main prize: the latest hi-tech computer gaming console from one of UEFA's partner sponsors. There's no big money on offer, probably because it would be difficult to organise, as there are entries from all across the globe.

HOW YOUR PLAYERS SCORE POINTS	POINTS
Game played, 60 minutes or more	2
Game played, less than 60 minutes	1
Goal scored by goalkeeper or defenders	6
Goal scored by midfielders	5
Goal scored by forwards	4
Assist	3
Clean sheet, goalkeeper or defender (must play at least 60 minutes)	4
Clean sheet, midfielder (must play at least 60 minutes)	2
For every two goals conceded by your goalkeeper or defenders	-1
Winning a penalty (does not count as an assist)	1
Giving away a penalty	-1
Penalty save	5
Penalty miss	-2
Every three saves	1
Yellow card	-1
Red card (includes any yellow card points)	-3

Note: Extra-time counts, but penalty shootouts do not.

So what's the secret?

With two points just for turning out for an hour, your players simply must be in the starting line-up. With defenders scoring six points for a goal and three for an assist, any stopper who is active in the opposition half of the field has to be top of your hit list. Seville's Daniel Alves helped pad his stats with a double-strike in one game against Swiss side Grasshoppers, which had him sitting proudly at the top of the list of defenders come the winter Champions League break.

There are various ways of looking at this one. If you support a team that regularly plays in the Champions League, then you may well know many of the players anyway and it's probably worth giving it a go. If your team flirts with Champions League qualification, then playing the game could make you even hungrier for European football and will make you better informed when all those transfer speculation stories surface in the tabloids over the summer. When your team is linked with Marseille's right-back, you might actually know who he is. If you're a fan of a Premiership also-ran whose aim every year is to avoid the drop, you can have a go to see how the other half lives, even though you know the players you are selecting will never grace your home ground. Still, it might make those European nights more interesting when Sky has all eight games on multi-screen. You know, those nights when filling in your tax return seems like more fun than watching Chelsea or Liverpool all-too-predictably nullify their second-rate Eastern European opposition and score a couple of goals from set-pieces. Just think, if you had Olympiakos defensive midfielder Ieroklis Stoltidis in your fantasy team, you might just want to switch over and see if he was living up to his reputation as being a deadly header of the ball from set-pieces and bagging you a few points. Or then again...

There is also a UEFA Cup format of the competition, which begins with the group stages of that competition.

Unlimited transfers are allowed until the teams lock down

prior to the group stages, then two are allowed between subsequent group games. With clubs placed in groups of five, it means they all get a week off, so, if you plan ahead and use your transfers wisely, you can swap players in and out when their teams are not in action.

Rules are identical, only that there are four lots of unlimited transfers instead of three in the Champions League. These are allowed after the group stages, and before the round of 16, quarter-finals and semi-finals.

Between the first and second legs of the knockout phase you are allowed one transfer and it's two before the final.

Again, prizes were a little disappointing in 2006–07. Match-day winners got something labelled a 'fan kit', which turned out to be what looked like a green towel and green football with the logo of a beer manufacturer on it. The company in question may claim to brew probably the best lager in the world and make similar boasts about imaginary nightclubs and flat-mates, but trust me, when it comes to this, you will never see a television advertisement saying 'C*****g, probably the best fan kits in the world' anywhere in the English-speaking world. The overall first prize was slightly better, it must be said: two tickets, travel and accommodation to the UEFA Super Cup match in Monaco, the traditional match-up between the winners of the Champions League and the UEFA Cup.

In this wonderful global age of 't'Internet' (as Peter Kay would say) you may find it appealing to be able to pit your wits against managers from all over the world. It is more than likely your rivals will come from Venezuela – that impoverished South American country had close to 18,000 entries last season, more than three times the number of another other nation. Explain that one!

You really do have to know your stuff – for instance, the highest-ranked goalkeeper at the start of the knockout stages was not Petr Cech (no surprise there because the Chelsea goalkeeper was out injured for much of the season), or Bayern Munich's Oliver Kahn or Real Madrid ace Iker Casillas, but Viktor Akinfeev of CSKA Moscow. Accordingly, more managers transferred him in and his price at the start of the game rose from 4.5 million euros to 4.8 million before CSKA were eliminated by Arsenal and Porto at the group stages.

Conversely, David Beckham's value dropped from 8.5 million to 7.7 million when he announced that he was signing for LA Galaxy and Real Madrid manager Fabio Capello responded by saying the Spice Boy would never play at the Bernabeu again.

Our verdict

If you haven't heard of Cristian Panucci, Philipp Lahm or Carles Puyol, it's probably best to stay clear, though it can broaden your knowledge of European football and you can impress (or bore) your mates with your knowledge of the opposition the next time Levski Sofia visit Stamford Bridge. The scoring system is simple enough, but the transfer profit system is confusing. It's all down to personal taste, really, but there's no harm having a go and if you do well in this one there is probably no Fantasy Football game you are not capable of winning. There is plenty to do, apart from during the three months' Champions League break over the winter, but, judging by the game's seemingly incredible popularity in South America, if you are looking for a Venezuelan pen-pal then this is definitely the one for you.

FANTASY LEAGUE PROFESSIONAL
Website: http://pro.fantasyleague.com

How the game works
All the managers get together at a suitable venue, such as someone's home or down the pub, and an auction is held for the best Fantasy Football talent the Premiership has to offer. A list of players is produced beforehand (this is available off the website) and managers take turns to pick a player from that list and open the bidding, which continues until everyone is done. The highest bid wins and the player concerned becomes the exclusive property of the winning manager and will appear in his team only over the coming season. One player at a time is bid upon and squads are assembled. Managers who break the bank early on and run out of money can fill in the remainder of their squads at the end by picking up players no one else wanted on free transfers.

The rules of the game are flexible and you set them yourselves. The chairman and members of each league agree on certain ground rules before bidding starts, covering such things as:

- How much money managers have to spend? (£50 million is reasonable.)
- How big are your squads? This can be between 11 and 18 players.

- Which formations are allowed? 4-4-2, 5-3-2, 4-5-1, 5-4-1 are all acceptable, but you may choose to go with just one of them, all four, or something in between.

- How many players from the same Premiership club? This can be up to three. Your players must play in the positions they appear in the league lists, so there's no playing Thierry Henry as a central defender to boost your points tally. Leagues can also choose to allow transfers (in which case an in-season transfer budget has to be agreed upon, as well as how many transfers are allowed and when), swap and loan deals, as well as the cut-off point near the end of the season when no more transfers are allowed. There is also the option of employing a fixed-squad option if they choose, which basically limits the number of players you can have in any one position. This stops bosses loading up with strikers, who score more points, and simply rotating them in and out as the chance arises.

What will it cost me?
It's not cheap. Entry fees in 2006–07 were £26 for a standard team, £32 for an interactive team and £42 for a premium team. The latter two versions give you access to a facility that allows you to conduct the auction online.

What can I win?
No money, just a gold medal. You could make it more interesting by having a bet with your mates, of course...

HOW YOUR PLAYERS SCORE POINTS	POINTS
Goal	3
Assist	2
Appearance (minimum of 45 minutes played, goalkeepers and defenders only)	1
Clean sheet (minimum of 75 minutes played, goalkeepers and defenders only)	2
Each goal conceded (goalkeepers and defenders only)	-1

Our verdict

Although there is no money involved (side-bets aside), this one can be a lot of fun, especially the auction itself, which can be a great social occasion and something that could turn into an annual event. But, with some people more considered than others in their choices, it can take a long time to conduct, so make sure that if you're in the pub you start early enough so that it's all done and dusted before the landlord kicks you out. Auctions, which can literally take hours, depending on how serious the managers are, can be sped up in a number of ways, such as limiting the budget bosses have available or forcing managers to up their bids by certain increments, like £500,000 or £1 million.

FANTASY LEAGUE AUCTION

Website: http://auction.fantasyleague.com

How the game works

You are given a budget of £75 million to pick a squad of 16 Premiership players in an online auction with your friends or work-mates. A league can be made up of anywhere between five and 12 managers. Your team must conform to one of two formations: 4-4-2 = one goalkeeper, four defenders (two full-backs and two centre-backs), four midfielders and two forwards; or 5-3-2 = one goalkeeper, five defenders (two full-backs and three centre-backs), three midfielders and two forwards.

In addition, there is a fixed-squad rule, which means whatever formation you choose your five spare players must be made up of one for each position, so managers employing a 4-4-2 system must have a 16-man squad comprising two goalkeepers, three full-backs, three centre-backs, five midfielders and three forwards. It's two goalkeepers, three full-backs, four centre-backs, four midfielders and three forwards if you're playing a 5-3-2 formation. Again, this prevents managers from loading up with strikers – the players who tend to accumulate the most points.

What will it cost me?

Entry was £20 per team in 2006–07.

What can I win?

As this game is just against your mates, there are no prizes.

Age limit
None.

Which games count?
Premiership only; players do not score points in cup competitions.

HOW YOUR PLAYERS SCORE POINTS	POINTS
Goal	3
Assist	2
Appearance (minimum of 45 minutes played, goalkeepers and defenders only)	1
Clean sheet (minimum of 75 minutes played, goalkeepers and defenders only)	2
Each goal conceded (goalkeepers and defenders only)	-1

So, if a defender plays 80 minutes and his side does not concede a goal, he gets three points, one for the appearance and an extra two for the clean sheet.

Transfers
Managers enter sealed bids online against the names of any player they are interested in. Bid increments are £250,000 and the minimum bid is £0. After the first round of offers is completed, the league chairman processes them and allocates players to the highest bidder. Subsequent rounds take place until all squads are filled. Play is then along the lines of the Guardian/Fantasy League Classic game, with unlimited substitutions allowed between games. The impressive

'Supersubs' option allows managers to make their changes up to ten days in advance and enables them to benefit fully from playing all 16 members of their squad.

Bosses are given an additional £25 million to spend on a maximum of 25 transfers throughout the season. There are 12 windows throughout the season, with managers able to swap a maximum of five players in one window.

The game uses what is called a 'Sealed Bids Engine', which allows managers to bid for players at any time up to the transfer deadline. When that deadline passes, it automatically checks all the offers and awards the player to the highest bidder. If bids are tied, the manager of the team lower in the league is awarded the player he is chasing.

Our Verdict

The online bidding process for your original squad and for transfers during the season works superbly, and is perfect if your mates are always out and about and it is proving impossible to get them all together under one roof. The Fantasy League Classic gameplay is also among the most satisfying out there, with a scoring system that is clear and simple. Although frequent changes to your squad on a daily basis are essential, these can be taken care of well in advance by the use of the Supersubs feature. The game may have no prize money, but all-in-all it is an impressive package, especially for those players who like having unique teams rather than squads that all contain the same nucleus of players.